# Jane Austen's Men

# Jane Austen's Men

HELEN AMY

First published 2024

Amberley Publishing
The Hill, Stroud
Gloucestershire, GL5 4EP

www.amberley-books.com



ISBN 978 1 3981 1043 4 (hardback)
ISBN 978 1 3981 1044 1 (ebook)



British Library Cataloguing in Publication Data.
A catalogue record for this book is available from the British Library.

1 2 3 4 5 6 7 8 9 10

Typesetting by SJmagic DESIGN SERVICES, India.
Printed in the UK.

# CONTENTS

# INTRODUCTION

This book is about the men in Jane Austen's life, her relationship with them and their importance to her, as well as some of the male characters in her novels.

Born in 1775, Jane Austen was the seventh child of the Reverend George Austen, Rector of Steventon and Deane in Hampshire, and his wife Cassandra. She lived at Steventon Rectory for the first twenty-five years of her life. The Austens were a happy, close-knit family. Having started writing as a child, by the age of eighteen Jane had filled three copy books with essays, plays and short stories. The many people she met at social functions provided her with excellent material for her writing; she became a careful and critical observer of people's foibles, weaknesses, manners and habits, and developed a fascination with the behaviour and motives of those around her.

The society in which Jane Austen lived and set her novels was a hierarchical one, in which everyone knew their place in the social order, and a patriarchal one, in which women were second-class citizens dependent on men. In this society boys received a classical education to prepare them for university and their future roles in the 'public' sphere running the country and as lawyers, clergymen, officers in the army and navy, and in business. Girls were given a limited education to prepare them for their future lives in the 'private' domestic sphere. The only real ambition for women of the higher classes was marriage and motherhood. This was believed to be the role God decreed for them and there was great pressure on women to marry. Those who failed to marry had to bear the stigma of being a spinster. The marriage market was highly competitive for women as there were not enough eligible young men to go round. This is why Mrs Bennet in *Pride and Prejudice* is so anxious for her daughters to find husbands.

In Georgian and Regency England polite society was governed by rules of behaviour and etiquette which were set out in conduct and advice literature. These rules dictated, for example, how men and women should dress, speak and behave in company. There were particularly strict rules regarding courtship. The importance of observing these rules is made very clear in Jane Austen's novels.

The novels are about life in Jane Austen's England from a woman's viewpoint. They are sometimes described as 'courtship novels' as they deal with the challenges, dilemmas and pitfalls encountered by the heroines in finding husbands. All the novels end happily with the marriage of the hero and heroine.

The first part of this book is about the real men in Jane's life. The primary sources used are Jane's letters and the letters and memoirs of members of her family. Although, no doubt, these men had negative character traits, these one-sided sources make little reference to them.

Unlike the real men, the fictional men who are the subject of the second part of the book are fully rounded. The Austen household was largely male. As well as her father and five brothers, boy pupils of her father lived in the rectory for much of Jane's childhood. This probably accounts for the insight and understanding which enabled her to create her realistic male characters.

A theme running through this part of the book is the importance of behaving like a gentleman. The title 'gentleman' originally referred to an educated man of the aristocracy or gentry who derived his income from property rather than by earning a living. By Jane Austen's time, a man's personal qualities and conduct could also determine if he was a gentleman. Men who worked in certain professions were also by this time regarded as gentlemen. These professions were the law, the church, the army, and the navy. Many of these men were the younger sons of the aristocracy who did not inherit under the rules of primogeniture and had to earn a living.

Another group of men – the newly rich – who had made their wealth through business were also accepted as gentlemen, but were often, like Mr Weston and Mr Cole in *Emma,* looked down on by the real gentry as upstarts.

There was yet another group, including men who made their living through trade or as apothecaries, doctors, or farmers, which was a step up in the social hierarchy. Jane Austen referred to these men as 'half-gentlemen'.

The novels show that some men born into or accepted into the gentry, like Mr Knightley, always behaved like gentlemen, while others, like Mr Darcy, did not always behave as they should do. The novels also show how some men who were not considered to be gentlemen, such as Robert Martin in *Emma,* behaved impeccably.

It is sometimes thought that Jane Austen wrote about real people, but this is incorrect. She used qualities and characteristics from people she knew when creating her characters, but they are all imaginary. She also took features from real places when creating her fictional localities, but these are also imaginary. Jane stated that it was her intention 'to create, not to reproduce'.

Jane Austen lived during a period of great upheaval when England was undergoing rapid transformation. The country was beginning to change from an agricultural into an industrial nation. New money was replacing the old inherited wealth and a new meritocratic system was replacing the old patronage. There were also stirrings of political discontent and social and industrial unrest. Many of these changes did not affect life in quiet rural Hampshire where Jane lived for much of her life, but they nevertheless form part of the backdrop to her life and novels. Also in the background was the long war between Great Britain and France, although this affected Jane's family more than many people as her brothers Frank and Charles were officers in the navy at this time.

For readers who are not familiar with the novels or who have not read them recently, I have included a summary of each one. Incorrect spellings and unconventional use of capital letters have not been changed or indicated.

# THE AUSTEN FAMILY

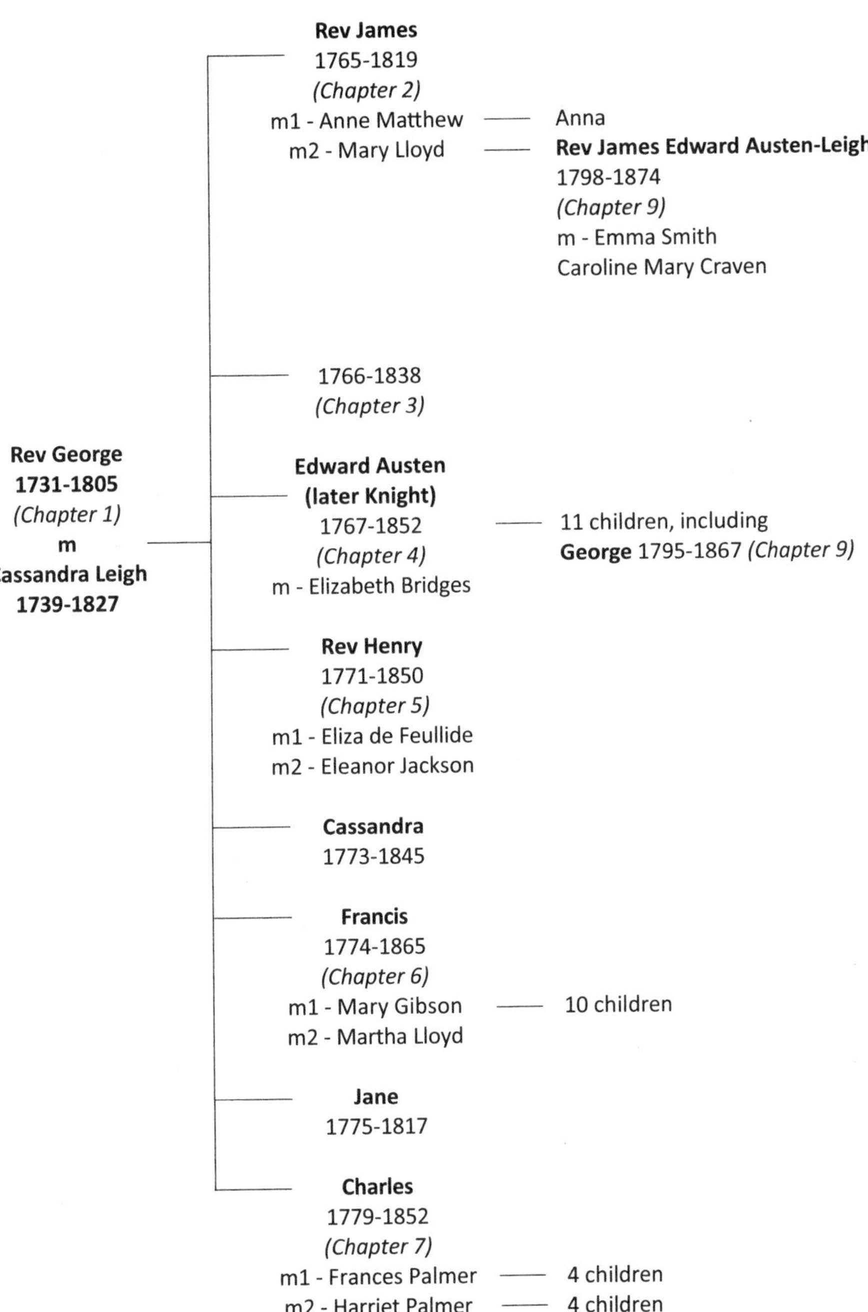

# PART 1

# THE MEN IN JANE AUSTEN'S LIFE

*Silhouette of Reverend George Austen, Jane's father.*

*Silhouette of Cassandra Austen, Jane's mother.*

*Silhouette of Cassandra Austen, Jane's sister.*

## 1

# GEORGE AUSTEN (FATHER)

George Austen, Jane's father, was born in 1731 in Tonbridge, Kent. He was the third child of William Austen, a surgeon, and his wife Rebecca, who had a son from a previous marriage. George's forebears came from the Tenterden and Sevenoaks area of Kent. One branch of the family made a considerable fortune in the clothing trade and, in the Tudor period, owned two manor houses – Grovehurst and Broadford, near Horsmonden. George came from a poorer branch of the family.

George had three sisters – Hampson born in 1728, who died at the age of two, Philadelphia, born in 1730 and Leonora in 1732. Rebecca Austen died not long after the birth of Leonora and, before long William married again. His second wife was Susanna Kelk, who lived in Tonbridge. This marriage did not last long, however, as William died eighteen months later. As their stepmother was unwilling to look after the orphaned Austen children, relatives of their parents stepped in to do so. George went to live with his aunt Jane Hooper and his sisters were taken in by other relatives.

Francis Austen, a wealthy uncle who was a lawyer in Sevenoaks, paid for George to attend Tonbridge School. Recognising his intelligent nephew's potential, Francis wanted to help him, despite having a large family of his own. George started at Tonbridge School when he was nine, and received the standard classical education given to boys of the aristocracy and gentry. George worked hard and did so well at school that he was awarded a scholarship to St John's College, Oxford, which he entered at the age of sixteen. At that time, Oxford and Cambridge Universities, the only universities in the country, had acquired a reputation for decadence and debauchery. Only a few lectures were held and there was little pressure to work. It was mainly students from wealthy families who were idle, but poorer students, many of whom became clergymen, generally worked harder. As he had to make his own way in life, George was a conscientious student and was determined to do well. He was awarded a Bachelor's degree in 1751 and a Master's degree in 1754. In 1753 George was also awarded a Smythe Exhibition, which had been instituted to allow poor former pupils of Tonbridge School to study at Oxford for holy orders, which led to his ordination as deacon and priest.

George's first clerical appointment was that of perpetual curate of Shipbourne in Kent and, at the same time, he was a master at his old school. George later returned to St John's College, where he was Assistant College Chaplain and Junior Proctor for the year 1759-60. As he was a tall, good-looking man with bright hazel eyes and wavy hair, George became known as 'the handsome Proctor'.[1] In 1760 he added to his academic achievements by obtaining a Bachelor of Divinity degree.

A year later George was presented with the living of Steventon in Hampshire by his wealthy second cousin, Thomas Knight, who owned extensive land and property in that county and in Kent. George decided not to take up this position immediately but left it in the hands of the curate, Thomas Bathurst, another cousin.

Possession of the living of Steventon meant that George could afford to get married, and it was not long before he met his future wife, Cassandra Leigh, the daughter of the Reverend Thomas Leigh, a former fellow of All Souls College, Oxford and retired rector of Harpsden in Oxfordshire. Cassandra was from a higher social class than George. One of her illustrious ancestors had been Lord Mayor of London in the reign of Queen Elizabeth, and she was related to the aristocratic Leighs of Stoneleigh Abbey in Warwickshire. It is not known where the young couple met, but it could have been in Bath, where Cassandra lived with her parents and sister, or in Oxford where she sometimes visited her uncle Theophilus Leigh, who was Master of Balliol College.

George and Cassandra married on 26$^{th}$ April 1764 at St Swithun's Church, Walcot, Bath. After the ceremony they set off for Hampshire where George was to take up his duties as Rector of Steventon. They did not move into Steventon Rectory straight away, as it needed renovation; the Austens' first marital home was the rectory of the neighbouring village of Deane. The living of Deane belonged to George's uncle Francis Austen, who had bought it, and the living of Ashe, with a view to his nephew taking over the first of the two to become vacant.

When the Austens moved into their new home they were joined by Cassandra's mother, who had recently been widowed, and a seven-year-old boy named George Hastings. The son of Warren Hastings, later the Governor-General of Bengal, George had been sent home to England to receive an education. It is not clear why the Austens were asked to care for him, but the arrangement was probably made through George Austen's sister Philadelphia Hancock, who lived in India and was a friend of Warren Hastings. Sadly, little George Hastings died of diphtheria soon after his arrival in England, much to the distress of the Austens, who had become attached to him.

George and Cassandra were a well-suited couple. Cassandra, who was sensible, practical, clever and witty, was the perfect wife for the placid, gentle, kind and scholarly George, who was a cheerful man with a positive outlook on life. Both possessed a good sense of humour. Being a woman, Cassandra was not as well educated as her husband, but she was, without doubt, his intellectual equal. As the daughter of a country clergyman, she was well prepared for her life as a rector's wife in rural Hampshire.

The Austens' first three children, James, George, and Edward, were born at Deane in 1765, 1766 and 1767 respectively. In the summer of 1768, with the renovation of Steventon Rectory finished, the family moved there. The lane between the two villages was then a rough cart track, made impassable for a carriage by deep ruts. Mrs Austen, who was not well, travelled to her new home on a feather bed placed on top of some soft items of furniture, in a waggon containing household goods.[2]

Steventon Rectory was a seventeenth-century brick building with a Georgian façade and a carriage drive in front. The front door with its latticed porch opened into two reception rooms; there were also seven bedrooms, three attic rooms, a study and kitchen. Behind the house were a bakery, dairy, brewhouse, well and water pump. George's study was at the back overlooking the garden. A path known as the 'church walk' led from the rectory garden to the church.

It was at Steventon Rectory that the remaining Austen children were born; Henry in 1771, Cassandra in 1773, Francis, known as Frank, in 1774, Jane in 1775 and Charles in 1779.

Sadly George, the Austens' second son, suffered from epilepsy and learning difficulties, and was probably deaf as well. At an early age he was placed in the care of a family in the nearby village of Monk Sherborne. It was a common practice in the eighteenth century for people with such disabilities to be removed from 'polite' society. George Austen paid for his son's care and his parents visited him regularly, but he was never a part of their family life.

Steventon, where the Austens lived for most of their married lives, was, and still is, a quiet village with winding country lanes and plenty of trees. The village consisted of the church, the rectory, the manor house, some brick and flint cottages and the surrounding farmland. The thirteenth- century church of St Nicholas and the rectory were located in an isolated position at one end of the village.

In addition to his clerical and pastoral duties, George looked after the rectory garden and orchard and worked on the glebe lands attached to the church. He also rented Cheesedown Farm in the north of the parish where he grew hay and wheat, and kept sheep and pigs. George was helped by two farm bailiffs but did a lot of the work himself. He enjoyed being a gentleman farmer.

The family's income came from George's stipend, from the tithes due to him as rector, and the sale of the farm produce that was surplus to his family's needs. In 1773, George's income was increased when he became rector of Deane. As Steventon and Deane were so close, with a combined population of 300, George was allowed by the Archbishop of Canterbury to hold the two livings in plurality. He looked after both parishes himself.

George further added to his income by educating a few sons of the aristocracy and gentry, alongside his own sons. This was a common practice among clergymen in the eighteenth century. George provided his sons and pupils with the typical male education of the time, based on the classics. According to his son Frank, his father was 'admirably calculated to the instruction of youth as he joined to an unusual extent of classical learning and a highly cultivated taste for literature in general, a remarkable suavity of temper and gentleness of manners.'[3] George's pupils boarded at the rectory, where they were looked after by his wife.

When his daughters returned from a girls' boarding school in Reading, George took over their education also. The education they had received at school placed great emphasis on the acquisition of good manners, social graces and ladylike accomplishments such as drawing, sewing and dancing. Academic learning was positively discouraged in girls, as it was considered unwomanly and unnecessary for their future lives in the domestic sphere. George and Cassandra Austen, however, were enlightened parents and wanted their daughters to have a proper education.

Cassandra and Jane studied English literature and history with their father and were allowed free rein in his library of over 500 books. This education was an excellent preparation for Jane's future career as a writer. Her love of literature and her wide reading is evident in her novels.

George Austen was a clergyman during a period of laxity and indifference in the Church of England. The majority of church livings were in the gift of wealthy landowners, the two universities and the crown, and were often given to men with the right connections but without a true vocation. They regarded the church as merely a way to make a living.

Despite his lucky connections, George Austen was a diligent and well-respected clergyman with a strong Christian faith. He lived among his parishioners, who were mostly agricultural labourers together with a few gentry families, and he took an active interest in their lives. His wife, and later their daughters, helped George with his pastoral duties by visiting the poor and needy villagers of Steventon and Deane, and making clothes for them.

Family life was very important to George Austen. He and his wife created a relaxed and happy home for their children, who were treated firmly but kindly. They were taught to live according to the tenets of the Christian faith, which included regular attendance at church and family prayers at home. In the words of George Austen's great grand-daughter, the Austen children were taught 'to do their duty to God and duty to man' and their lives revolved round these 'twin poles'.[4]

The Austens liked doing things together, including reading aloud to each other in the evenings and writing amusing puzzles in verse, which they referred to as 'charades' and 'conundrums'. The younger members of the family and George's pupils enjoyed putting on amateur dramatic performances for friends and family to watch.

A letter George Austen wrote to his son Frank when he embarked on his career in the navy gives an insight into the values and duties he taught his children, and shows the high standards he observed himself. George urged Frank to remember his religious duties, to treat others kindly, to behave respectfully to his commanding officers, to be 'active' and 'ready' to obey orders, and to treat his inferiors well. He also emphasised the importance of 'good humour', 'sobriety', 'prudence' and the necessity of 'carefully avoiding every appearance of selfishness'.[5]

George had a very close relationship with his daughter Jane. They had a similar positive outlook on life and sunny disposition. Jane's love and respect for her father is evident in her letters to her sister and other family members. It was George who recognised Jane's writing talent early on, supported her in her earliest attempts at writing and continued to do so. He bought her at least one of the three copy books in which she wrote what became known as her 'juvenilia'. One of Jane's early pieces, a play entitled 'The Mystery: An Unfinished Comedy', was dedicated to her father with mock solemnity, in the style of writers of the day. He bought Jane a portable mahogany writing desk from a shop In Basingstoke in December 1794, possibly for a birthday present, and Jane took this with her when she went on long journeys.

When Jane completed writing *First Impressions,* which was later published as *Pride and Prejudice,* her father sent the manuscript to the well-known London publisher Thomas Cadell with the following letter:

> Sir
>
> I have in my possession a manuscript novel comprising 3 vols; about the length of Miss Burney's 'Evelina.' As I am well aware of what consequence it is that a work of this sort shd. make its first appearance under a respectable name, I apply to you. I shall be much obliged therefore if you will inform me whether you choose to be concerned in it, what will be the expense of publishing it at the author's risk, and what you will venture to advance for the property of it, if on perusal it is approved of. Should you give any encouragement, I will send you the work.
>
> I am, Sir, your humble servant,
>
> George Austen

Cadell responded by returning the letter endorsed with the curt message 'declined by return of post'.[6] It is not known if Jane was aware of her father's action and if she was disappointed by the rejection. If she was, it did not discourage her from writing. It was, in fact, a lucky rejection as it allowed Jane to revise and polish the work, turning it into one of the world's greatest novels.

George Austen was a great reader and passed on his love of reading to all his children. George's large library contained the works of contemporary poets such as William Cowper and the novels of authors such as Tobias Smollett, Henry Fielding and Samuel Richardson, as well as copies of popular Gothic novels, the craze for which Jane satirised in *Northanger Abbey*. George kept up to date with local news by reading the *Hampshire Chronicle,* which also contained news of the war with France, agricultural prices and advertisements. Another of George's interests was the study of astronomy. He owned a small astronomical instrument, which he kept in a black shagreen case.

George and Cassandra Austen had a busy social life. Their social circle included the type of large landowners and lesser gentry who feature in Jane's novels. These people were traditional Tories like themselves – mostly the sort of cultured, well-connected people who shared their values. A few of their friends were members of the 'nouveaux riches' who had risen up the social scale into the gentry through trade and business. They met at formal assemblies, parties, balls, dinners and, with the lesser gentry, they visited one another at home. One event to which the Austens were always invited was the annual ball given by Lord Portsmouth, a former pupil of George's, at Hurstbourne Park, his grand country house near Whitchurch in Hampshire.

Although by no means as well off as other members of the local gentry, the Austens were accepted on equal terms by them. This was partly because George was an educated man with an important position in the community and also because of their relationship with Thomas Knight, who owned all the property in Steventon and much of the surrounding land. The Austens were looked up to and accorded a similar status to that of lords of the manor. Mrs Austen's aristocratic lineage and her connections in the academic world also made them acceptable.

George was part of the local farming community with whom he came in regular contact. He participated in events in the farming calendar, such as the ploughing matches held on Plough Monday, and harvest celebrations. George was friendly with Lord Bolton of nearby Hackwood Park, with whom he shared an interest in pigs. Hugh Digweed was another farmer friend, with whom he attended the local livestock auctions. They pooled their money to buy twenty or thirty sheep. When they returned to Steventon, the first half of the flock to run out of the pen were considered as belonging to the rector.

George and Cassandra Austen did not spend all their time in north Hampshire. They often travelled around the country to visit relatives, usually accompanied by their daughters. Travel was easier than earlier in the century, due to improvements in roads and transport. On the Austen side of the family, they visited the Walters and the Hancocks. William Hampson Walter was George's older half-brother, who lived with his wife Susannah and their family in Kent.

In 1788, George and Cassandra Austen took their daughters to visit their father's Austen and Walter relations in Kent. On the way home they stopped in London to see George's sister Philadelphia Hancock and her daughter Eliza, who had returned from India. In a letter to her cousin Philadelphia Walter, written a few days later, Eliza asked: 'What did you think of my uncle's looks? I was much pleased with them, and if possible he appeared more amiable than ever to me. What an excellent and pleasing man he is; I love him most sincerely.'[7]

George loved his niece most sincerely in return and some years later, after she had fled to England from revolutionary France with her mother and young son, they were welcomed to the rectory for lengthy stays.

The Austens also kept in touch with Mrs Austen's family. They visited her brother James Leigh-Perrot and his wife Jane, who had homes in Berkshire and Bath, and her sister Jane Cooper, who also lived in Bath with her husband and family. They visited Mrs Austen's cousin, the Reverend Thomas Leigh, in Adlestrop, Gloucestershire. When travelling beyond Hampshire the Austens went by public stage-coach or by post-chaise, stopping overnight at an inn when necessary. They had their own carriage for local travel.

By the end of the 1790s, the Austen sons had all left home. James was a clergyman married to his second wife Mary, and father of two children. Edward had been adopted as a sixteen-year-old by his father's childless cousin, Thomas Knight II, to be his heir. In 1797 he had come into his inheritance and moved into Godmersham House, near Canterbury, with his wife and young family. Henry was a lieutenant in the Oxfordshire Militia and, in 1797, married his widowed cousin Eliza. Frank and Charles were both progressing in their naval careers. Cassandra and Jane, as unmarried dependent daughters, were still living with their parents. Sadly, Cassandra's clergyman fiancé died in the West Indies early in 1797 while serving as private chaplain to his kinsman Lord Craven, who was Colonel of the Regiment of Foot in Lord Abercrombie's army.

In December 1800, having enjoyed thirty-two years living a contented life that revolved around his family, his clerical duties, his parishioners and running his farm, George Austen made the sudden decision to retire and move to Bath. Jane was so shocked to hear this that she fainted. Both Jane and Cassandra were very attached to their childhood home and the Hampshire countryside, but they were not consulted about the move. They had no choice but to go wherever their parents took them. The blow was softened by the promise of holidays in the west country and Wales.

The plan was for George to retain the living of Steventon, employ James to be his curate and find a new rector for Deane. Jane suspected that her sister-in-law Mary may have played a part in her father's sudden decision to retire. She was eager for James to succeed him as he was next in line to inherit the living of Steventon under the terms of the will of Thomas Knight. George's 500 books and Jane's piano were sold prior to the move to Bath. Before they left, the Austens received farewell visits from friends, neighbours and parishioners who were all sorry to see them go.

There were several possible reasons why George and his wife chose Bath for their retirement location. They were familiar with the city and knew a number of people who lived there, as well as the Leigh-Perrots. It was also full of retirees and catered for old people. Another consideration may have been that Bath was a renowned hunting ground for husbands and they may have seen a move there as a last chance for their daughters, who were already in danger of being written off as old maids, to find suitable partners.

The Austens left Steventon in early May. Mrs Austen and her daughters went to visit Martha Lloyd, sister of Mary Austen and a friend of Jane and Cassandra, who lived at Ibthorpe in Berkshire with her mother. George went to London and then to

Godmersham with Frank. After two days at Ibthorpe, Mrs Austen and Jane went on to Bath leaving Cassandra behind. They reached Bath in the early evening and went straight to the Leigh-Perrots' home at 1, Paragon, where they planned to stay while looking for suitable, reasonably priced accommodation.

At the end of the month, by which time George and Cassandra had arrived, the Austens took out a lease on 4, Sydney Place, opposite Sydney Gardens in the lower part of the city, not far from its centre. While their new home was being decorated it is thought they went on holiday to Sidmouth in Devon.

In April 1802, James, Mary and his daughter Anna visited his parents and sisters in Bath. In later life Anna recalled this visit and recorded that her grandparents 'seemed to enjoy the cheerfulness of their Town life, and especially perhaps the rest which their advancing years entitled them to, which, even to their active natures, must have been acceptable.'[8] Anna also recorded the following memory of her grandfather's appearance at the time:

> When I have the most perfect recollection of him he must have been getting on hard, as people say, for 70. His hair in its whiteness might have belonged to a much older man; it was beautiful and glossy, with short curls above the ears ... I can well remember at Bath, where my Grand Father latterly resided, what notice he attracted, when on any public occasion he appeared with his head uncovered.[9]

A miniature portrait of the still handsome George, which was painted the year before, fits with this description.

In 1802 and 1804 the Austens enjoyed at least two more holidays in the west country and Wales. On the holiday to

Lyme Regis in the summer of 1804 they were joined by their son Henry and his wife Eliza. Jane later used her knowledge of Lyme Regis when creating the setting for much of the action in *Persuasion*. Some time in September, Henry, Eliza and Cassandra left for Weymouth while Jane stayed on at Lyme with her parents. A letter Jane sent to Cassandra shows how much they enjoyed themselves bathing in the sea and visiting the Assembly Rooms where they mixed with the 'quality at Lyme'. Jane described a ball which she attended with both her parents.

> The Ball last night was pleasant, but not full for Thursday. My Father staid very contentedly till half past nine – we went a little after eight – & then walked home with James [a servant] & a Lanthorn, tho' I believe the Lanthorn was not lit, as the moon was up... My Mother & I staid about an hour later.[10]

Following this holiday, the Austens moved to 3, Green Park Buildings East where, on 21st January of the following year, George Austen died. He had been unwell for a while but his death was both sudden and unexpected. Jane wrote the following letter to her brother Frank, who was on board HMS *Leopard* at Dungeness, informing him of their loss.

> My dearest Frank,
> I have melancholy news to relate, & sincerely feel for your feelings under the shock of it. – I wish I could better prepare You for it. – But having said so much, Your mind will already forestall the sort of Event which I have to communicate. – Our dear Father has closed his virtuous & happy life, in a death almost as free from suffering as his Children could have wished. He was taken

ill on Saturday morning, exactly in the same way as heretofore, an oppression in the head with fever, violent tremulousness, & the greatest degree of Feebleness. The same remedy of Cupping, which had before been so successful, was immediately applied to – but without such happy effects. The attack was more violent, & at first he seemed scarcely at all relieved by the Operation. – Towards the Evening however he got better, had a tolerable night, & yesterday morning was so greatly amended as to get up & join us at breakfast as usual, walk about with only the help of a stick, & every symptom was then so favourable that when Bowen saw him at one, he felt sure of his doing perfectly well. – But as the day advanced, all these comfortable appearances gradually changed; the fever grew stronger than ever, & when Bowen saw him at ten at night, he pronounc'd his situation to be most alarming. – At nine this morning he came again – & by his desire a Physician was called; – Dr Gibbs – But it was then absolutely a lost case – Dr Gibbs said that nothing but a Miracle could save him, and about twenty minutes after Ten he drew his last gasp. – Heavy as is the blow, we can already feel that a thousand comforts remain to us to soften it. Next to that of the consciousness of his worth & constant preparation for another World, is the remembrance of his having suffered, comparatively speaking, nothing. – Being quite insensible of his own state, he was spared all the pain of separation, & he went off almost in his Sleep. – My Mother bears the Shock as well as possible; she was quite prepared for it, & feels all the blessing of his being spared a long illness. My Uncle and Aunt have been with us, & shew us every imaginable kindness. And tomorrow we shall I dare say have the comfort of James's presence, as an Express has been sent to him. – We write also of course to Godmersham & Brompton. Adieu my dearest Frank. The loss of

> such a Parent must be felt, or we should be Brutes. – I wish I could have given you better preparation – but it has been impossible.
>
> Yours Ever Affecly
>
> J.A.[11]

A second letter had to be sent the following day, as Frank's ship had moved to Portsmouth before he could have received the first one. Jane added a few more sentences, including: 'His tenderness as a Father who can do justice to? ... The Serenity of the Corpse is most delightful! – It preserves the sweet, benevolent smile which always distinguished him.'[12]

George Austen's death marked the end of a good and worthwhile life, dedicated to the service of others. He was much lamented by his family, friends and former parishioners. George was buried in the crypt of St Swithin's Church, Walcot, the church in which he was married over forty years earlier. The inscription on his burial stone reads:

> Under this stone rest the remains of the Rev George Austen, Rector of Steventon and Deane in Hampshire, who departed this life the 21st January 1805, aged 73 years.

Among George's personal belongings were his small astronomical instrument in a black shagreen case and a pair of scissors, which were sent to Frank. Sadly, George did not live long enough to witness the literary success of his talented daughter Jane – a talent which he had recognised so early and did his best to encourage.

Following her husband's death, Mrs Austen, her daughters and their friend Martha Lloyd, who had joined their household, only remained in Bath for another year and a half. They moved to

Southampton where they shared a house with Frank and his wife Mary.

In 1809 they moved again to a cottage in Chawton, Hampshire, which belonged to Edward Austen. It was there that Jane revised her three early novels for publication and wrote her later novels. Jane remained there until the last two months of her life. Mrs Austen lived there until she died at the age of eighty-seven in 1827 and Cassandra lived there until her death in 1845. Both are buried in the churchyard of St Nicholas Church, Chawton.

Steventon Rectory, where George Austen, his wife and family had enjoyed so many happy years, was demolished in 1824. All that now remains of it are an old well and an iron water pump. A new rectory was built on the hill opposite for George's nephew William Knight, who was then rector.

THE REV. JAMES AUSTEN

*James Austen, Jane's brother.*

## 2

# JAMES AUSTEN

James, the eldest child of George and Cassandra Austen, was born at Deane Rectory on 13th February 1765. He was privately baptised on the day of his birth and publicly baptised on 17th March. As soon as he was weaned James was sent to be cared for by a woman who lived in the village, thought to have been Elizabeth, wife of John Littleworth, who was known locally as Nanny Littlewart. The Austens' subsequent babies were all sent out to be cared for in the same way. This was a common custom among the gentry at that time. The baby was visited by one of its parents every day and was frequently brought to them at the rectory, but the cottage was the baby's home until he could walk and talk.

James, who was known as Jemmy during his childhood, received his earliest education from his mother. In the eighteenth century it was the mother's responsibility to provide her children with basic literacy skills, religious instruction, and moral guidance. James was then taught by his father alongside his pupils. George Austen was unable to make any financial provision for his sons, so they had to be educated for a professional career. James liked learning and was a diligent student. He also enjoyed the company of his fellow pupils, one of whom, Fulwar Craven Fowle, became a close friend.

From an early age James loved the outdoors and liked to follow the local hunt. As relatives of Thomas Knight, who owned all the land around Steventon, the Austen boys were allowed to hunt freely. James acquired a love of the countryside and when he was older, he expressed this by writing pastoral poetry in the style of Thomas Gray's famous *Elegy in a Country Churchyard*.

James, who grew into a tall and handsome young man, was of a serious, contemplative disposition and was the scholar of the family. Although he was quite cheerful when younger, James was later subject to periods of melancholy and had a rather negative outlook on life.

George Austen was such a good teacher that James went to Oxford University at the precocious age of fourteen. He went to St John's College, his father's old college, on a Founder's Kin Scholarship, for which he was eligible because an ancestor of his mother was related to the founder of the college.

When he arrived at Oxford, James was invited to dinner by his great-uncle Dr Theophilus Leigh, who was Master of Balliol College. Before he sat down to eat, James, being unaware of university customs, was about to remove his academic gown as if it was an outdoor coat. He was stopped by the learned doctor, who said with a wry smile, 'Young man, you need not strip: we are not going to fight.'[1]

James worked hard at university because of his love of learning and also because, like his father, he had to make his own way in the world. He sometimes neglected his studies, however, to indulge his passion for hunting, as he described in the following excerpt from one of his poems.

> For there in early days, a truant oft
> From Alma Mater's discipline & rule,
> In spite of imposition, & the frown
> Of angry Dean, or Tutor grave & wise,
> I've dashed through miry field & boggy lane,
> Led by the musical & cheering notes
> Of the loud echoing pack, full many a mile.[2]

In December 1782, when James was home from university for Christmas, the younger members of the Austen family put on an amateur theatrical performance. So great was the interest in the theatre at this time that many families put on such productions in their homes.

The first play performed by the Austens was the tragedy *Matilda* by Thomas Francklin. James wrote his own prologue and epilogue, which were read by his brother Edward and Tom Fowle, one of his father's pupils. The play was performed to an audience of family and friends. This was the first of a series of plays put on over the next six years. They were performed in the rectory dining room in winter and in George Austen's tithe barn in summer. As well as writing prologues and epilogues for the plays, James organised the productions.

Jane used her memories of these family theatricals when she wrote *Mansfield Park*. The performance which the young Bertrams and their friends were planning to put on is an important part of the novel's plot.

Despite his extra-curricular activities, James did well at Oxford University and was awarded his Bachelor of Arts degree in 1783 when he was only eighteen. He then remained at Oxford to become a Fellow of St John's College, with the plan of eventually becoming a clergyman.

In November 1786, James made a trip to the Continent, going first to France where he probably stayed with his cousin Eliza's husband, the Comte de Feullide. He also visited Spain and Holland before returning to England in the autumn of 1787. On his return James spent some time at Steventon, where he helped his father who was tutoring Cassandra and Jane. James had a considerable knowledge of English literature, which made him the perfect mentor for his sisters. In particular, he helped to direct Jane's reading.

In December of that year, James was ordained a deacon at Oxford by the Bishop of St David's. The following year he received his Master's Degree and in July was appointed curate of Stoke Charity, a small village in Hampshire. He continued to live in Oxford as this was only a nominal, non-residential appointment.

During his remaining time at Oxford, James launched the publication of a weekly magazine named *The Loiterer*, for the students and lecturers of the university. This magazine was in the style of *The Spectator* and *The Rambler*, the satirical periodicals published by Joseph Addison and Richard Steele and, like theirs, its intention was to bring about reform through ridicule. Its editor stated that it would provide a sketch of the manners, character and amusements at Oxford.

*The Loiterer* was published weekly from January 1789 until March 1790. As well as editing the magazine, James wrote many of the articles in it, with contributions from his brother Henry, who was by then an undergraduate at St John's College, and other students. The articles were on a variety of subjects including *The Disadvantages Arising From Misconduct at Oxford* and *The Medicinal Virtues of Port Wine. The Loiterer* also published spoof advertisements, such as the following one written by James.

> Wanted – A Curacy in a good sporting country, near a pack of foxhounds, and in a sociable neighbourhood; it must have a good house and stables, and a few acres of meadow ground would be very agreeable. – To prevent trouble, the stipend must not be less than £80. The Advertiser has no objections to undertaking three, four or five Churches of a Sunday, but will not engage where there is any weekly duty. Whoever has such a one to dispose of, may suit themselves by sending a line, directed to be left at the Turf Coffee House.[3]

James finally left Oxford in March 1790 and in the following month he was appointed curate of Overton, a village in Hampshire not far from Steventon. This was a proper position, requiring residence and responsibility for the parishes of Overton and nearby Laverstoke. In many ways, the spoof advertisement James had written for *The Loiterer* could have been used to advertise his new appointment. Once installed at Overton, James soon became part of the local community and began to hunt with the local Kempshott pack.

It was around this time that James met his first wife, Anne Mathew. Anne, who was five years his senior, was the daughter of General Edward Mathew and his wife Jane, who was the daughter of the 2nd Duke of Ancaster. They lived in the old manor house in the village of Laverstoke, a few miles from Overton. James, as a lowly country curate, was well below Anne in social status, but her parents did not object to the match.

General Mathew had served in the Coldstream Guards and seen action in Europe and America. He had also been equerry to King George III from 1762 to 1776. His final appointments were as Commander-in-Chief of the Windward and Leeward Islands in the West Indies, and then Governor of Grenada.

Anne was one of three sisters, who were described by her sister-in-law Jane as having 'large dark eyes and a good deal of nose'.[4] She and James were married at Laverstoke on 27th March 1792, in a service conducted by his father. By this time James had been presented with the living of Sherborne St John by William Chute, Member of Parliament for Hampshire, with whom he had become friends through their shared love of hunting.

For the first few months of their marriage, James and Anne lived at Court House, in Overton. Then, when James became his father's curate, they moved to Deane Rectory. Despite holding multiple clerical positions James was, like his father, a conscientious clergyman, with a strong Christian faith and a genuine vocation.

On their marriage General Mathew gave his daughter and son-in-law a generous allowance of £100 a year. Later, he bought the chaplaincy of the 86th Regiment of Foot as a sinecure for James. After paying for a deputy, the remainder provided a further source of income. The Leigh family presented James with the livings of Cubbington and Hunnington in Warwickshire. Like the living of Stoke Charity, these were only nominal appointments, which added to James' and Anne's income. With all these sources of income, James could afford a pack of harriers for himself and a carriage for his wife.

Just over a year after their marriage Anne gave birth to a daughter. Jane Anna Elizabeth, always known as Anna, was born after a difficult pregnancy. Her mother-in-law got out of bed in the middle of the night and walked along the dark country lane to Deane, with a lantern, to be with Anne during her labour. The baby was baptised a few weeks later, for which occasion her Aunt Jane wrote *Miscellaneous Morsels,* which she dedicated to her new niece with the advice: 'If you seriously attend to them, You will derive from them very important Instructions, with regard to your Conduct in Life.'[5]

When James had any time left over after performing his clerical duties, he liked reading. Like his father and sister Jane, he read novels and history books. In the words of his mother James possessed 'Classical Knowledge, Literary Taste, and the power of Elegant Composition he possessed in the highest degree.'[6] He was also interested in science and, according to one of Jane's letters, he read Dr Jenner's pamphlet on cowpox.

Sadly, James' and Anne's marriage did not last long as Anne died suddenly in May 1795. She had just finished eating a meal when she was taken ill. A doctor was called but there was nothing he could do, and Anne died a few hours later. According to the doctor she had probably suffered a ruptured liver. Anne was buried in the churchyard of St Nicholas Church, Steventon, and a memorial tablet was erected in the south side of the chancel. The words on the tablet refer to 'the Innocency of her Heart, Simplicity of her Manners, And amiable, unspotted Tenour of Her Life, in every Relation' and her 'Christian Fortitude'.

Anna was only two when her mother died and not surprisingly for some time afterwards she kept asking for her. As James was struggling to deal with his own grief, he sent his daughter to Steventon Rectory to be comforted and cared for by her grandparents and aunts. A little cherrywood chair was bought for Anna to use at the rectory. Later, all that Anna could remember of her mother was a figure in a white dress. General Mathew continued to pay James the allowance of £100 a year, so that he had enough money to pay for Anna's education and maintenance. Anna remained at Steventon Rectory for nearly two years. During this time, she developed a close relationship with her aunts, and they continued to be close as she grew up.

After his wife's death, James was a constant visitor at Steventon Rectory and frequently escorted his mother and sisters to balls at the Basingstoke Assembly Rooms. Jane commented on the improvement in his dancing. He seemed to be on the lookout for another wife, partly because he wanted Anna to have a mother figure in her life.

The first woman James showed a romantic interest in was Lady Catherine Powlett, the daughter of the 6th Duke of Bolton, who lived at Hackwood Park near Basingstoke. James wrote her a sonnet in which he likened her to the goddess Venus, but the poem did not have the desired effect, as the lady did not return his feelings.

In 1796 James briefly courted his widowed cousin Eliza de Feuillide, but it seems that this was little more than a flirtation to the vivacious and extrovert Eliza. She never really considered marrying the serious and sometimes melancholy James. Apart from their incompatible characters, Eliza was put off by the fact that he was a clergyman. It is surprising that James ever considered that the pleasure-loving Eliza would have made him a suitable wife.

James next turned his attention to two women called Mary. One was Mary Harrison, who lived in Andover, and the other was Mary Lloyd – he chose the latter. Mary was the daughter of the Reverend Noyes (or Nowis) Lloyd, the late incumbent of Emborne in Berkshire, and his wife Martha Craven Lloyd. Mrs Lloyd became a tenant of George Austen when she moved into the recently vacated Deane Rectory in the spring of 1789. Her daughters Martha and Mary moved in with her. A third daughter, Eliza, had married her cousin Fulwar Craven Fowle, a former pupil of George Austen and friend of James. Cassandra and Jane Austen became friends with the Lloyd sisters, and they were particularly close to Martha.

James proposed to Mary after getting to know her better when she stayed at Steventon Rectory in the autumn of 1796. Mary accepted the proposal, much to his mother's delight. Mrs Austen's pleasure is evident in the following paragraph from a letter to her future daughter-in-law:

> Mr Austen & Myself desire you will accept our best Love, and that you will believe us truly sincere when we assure you that we feel the most heartfelt satisfaction at the prospect we have of adding you to the Number of our very good Children. Had the Election been mine, you, my dear Mary, are the person I should have chosen for James' Wife, Anna's Mother, and my Daughter, being as certain, as I can be of anything in this uncertain world, that you will greatly increase and promote the happiness of each of the three[7]

Eliza was also pleased to hear about the engagement. In a letter to her cousin Philadelphia Walter. She wrote:

> James has chosen a second Wife in the person of Miss Mary Floyd [sic] who is not either rich or handsome, but very sensible & good-humoured... Jane seems much pleased with the match, and it is natural she should, having long known and liked the Lady.[8]

Mary was badly scarred by smallpox, as James' friend William Chute's mother noted when he took her to meet the Chute family. In a letter to her sister Mrs Chute wrote: 'She is perfectly unaffected, and very pleasant; I like her. Was it not for the smallpox which has scarred and seamed her face dreadfully, her countenance would be pleasing; to my near-sighted eyes at a little distance she looked to advantage.'[9]

James and Mary were married at Hurstbourne Tarrant in Hampshire on a snowy day in January 1797. James recorded the event in the following poem addressed to Mary:

> Cold was the morn, & all around
> Whitened with new fallen snow the ground,
> Yet still the sun with cheering beam,
> Played on the hill, and vale, and stream,
> And almost gave to winter's face
> Spring's pleasing cheerfulness and grace.[10]

After her marriage Mary moved back to Deane Rectory, where she had previously lived with her mother and sister, and four-year-old Anna returned to her father's home.

Unfortunately, Mrs Austen had been too hasty in predicting that Mary would increase the happiness of her family. Sadly, Mary's marriage to James brought out an unpleasant side to her character, which had previously been hidden, and she did not turn out to be either a good or kind stepmother to Anna. As a result, Jane's pleasure at the marriage between her brother and her friend turned to sadness and disappointment. Not long after their marriage, Mary began to resent James' closeness to his family and objected to his frequent visits to Steventon Rectory. For a while she stopped these visits but, as Jane noted in a letter to her sister, he occasionally defied her: 'James seems to have taken to his old Trick of coming to Steventon inspite [sic] of Mary's reproaches, for he was here before Breakfast, & is now paying us a second visit.'[11]

This was the start of Mary's increasingly overbearing and dominating behaviour. Mary, who had a strong character, exerted more and more control over her weaker husband. Jane noted how this changed her brother's character and he was no longer the cheerful and pleasant person he had once been. She noticed that James seemed to allow his wife to control him and made no attempt to assert himself. Mary could be sharp and brusque in manner. The emergence of these negative character traits in Mary spoilt her longstanding friendship with Jane and affected Jane's relationship with her brother. It was also regrettable because, as Jane's letters show, Mary could be kind and thoughtful. Despite his wife's faults, particularly her dominating behaviour, James was devoted to her.

In November 1798, James' and Mary's first child, James Edward, was born. On this occasion Mrs Austen did not walk through the country lanes at night to attend her daughter-in-law's confinement, as she had done when James' first wife was in labour. Mrs Austen was so worried that she asked not to be informed until after the event. This may have been because two neighbours had recently died in childbirth. This information was wisely kept from Mary and the baby arrived safely.

The new baby was christened at James' church in Deane, on the first day of 1799. Although he was christened James Edward, he was always known in the family as Edward, to distinguish him from his father. James Edward would one day write the first biography of his famous aunt.

Jane's disappointment in Mary's behaviour increased when, in December 1800, her father made the sudden decision to retire and move to Bath. Only a few weeks earlier, George Austen had been planning changes in the rectory garden, including the planting of new trees. As mentioned earlier, Jane suspected that Mary had put pressure on her father to retire. James was due to inherit the living of Steventon on his father's death and Jane thought that Mary could not wait for this to happen, as she was eager to move into Steventon Rectory, which was more spacious than her current home. If Mary's intention had been for James to take over as Rector of Steventon she did not succeed, as her father-in-law decided to retain the living and pay his son to be his curate, though he did move into the rectory.

Jane was so upset with Mary that she declined an invitation to a party held to celebrate her and James's fourth wedding anniversary. Jane was also displeased when preparations were being made for the move to Bath. Mary and a group of local ladies turned up at the rectory to inspect her mother's poultry, with a view to buying them. Jane reported this in a letter to her sister: 'Soon afterwards a party of fine Ladies issuing from a well-known, commodious green Vehicle, their heads full of Bantam-Cocks and Galinies (hens), entered the house'[12]

The 'commodious green vehicle' was James's and Mary's carriage. Jane went on to write, with more than a hint of bitterness:

> My father's old Ministers are already deserting him to pay their court to his Son; the brown Mare, which as well as the black was to devolve on James at our removal, has not had patience to wait for that, & has settled herself even now at Deane ... everything else, I suppose, will be seized by degrees in the same manner.[13]

Jane was also angry that some of the items in the rectory, which James and Mary wanted to buy, were valued at less than she expected. In a letter to Cassandra, she wrote 'The whole World is in a conspiracy to enrich one part of our family at the expence [sic] of another.'[14]

Another unpleasant trait of Mary's was her resentment towards people who reminded her of James's life before their marriage. She never liked her husband's cousin Eliza because he had once courted her. Mary never invited Eliza to her home and would not allow Anna to accept invitations to stay with her and her husband, James's brother Henry. Mary held a grudge against Eliza until the day the latter died.[15] Mary also showed resentment towards Anna, and she made her feel unwelcome in her father's home.

Unforgivably, James allowed his wife's behaviour to influence his own and he treated Anna less favourably than he treated his children by Mary. James wrote poems expressing his love for these children, but he did not write so much as a line about Anna.[16] He also never spoke to Anna of the mother she had lost, whose name was never mentioned, presumably to appease Mary.

To her great credit, Anna was always a dutiful daughter to James and spoke affectionately of him, and she was also respectful of her step-mother. Fortunately, Anna remained close to her two aunts Cassandra and Jane and could always go to them for acceptance and affection.

Jane noticed that her brother and sister-in-law, who often pleaded poverty, made a show of giving, but only once their own needs were covered. After his marriage, James became more interested in money and less generous than he had been before. Mary's meanness was one of the things that led to a strained relationship with Jane.

James worked diligently as his father's curate at Steventon for nearly five years, until on January 21st 1805 George Austen died suddenly and unexpectedly. On hearing the news, James hurried to Bath to be with his mother and sisters. He tried to persuade his mother to return with him to Steventon, but she refused.

James now became Rector of Steventon and the income from the living passed to him. This left Mrs Austen and her daughters in a precarious financial position. As a result, James and all his brothers pledged an annual sum according to their means to support them, except Charles, who could not afford to contribute.

In June 1805, James and Mary's daughter Caroline Mary Craven was born. Anna was taken to Godmersham by her grandmother and aunts just before Caroline's birth, presumably to help Mary. James's time was now filled with his clerical and parental duties.

James and Mary were better-off financially when he became Rector of Steventon, with his stipend and other income due to him as rector. At the end of 1805, General Mathew died and his allowance for Anna ceased. This was soon replaced by an allowance from James's uncle James Leigh-Perrot, of whose estate he was trustee and from whom he expected an inheritance. For this reason, James and Mary were careful to remain on good terms with the Leigh-Perrots. Jane was astonished to calculate that her brother's income was then £1,100 a year, after paying his curate.

James and Mary often travelled to other parts of the country to visit relatives. In 1802 they went to Bath with Anna and, presumably, three-year-old Edward, although there is no record of him going. This must have been an uncomfortable time for Jane, given her suspicion that Mary was responsible for her father's sudden decision to retire. This was the visit, described in the first chapter, which Anna recalled many years later, including her memory of her still handsome grandfather.

In January 1807, James, Mary and eighteen-month-old Caroline visited his mother and Jane at Southampton. Cassandra was at her brother's home Godmersham House in Kent, so Jane was left to look after and entertain them without her sister's help.

The weather was bad, so James, who hated to be confined indoors, was irritable and restless. Jane suggested reading aloud together in the evenings, but Mary objected to the books chosen. Jane could not wait for her guests to leave. She wrote to Cassandra expressing her relief at their departure: 'When you receive this, our guests will be all gone or going; and I shall be left to the comfortable disposal of my time, to ease of mind from the torments of rice puddings and apple dumplings, & probably to regret that I did not take more pains to please them all.'[17]

Jane told her sister that Mary had asked her to return with them to Steventon. 'I need not give my answer,' she added. In her next letter to Cassandra Jane referred to her brother's visit again, and her frustration at the change in him since his marriage to Mary is evident:

> I am sorry & angry that his Visits should not give one more pleasure; the company of so good & so clever a Man ought to be gratifying in itself; – but his Chat seems all forced, his Opinions on many points too much copied from his Wife's, & his time here is spent I think in walking about the House & banging the Doors, or ringing the Bell for a glass of Water.[18]

In the summer of 1808, James, Mary and their two children went to stay with his brother Edward, his wife Elizabeth and their children at Godmersham House. Anna, who had recently caused some consternation by having her hair cut short, was left behind at Southampton with her grandmother and Aunt Cassandra. Jane went with James and Mary, so her brother rode there on horseback to make space for her in their carriage.

In a letter to her sister, Jane described their two brothers riding around Edward's estate together and enjoying each other's company. James conducted a service at Godmersham church one Sunday. James Edward played happily with his cousins, but Caroline, who was only three years old, did not enjoy herself so much, and she later recalled that she was not very happy in a strange house.

There was plenty for them all to do on the Godmersham estate, and plenty of Edward's neighbours and friends for them to meet. There were also trips to Canterbury, and Edward took James to Sandling Park near Hythe, the home of his brother-in-law, which Jane described as 'a nice scheme for James as it will show him a new & fine County.' In a letter to Cassandra she wrote: 'Edward certainly excels in doing the Honours to his visitors, & providing for their amusement.'[19] The visitors returned home, after a busy and enjoyable visit, in early July.

The last of the family visits undertaken by James and Mary of which details were recorded took place in August 1809. They went with James Edward and Caroline to Stoneleigh Abbey, in Warwickshire, to stay with James's mother's cousins, the Reverend Thomas Leigh and his sister Elizabeth. Many years later, Caroline recorded this visit in her *Reminiscences*. She was impressed with the old abbey and remembered enjoying her time there:

> I think I was very happy at Stoneleigh. Nobody teized [sic] me, or wanted me much in the parlour, and I had the range of the house, with Betsy [a servant] for my companion. The size of the rooms and the antique appearance of some of them impressed me very much. I delighted chiefly in the picture gallery, as it was called, tho' not many pictures were there; but in it stood a spinett [sic], so old and uncared for, that I was allowed to play on it as much as I pleased. From the gallery, a double flight of stone steps descended into the garden.[20]

Caroline also remembered day excursions to Warwick Castle, Guy's Cliff, Combe Abbey, and Kenilworth. On their way home James and Mary called on family friends in Berkshire.

Anna made life difficult for her father and stepmother during her teenage years; not surprisingly, considering the way she had been treated, Anna developed a rebellious streak. In 1809, at the age of sixteen, she became engaged without her father's consent to Michael Terry, a Cambridge-educated clergyman, who lived in the nearby village of Dummer. Michael, who had the prospect of a comfortable living, belonged to a respected and well-connected family. Despite these advantages, James and Mary did not consider him a suitable match for Anna. They may have been worried about the age gap, as Michael was eighteen years older than Anna. To separate the couple, Anna was sent to Godmersham.

A few weeks later, Michael's sister appealed to James and Mary to reconsider their opposition to the engagement, and Cassandra also spoke out on Anna's behalf. As a result, Michael was allowed to go to Godmersham to see Anna. After returning home, Anna went to stay with the Terry family and while there, she decided to break off the engagement. This caused her father and stepmother much embarrassment and made it awkward for them to meet the Terrys, whom they knew socially.

To relieve the friction at home, Anna often went to stay with her grandmother and aunts, who now lived in the village of Chawton, fifteen miles from Steventon. It was good for her to have their support and guidance, in view of her poor relationship with her stepmother.

James and Mary took an interest in Jane's writing. After *Sense and Sensibility* was published in 1811, James sent his sister the following poem. It was addressed to 'Miss Jane Austen, the reputed author of *Sense and Sensibility*, a novel lately published'.

On such Subjects no Wonder that she shou'd write well,
In whom so united those Qualities dwell;
Where 'dear Sensibility,' Sterne's darling Maid,
With Sense so attempter'd is finely pourtray'd.
Fair Elinor's Self in that Mind is exprest,
And the feelings of Marianne live in that Breast.

Oh then, gentle Lady! continue to write,
And the Sense of your Readers' t'amuse and delight.[21]

The poem, written in a disguised hand, was signed 'A Friend'. James was easily identified as the author, both by the Alton postmark and because he was the poet of the family.

In June 1812, Mrs Austen and Jane went to stay at Steventon Rectory for two weeks. Mrs Austen had decided that she was now too old to stay away from home. Having made this decision she chose that her last visit would be to James and Mary at Steventon Rectory, which had been her home for most of her married life.

James continued to enjoy his life, devoted to his parishioners and his family. Unfortunately, he still had worries concerning Anna. In 1813 she became engaged again, this time to Ben Lefroy, the son of Jane's late friend Anne Lefroy. Although Ben was a pleasant young man and was in many ways a good match for Anna, he had not yet decided on a career. There was concern that he would be unable to support Anna and a family.

After the engagement was announced, Anna was sent to stay with her grandmother at Chawton for three weeks, suggesting that all was not well at home. The matter was resolved when Ben decided to become a clergyman. He and Anna were married in November 1814 at Steventon Church. James gave away his daughter and Caroline was a bridesmaid.

Anna and Ben went to live in Hendon, then a country village outside London. All the anxiety and friction in the family came to an end with Anna's marriage. There was much relief that Anna was settled and happy. In August 1815, to the delight of her grandmother and aunts, Anna and Ben moved to Alton, a few miles from Chawton.

In 1816 James suffered a financial blow. His brother Henry was declared bankrupt, due to the difficult economic conditions following the Napoleonic Wars. This led to the end of his banking career and the closure of an army agency he had set up in 1801. Henry also lost his position as Receiver General of Oxfordshire, which he had held since 1813. James, who had stood surety for the army agency, lost several hundred pounds.

James suffered a further blow the following year when his uncle James Leigh-Perrot died. As James was sole trustee of his wealthy uncle's estate, on hearing the news he and Mary went to the Leigh-Perrots' home in Berkshire, leaving Caroline with Anna at Alton. James had expected to inherit some money on his uncle's death but was disappointed to discover that his uncle had left his entire estate to his wife for her lifetime, and he was only a reversionary heir. In fact, because James died before Jane Leigh-Perrot, he did not benefit at all from his uncle's will. His interest in the estate eventually passed to his son.

On 24th May 1817, Jane, who had been unwell since the start of the previous year, left her home in Chawton to go to Winchester to be near her doctor. She was accompanied by her sister Cassandra. It is thought that her illness was either Addison's Disease or some form of lymphoma. James and Mary lent them their carriage for the journey, so that they could travel in comfort. Jane was grateful for this kindness. In a letter to a friend, she wrote: 'That's a sort of thing which Mrs J. Austen does in the kindest manner,' and then added 'But still she is in the main not a liberal [generous]-minded Woman.'[22]

Jane and Cassandra stayed in lodgings at 8, College Street, just behind the cathedral. Over the next few weeks James visited his sister several times, although he was himself unwell with a digestive complaint. He and his brother Henry, who had recently been ordained, went to provide spiritual comfort and to administer Holy Communion, while Jane was still able to participate.

On 6th June, Mary went to Winchester to help Cassandra nurse Jane. Apart from one brief return home, Mary remained with her sisters-in-law until Jane died. Jane was grateful to Mary and thanked her for being such a 'kind sister' to her.[23] This suggests that, despite their strained relationship, Jane recognised and appreciated Mary's strengths.

James visited Jane for the last time the day before she died, but he was too unwell to attend her funeral held in Winchester Cathedral on 24th July. His son James Edward went to represent him. As it was not customary for women to attend funerals in the early nineteenth century, Cassandra and Mary remained in College Street. They returned home the next day.

After Jane's death, James wrote a poem about her in which he refers to her 'Fancy [imagination] quick,' her 'wit which never gave offence,' her 'Temper even calm and sweet' and her 'real and genuine worth.' He imagined her being accompanied to heaven by 'seraphs'.[24] This idealised picture of Jane was written in the early days of grief. Jane herself would not have agreed with some of the sentiments expressed.

James outlived his sister by just two and a half years. He had suffered from digestive problems for several years – there is a reference in one of Jane's letters to him being on a restricted diet of bread, meat and water. It was this complaint that had prevented him from attending Jane's funeral.

In September 1817, James had a serious attack of his illness. Mary recorded in her diary, 'Austen seized with pain in his Bowels

& took to his bed.'[25] When he was recovering, James was taken to Worthing for a break to see if a change of air helped but, unfortunately, this brought him no benefit.

James' health deteriorated further over the following year. He had planned to go to Wales to enjoy the scenery of the Wye Valley, but his illness prevented him from travelling that far. He went instead to the New Forest, stopping on the way for one night with his mother at Chawton. This holiday was also cut short because it was too much for him.

In the summer of 1819 James went to London to seek the medical advice of Dr Southey, the brother of the poet Robert Southey. He was accompanied by Mary and Caroline, who wrote in her *Reminiscences*:

> Dr Southey came, and was in regular attendance, and at first he gave encouragement... His visits I think were agreeable to the patient. We stayed in London a fortnight but my father longed to be at home again, and Dr Southey did not urge any further stay. He must have seen he could do no good – so we departed.[26]

Before long James could not go out in a carriage, as he could not bear the motion. He could go no further than the garden, where he sat in a sheltered spot in a bath-chair. As James's condition grew worse, Anna and other members of his family visited, but only one at a time. He also received visits from the Reverend Davis, who had taken over his duties as Rector of Steventon.

James' condition continued to deteriorate throughout the autumn of 1819. He died on 13th December with Mary, James Edward, and Caroline at his side. His funeral, which took place on Saturday 18th December, was attended by his son and his brothers. James was buried in the churchyard of St Nicholas Church, Steventon, where he had been rector for eighteen years. A commemorative tablet was later placed in the north side of the chancel, on which was written the following words and a long poetical tribute by his son.

To the Memory of
The Revd James Austen
Who succeeded his father the Revd George Austen
As Rector of this Parish
And died Dec 13th, 1819 aged 53 years
This monument and the stone which covers his grave in the
churchyard were erected by his widow and children.

The final words of James Edward's tribute read:

Rest earliest friend for thee whose cares are o'er.
Dear as thy presence was, we grieve no more;
Well-taught by thee our hearts can heavenward rise;
We dare not sorrow where a Christian lies.

Shortly after James's death, his wife and two children vacated Steventon Rectory. Henry Austen moved in to hold the living until his nephew William, Edward's son, was old enough to take over. Mary, James Edward, and Caroline moved to Berkshire, where they lived in a series of rented houses in the Newbury area.

When James Edward received his Leigh-Perrot inheritance on the death of his great-aunt in 1836, he could afford to assist his mother financially and rent a comfortable house for her and his sister at Speen. Mary died in August 1843 at the age of 72, from what was described as an 'apoplectic seizure'.[27] She was buried beside her husband in the churchyard of Steventon Church and a memorial tablet was erected in the chancel to their 'good and affectionate mother' by James Edward and Caroline.

## 3

# GEORGE AUSTEN (BROTHER)

George, the second son of George and Cassandra Austen, was born on 26th August 1766 at Deane Rectory. He was privately baptised on the day of his birth and publicly baptised on 29th September. George was weaned early and sent to live for the first year of his life with the same foster mother as his brother James.

Family letters reveal that George's parents were concerned about him as he began to suffer from fits at a very young age. It appears that there was a little improvement in his condition and then he deteriorated further. On 2nd July 1770, in a letter to his sister-in-law Susannah Walter, George Austen wrote: 'God knows only how far it (George's improvement) will come to pass, but from the best judgement I can form at present, we must not be too sanguine on this head; be it as it may, we have this comfort, he cannot be a bad or a wicked child.'[1]

A few months later Cassandra Austen informed Susannah that George 'seems pretty well, tho' he had a fit lately; it was near a twelvemonth since he had one before, so was in hopes they had left him, but must not flatter myself so now.'[2]

As previously mentioned, George suffered from epilepsy, learning difficulties and was probably deaf too. He was cared for by a family who lived in the nearby village of Monk Sherborne. There is no mention of George in Jane's letters, and he is only briefly mentioned in other family records.

George lived with his carers until he died from dropsy in 1838, at the age of 72. He is buried in an unmarked grave in the churchyard of All Saints Church, Monk Sherborne.

*Thomas Knight II, Edward Austen's adoptive father, painted by George Romney.*

*Catherine Knight, Edward Austen's adoptive mother, painted by George Romney.*

*Edward Austen being handed over to his adoptive mother. A silhouette by the London artist William Wellings.*

# 4

# EDWARD AUSTEN

Edward, the third son of George and Cassandra Austen, was born at Deane Rectory on 7th October 1767 and was privately baptised the same day. His public baptism took place on 22nd November. 'Neddy', as he was known as a child, moved to Steventon Rectory the following year with his parents and two older brothers.

Edward enjoyed playing in the rectory garden with his brothers and, like them, was keen on field sports. He was educated by his father alongside his brothers James and Henry, and his father's pupils. Unlike his brothers, however, Edward did not go on to university but followed a different path.

In the summer of 1779, Thomas Knight II, the son of George Austen's wealthy kinsman and benefactor, visited Steventon Rectory with his new wife Catherine. Mrs Knight was the daughter of the Reverend Dr Wadham Knatchbull, Prebendary of Durham and vicar of the parish of Chilham and Molash in Kent. The Knights, who were on their wedding tour, stopped at Steventon so that Catherine could be introduced to her new relatives.

During their stay the Knights took a liking to twelve-year-old Edward, who was a charming, good-natured and cheerful boy. They were so impressed by him that they asked him to accompany them on the rest of their tour. The couple felt such an affection for Edward that the following year they wrote to his father to ask if he could spend the summer with them at Godmersham House in Kent, which Thomas had recently inherited on the death of his father.

At first, George Austen was reluctant to allow his son to go because his was concerned about the impact a long absence would have on his education. Mrs Austen, being a practical and sensible woman, and knowing that Edward was not as academic as his brothers James and Henry, persuaded her husband to change his mind. She realised the potential benefits of agreeing to the request.

Edward set off on the long journey to Godmersham accompanied by Thomas Knight's coachman, who had been sent to fetch him. He rode all the way from Steventon to Godmersham on the pony which the coachman had brought with him, with the coachman on horseback beside him. At the end of the summer, Edward returned home and resumed his education.

Some time before 1783, George and Cassandra Austen received another letter from the Knights, one which would have a lasting impact on the Austen family. It had become apparent that after four years of marriage, the Knights were unlikely to have a child of their own. As the owners of valuable and extensive land and property in Kent and Hampshire, they were anxious to find someone to inherit their estates and wealth, and they had chosen Edward Austen. The Austens granted permission for them to adopt their son, but again, not without some hesitation on the part of George Austen.

The formal adoption of the sixteen-year-old Edward was recorded in a silhouette by the famous artist William Wellings. This shows George handing over his son to Catherine Knight, watched by Thomas Knight and his sister Jane. The Knights also commissioned a portrait of Edward, dressed in a blue jacket and white shirt, to mark the occasion. Edward agreed to adopt the name of Knight when he came into his inheritance, although this did not happen until the death of Mrs Knight in 1812. Years later, Mrs Knight told Edward that ever since his adoption she had felt for him 'the tenderness of a mother'.[1]

Her brother Edward's adoption at the age of sixteen may have given Jane the idea, years later, of creating two characters who were not brought up by their birth parents. In *Mansfield Park,* Fanny Price is brought up by her aunt and uncle, Lord and Lady Bertram, to help her parents who are bringing up a large family in an overcrowded home. Fanny's life, like Edward's, is transformed as a result of being taken into the home of her wealthy relatives.

In *Emma,* Frank Churchill was handed over by his widowed father to be brought up by his wealthy uncle and aunt. When Isabella Knightley comments that 'There is something so shocking in a child's being taken away from his parents' natural home,' was she voicing Jane Austen's opinion of her brother's adoption, even though Edward's experience was a happy one?

The Knights sent Edward on a Grand Tour of Europe to see the classical sights in 1786. This was a fashionable way for the sons of the English upper class to finish their education. Edward spent one year in Switzerland and then went to Dresden, where he was received at the Court of Saxony. Edward met many other young aristocrats on his tour, which concluded with a visit to Rome.

While he was there, a full-length portrait was painted of Edward, which shows a tall, rosy-faced, handsome young man with powdered hair and wearing fashionable clothes. To show that he had seen the classical sights, the artist included part of a marble frieze and a Corinthian capital in the picture. Edward returned home in 1788, when he settled down to learn the skills needed to manage the Knights' properties and estates that he would eventually inherit.

Among Edward's neighbours at Godmersham were Sir Brook Bridges, 3rd Baronet, and his wife Fanny, who lived at Goodnestone Park, near Wingham. Edward met and fell in love with their daughter Elizabeth, who was six years younger than him. Elizabeth had attended an exclusive boarding school known as the 'Ladies' Eton' in Queen Square, Bloomsbury.

The engagement of Edward and Elizabeth was announced in March 1791. In a letter to a relative informing her of the engagement, Lady Bridges wrote:

> We had for some time observed a great attachment between Mr Austin (sic) (Mr Knight's Relation) and our dear Elizth; and Mr Knight has, in the handsomest manner, declared his entire approbation of it (their engagement); but as they are both very young, he wish't it not to take place immediately, and as it will not suit him to give up much at present, their Income will be small, and they must be contented to live in the Country, which I think will be no hardship to either party, as they have no high Ideas, and it is a greater satisfaction to us than if she was to be thrown upon the world in a higher sphere, young and inexperienced as she is. He is a very sensible, amiable young man, and I trust and hope there is every prospect of Happiness to all parties in their union.[2]

A miniature portrait of Elizabeth by the famous miniaturist Richard Cosway shows that she was a very pretty, fair-skinned young lady with large eyes, a clear complexion, and a lot of wavy hair. The young couple were married in December 1791 at Godmersham, in a double ceremony with Elizabeth's sister Sophia, who married William Deedes of Sandling, near Maidstone.

After their wedding, Edward and his bride went to live at Rowling, a small Georgian house belonging to Elizabeth's parents on their estate at Goodnestone. Edward and Elizabeth's first child, Frances, always known as Fanny, was born at Rowling in January 1793. She was followed rapidly by Edward, George, and Henry.

Both of Edward's sisters visited him, Elizabeth, and their children at Rowling. When Jane visited in September 1796, she complained in a letter to Cassandra about the 'dreadful hot weather' in Kent which 'keeps one in a continual state of Inelegance'.[3] She went to Goodnestone to dine with Elizabeth's family. After dinner and some country dancing, Jane and Elizabeth walked home 'under the shade of two Umbrellas'.[4]

In 1794, Edward's adoptive father Thomas Knight died. The whole of the Knight estates in Kent and Hampshire became Edward's, subject to the life interest of Mrs Knight. Three years later, Mrs Knight handed over the estates to Edward, retaining an annual income of £2,000. She went to live in Canterbury in a house named 'White Friars'.

Initially, Edward was worried about taking over the estates. He expressed his concerns in a letter to Mrs Knight:

> I am confident we should never be happy at Godmersham whilst you were living at a smaller and less comfortable

> House – or in reflecting that you had quitted your own favourite Mansion, where I have so often heard you say your whole Happiness was center'd, and had retired to a residence and style of Living to which you have been ever unaccustomed, and this to enrich us.[5]

Mrs Knight wrote a very affectionate reply:

> If anything were wanted, my dearest Edward, to confirm my resolution concerning the plan I propose executing, your Letter would have that effect; it is impossible for any person to express their gratitude and affection in terms more pleasing than you have chosen, and from the bottom of my heart I believe you to be perfectly sincere when you assure me that your happiness is best secured by seeing me in the full enjoyment of every thing that can contribute to my ease and comfort, and that happiness, my dear Edward, will be yours by acceding to my wishes... Many circumstances attached to large landed Possessions, highly gratifying to a Man, are entirely lost on me at present; but when I see you in the enjoyment of them, I shall, if possible, feel my gratitude to my beloved Husband redoubled, for having placed in my hands the power of bestowing happiness on one so very dear to me.[6]

Soon after this exchange of letters, Edward, Elizabeth, and their four children moved into Godmersham House. It was a grand Palladian style house with a beautiful classical interior, which had been built by Thomas Knight I in 1732. The following description of Godmersham House and park gives some idea of the vast land and property Edward inherited in Kent.

> It lies in the beautiful Stour valley, a situation healthy and pleasant to the extreme, the River Stour glides through it from Ashford, in its course towards Canterbury; Godmersham House and park are the principal objects in it, both elegant and beautiful, the Ashford high road encircles the east side of the park, along which there is a sunk [fence], which affords an uninterrupted view of the whole of it, and adds greatly to the beauty of this elegant scene, and leads through the village of Godmersham close to it, the whole village which contains about twenty houses, belongs to Mrs Knight, excepting one house, as does the greatest part of the parish, excepting the lands belonging to the dean and chapter of Canterbury. There are about twenty more houses in the parish, and about two hundred and forty inhabitants in all. The church, and vicarage, a neat dwelling pleasantly situated, stand at a small distance from the village, on the left side of the road, with the antient [sic] manor-house near the former, close to the bank of the river; the meadows in the vale are exceeding fertile, the uplands are chalk, with some gravel among them, the hills rise high on each side, those on the west being the sheep walks belonging to Godmersham-house, the summits of which are finely cloathed [sic] with wood, at proper intervals; the opposite ones are the high range of unenclosed pasture downs of Wye and Brabourne.[7]

Edward also inherited the whole of the village of Steventon in Hampshire and the surrounding land, as well as Chawton House, which was always referred to as Chawton Great House by the Austens. It was a Tudor mansion, with mullioned windows and an impressive porch, situated on rising ground in the village of Chawton, overlooking the grey stone church of St Nicholas. Being a practical man with a good head for business, Edward was ideally suited to the responsibilities he was taking on as the owner of two large country houses and vast tracts of land.

Edward kept in close contact with his birth family, despite now moving in a higher social sphere than them. It gave him pleasure to share his great good fortune with them. The Austens always received a warm welcome at Godmersham House, and Edward and Elizabeth made sure they enjoyed their stay.

In August 1798, George and Cassandra Austen and their two daughters made their first visit to Godmersham. Edward proudly showed his family his new home and its landscaped grounds, which included two summerhouses, one in the form of a Greek temple and the other a Gothic hermitage. There was also a river walk and bathing house. A path led through the park to the little church of St Lawrence the Martyr. As a fellow farmer, George Austen took a great interest in Edward's sheep and pigs.

Elizabeth gave birth to her fifth baby, a boy named William, while the Austens were at Godmersham. When her parents and Jane left for home on 24th October, Cassandra stayed behind to help as Elizabeth was still recovering from her confinement.

After their first visit to Godmersham, Jane and Cassandra always went there separately. Cassandra's visits, like her first one, usually coincided with Elizabeth's confinements so that she was at hand to help. Cassandra became close to Elizabeth, which was natural as Edward, who resembled her physically, was Cassandra's favourite brother.

In 1799, Edward became unwell, probably with gout, and on 16th May he set off for Bath, the famous health spa, to take the waters in the hope of a cure. He was accompanied by Elizabeth, their two eldest children Fanny and Edward, Mrs Austen, and Jane. They arrived in Bath on the wet afternoon of the following day and all they could see from their carriage were umbrellas. As soon as they arrived Jane wrote to her sister to report on their journey, which 'went off exceedingly well,' and to describe their lodgings at 13, Queen Square, near the famous Royal Crescent:

> We are exceedingly pleased with the House ... I like our situation very much ... the prospect from the Drawing room window at which I now write, is rather picturesque, as it commands a perspective view of the left side of Brock Street, broken by three Lombardy Poplars, in the Garden of the last house in Queen's Parade.[8]

The arrival of Edward and Elizabeth Austen from Godmersham House in Kent and their relatives would have been announced in the list of arrivals published in Bath newspapers and recorded in the visitors' books at the various venues they visited.

While Edward took the waters and consulted doctors the rest of the party enjoyed the pleasures and entertainments on offer, including the theatre, a concert, a gala at Sydney Gardens to honour the king's birthday, and shopping in the fashionable emporia of Milsom Street. Jane particularly enjoyed the gala and fireworks, which she described to Cassandra as 'really beautiful, & surpassing my expectation; – the illuminations too were very pretty.'[9]

The Austens also joined James and Jane Leigh-Perrot at various functions and gatherings and drank tea with them at their home. In a letter to her sister dated 2nd June, Jane wrote: 'He [Edward] was better yesterday than he had been for two or three days before... He drinks at the Hetling Pump, is to bathe tomorrow, & try Electricity on Tuesday.'[10]

The Austens returned home on 26th June after an enjoyable stay and with Edward's health restored. They took with them two black carriage horses he bought while in Bath.

Edward and Elizabeth, like other country house owners and their wives, worked in partnership. Edward was responsible for looking after Godmersham House and the surrounding estates, and ensuring that his Hampshire properties and estates were well cared for by his estate manager in his absence. Being a practical man, Edward was ideally suited to the responsibilities of a country house owner. Although he had farm bailiffs to help him, he took an active part in hay-making, pig-breeding, poultry-keeping and other aspects of farming. Being an easy-going and affable man, he got on well with people he did business with. His kindness and generosity towards his employees, tenants, and the local villagers made him popular.

Like many country house owners Edward carried out improvements to his houses and parkland. He used his knowledge of classical architecture and landscapes acquired on the Grand Tour when making improvements. To add to his many responsibilities, Edward was also a magistrate, leader of the local militia during the Napoleonic Wars and High Sheriff of Kent. As a magistrate, he made frequent trips to Canterbury to visit the county bench and to inspect the jail. Jane accompanied him on one such visit and, in a letter to Cassandra, she wrote: 'He went to inspect the Gaol, as a visiting Magistrate, & took me with him. – I was gratified – & went through all the feelings which People must go through I think in visiting such a Building.'[11]

Elizabeth Austen was a capable and energetic woman who skilfully performed the many tasks involved in running a large country house. According to Anna Austen she was 'a very lovely woman, highly educated... Her tastes were domestic; her affections strong, though exclusive, and her temper calculated to make Husband and children happy in their home'[12] Her responsibilities included running the household, which involved the supervision of a large team of servants, managing a large household budget, overseeing the care of her children and being involved in their early education, as well as being a hostess to guests and visitors. Godmersham House was always busy. In Jane's words, 'In this House there is a constant succession of small events, somebody is always going or coming.'[13] Some of these people were members of Edward's and Elizabeth's large social circle making social calls.

One of Elizabeth's most onerous tasks was hosting social events, such as dinners and house parties. The aristocracy entertained on a lavish scale and Elizabeth had to plan events, supervise the preparations, and receive and entertain guests. She also put on four social events a year for her servants, estate workers and tenants, as well as performing charity work in the local community.

Elizabeth, who endured eleven pregnancies and confinements in less than sixteen years, was a loving and diligent mother. As her daughter Fanny's diary reveals, she managed to find time to take part in her children's games and activities. As well as this heavy workload, Elizabeth supported Edward in his various roles and was probably involved in the improvements to Godmersham House and estate. She also involved her daughters in her charity work in the local community.

Edward found time to be with his children. Jane noted the charming way her brother had with children. His nephew James

Edward remembered that he possessed 'a spirit of fun and liveliness, which made him especially delightful to all young people.' He described his uncle as a 'very amiable man, kind and indulgent to all connected with him.'[14]

When he was not fulfilling his duties as a country house owner Edward participated in country sports, often with any of his brothers who were staying at Godmersham. Edward brought his sons up to enjoy hunting, shooting, and fishing. When Edward's son returned from a trip to Scotland with his Uncle Henry in 1813, Jane noted that he did not appear to have enjoyed the Scottish scenery as much as his uncle. In a letter to Cassandra, she wrote: 'Edward is no Enthusiast in the beauties of Nature. His Enthusiasm is for the Sports of the field only ... we must forgive his thinking more of Growse [sic] & Partridges than Lakes and Mountains.'[15] Edward also played cricket with his sons, which was becoming a popular sport.

Jane's letters to her sister provide a fascinating insight into life at Godmersham. She loved staying there, particularly enjoying the luxurious surroundings, fine food, the social events, and trips to Canterbury. Jane described Kent as 'the only place for happiness. Everybody is rich there,' which she compared to Hampshire 'where People get so horridly poor and economical.'[16]

In her letters Jane made many observations about the people she met in Kent. She was always on the lookout for raw material for her writing. Her visits there gave her an insight into life in a grand country house, which was particularly useful when writing *Mansfield Park*. When she went to Godmersham, Jane took whichever novel she was writing with her. According to her niece Marianne, Jane

> … would sit quietly working [doing needlework] beside the fire in the library, saying nothing for a good while, and then would suddenly burst out laughing, jump up and run across the room to a table where pens and paper were lying, write something down, and then come back to the fire and go on quietly working as before.[17]

Without her brother's great good luck in being adopted by Thomas and Catherine Knight and his hospitality, Jane would have been deprived of the valuable source of material which Godmersham provided.

Edward was very generous with his time. In September 1805 he, Elizabeth and Fanny went on holiday to Sussex with his mother and sisters. They went first to Battle and then on to Worthing where, according to Fanny's diary, they enjoyed long walks and swimming in the sea. When Chawton Great House was vacant between lettings, Edward held family gatherings there. At the first of these, in September 1807, Edward and his family were joined by his mother and sisters, James, Mary and their children. This was the first time that Edward's children had been to the house and they had great fun exploring it. In a letter to her former governess Fanny wrote:

> This is a fine large old house, built long before Queen Elizabeth I believe, & here are such a number of old irregular passages … that it is very entertaining to explore them, & often when I think myself miles away from one part of the house I find a passage or entrance close to it, & I don't know when I shall be quite mistress of all the intricate, & different ways.[18]

Fanny was intrigued by all the portraits of 'the Knights and all the old families that have possessed the estate.' She also liked the trees surrounding the house which made it 'pretty'.[19] The house party lasted ten days.

It may have been during this visit that Edward's niece Anna got to know him well enough to be able to recall later that his 'disposition' was 'sweet and yielding' and that 'his whole character [was] so opposed to contention of every kind that he could never have been, under any circumstances, an irritable or discontented man.'[20] Caroline Austen's memories of Edward telling 'amusing stories'[21] to his nephew and nieces probably also date back to this time.

At the end of September 1808 Cassandra went to Godmersham to attend her sister-in-law Elizabeth during her eleventh confinement, as she had with previous ones, and to help to run the house and care for the children while she recovered. When Cassandra arrived on 28th September the baby, Brook John, had already been born. Cassandra wrote home to announce the baby's arrival and to report that Elizabeth and her baby were both well. Elizabeth continued to make a good recovery so it was a great shock when, on 10th October, she suddenly became ill and died. Her daughter Fanny described what happened in her diary: 'Oh! The miserable events of this day! My mother, my beloved mother torn from us! After eating a hearty dinner, she was taken violently ill and expired (may God have mercy upon us) after half an hour!!!!'[22]

Mrs Austen, Jane and Martha were informed of the tragedy by James and Mary. This was followed by a detailed letter from Cassandra, to which Jane replied:

> We have felt, we do feel for you all – as you will not need to be told – for you, for Fanny, for Henry [Bridges], for Lady Bridges &

> for dearest Edward, whose loss and whose sufferings seem to make those of every other person nothing. – God be praised! that you can say what you do of him – that he has a religious Mind to bear him up, & a Disposition that will gradually lead him to comfort.[23]

She concluded by saying, 'Tell Edward that we feel for him & pray for him!'[24]

Jane was worried about Edward and his motherless children. She was particularly concerned about the effect of her mother's death on Fanny. As the eldest daughter, she would have to support her father and take on her mother's role as mistress of a grand country house at the age of sixteen, as well as helping to care for her ten younger siblings. The death of her mother was the end of Fanny's childhood.

Not long after Elizabeth's death, Edward offered his mother, sisters, and Martha Lloyd a new home. Frank Austen and his wife Mary had recently moved to Alton, and they had been considering a move themselves. Edward offered them the choice of two cottages – one in Wye close to Godmersham and the other was Chawton Cottage, on his Hampshire estate. They chose the latter. Jane's excitement at moving back to her native county is evident in her letters to her sister. In a letter dated 27th-28th December 1808, she wrote: 'Yes, yes we *will* have a Pianoforte, as good a one as can be got for 30 Guineas – & I will practise country dances, that we may have some amusement for our nephews & nieces, when we have the pleasure of their company.'[25]

Chawton Cottage, which had previously been the home of Edward's estate manager, was an L-shaped, two-storey, brick building, with a tiled roof and sash windows. Despite its name, it was quite a large house with plenty of space for the Austens,

Martha and their servants. It was situated on a corner plot in the village of Chawton, within walking distance of Chawton Great House. Edward paid for a few alterations and improvements to make 'The Cottage,' as it was called, a comfortable home, and provided a donkey carriage that was kept in a small outhouse as transport for his elderly mother.

The move to Chawton was very important for Jane. After eight unsettled years in Bath and Southampton, during which she had written very little, her new permanent home in her beloved Hampshire countryside gave her the peace and stability she needed to resume writing. It was here that she revised her first three novels and wrote three more. It was Edward's generous gift of Chawton Cottage which enabled this to happen.

Edward, like the rest of the Austen family, was proud of Jane's literary achievements. Jane noted the opinions of her family and which of her novels they each liked best. Edward particularly liked *Mansfield Park,* although he thought it was not so clever as *Pride and Prejudice.*[26] He pointed out a blunder Jane made in *Emma.* Referring to the strawberry picking party at Donwell Abbey he said: 'Jane, I wish you would tell me where you get those apple-trees of yours that come into bloom in July.[27]

Catherine Knight, Edward's adoptive mother, died in October 1812. Having become the sole owner of the Knight estates and properties, Edward adopted the coat of arms and surname of Knight. Fanny was not at all happy about the name change and wrote indignantly in her diary: 'Papa changed his name … in compliance with the will of the late Mr Knight, and we are therefore all Knights instead of dear old Austens. How I hate it!!!'[28] Jane's response to the name change was 'I must learn to make a better K.'[29]

When his tenants moved out of Chawton Great House in 1812, Edward began to use it as a second home for his family. In April of the following year, Edward and his entire household moved into Chawton Great House while Godmersham House was redecorated. There was much to-ing and fro-ing between the house and Chawton Cottage. In a letter to Frank, written during Edward's stay, Jane wrote: 'We go on in the most comfortable way, very frequently dining together, & always meeting in some part of every day. – Edward is very well & enjoys himself as thoroughly as any Hampshire-born Austen can desire. Chawton is not thrown away upon him![30]

During her stay at Chawton, Fanny's already close relationship with her Aunt Jane became closer still. Fanny recorded in her diary that she and Jane spent 'delicious times together'.[31] It was good for Fanny as she grew into a young woman to have an affectionate, supportive mother figure to turn to, and Jane must have been a great help to Edward. After Fanny returned home, she and Jane began to write letters to each other.

The visit to Chawton lasted longer than planned, because it took so long for the paint to dry at Godmersham House. When Edward and his household finally left in September, he went with three of his daughters and Jane to visit his brother Henry in London. Jane was amused at the sight of the party setting off for Kent in a variety of vehicles. In a letter to Frank, she wrote: 'It puts me in mind of the account of St Paul's Shipwreck, where all are said by different means to reach the Shore in safety.'[32]

Edward often paid visits to Henry in London and that of September 1813 was typical. Henry had just moved into rooms above his business in Henrietta Street, Covent Garden. Henry's guests had a long list of places to see and things to do in London, including a visit to the dentist for the three young ladies. Henry took them to the theatre several times and Jane, Edward and his daughters went shopping. At Wedgwood's shop Edward and Fanny ordered a purple and gold dinner service decorated with the Knight family crest.

In the summer of 1814, peace celebrations were held across the country to mark the end of the war with France. Edward and his family were staying at Chawton Great House at the time and Fanny took her grandmother to see the illuminations in Alton. She then went with her father to London, to join Henry and Cassandra and take part in the celebrations there. They watched a parade of sovereigns and generals of Britain's allies, who were on a state visit to London.

In the autumn of that year, a claim was made on Edward's Hampshire estate by some heirs at law (heirs by right of blood) of the Knight family. The plaintiffs were Mr and Miss Hinton of Chawton Lodge and James Baverstock, a brewer who lived in Alton. Edward risked losing a considerable amount of property, including Chawton Cottage, and two thirds of his annual income.[33] Unsurprisingly, this caused much anxiety to the Knight and Austen families, and it took several years to resolve.

Sometimes Edward and one or two of his children stayed at Chawton Cottage, where they were always welcome visitors. In May 1816, when Jane was very unwell, Edward and Fanny stayed at the cottage for three weeks. This visit was good for both Jane and Cassandra, who was running the household with Martha's help, as well as caring for her elderly mother and Jane. They helped to keep Jane's spirits up when her health was failing, and Cassandra was always pleased to spend time with her favourite brother.

In July 1817, when Jane was critically ill in Winchester, Edward went to Chawton Cottage to be with his mother. There is no record of him visiting Jane at this time, but he was one of the mourners at her funeral, which took place in Winchester Cathedral on 24th July. When Edward, often with one of his children, visited his mother, Cassandra, and Martha after Jane's death, they were aware of the sad atmosphere. Chawton Cottage was not the same without Jane.

In April 1818, the lawsuit against Edward which had been dragging on for several years was finally concluded when Edward paid the significant sum of £15,000 to the other party. A large area of Chawton Park wood was cut down and the timber sold to raise this sum.[34] It was a great relief when this matter was finally settled.

All of Edward's children moved away from Godmersham except for Marianne, who became mistress of the house when in 1820 Fanny became the second wife of Sir Edward Knatchbull of Merstham-le-Hatch in Kent.

Three of Edward's sons went to Oxford University and one to Cambridge. The eldest, Edward, took up residence at Chawton Great House in 1826, as caretaker for his father, and on his father's death inherited all the Knight properties and estates. He remained at Chawton. The remaining brothers all had professional careers. Two of them, William and Charles, entered the Church. William became Rector of Steventon and Charles became Curate of Chawton. All the brothers, except Charles, married. Four of Edward's daughters made good marriages. Marianne remained at Godmersham and looked after her father. She became known to her many nephews and nieces as 'Aunt May'.

By 1828 Cassandra was the sole occupant of Chawton Cottage, apart from her servants. Her mother had died the year before and Martha had recently moved out on becoming Frank Austen's second wife. Cassandra was never short of company, however, as her nephews Edward and William Knight and their families and her nephew Charles all lived nearby. It was also easier for Cassandra to visit Edward at Godmersham, now that she no longer had to look after her mother.

In March 1845, Cassandra suffered a stroke while staying at her brother Frank's house near Portsmouth. She died a few days later, on 22nd March. Her body was taken back to her home in Chawton where she was laid to rest beside her mother in the churchyard of St Nicholas Church. It seems that Edward did not attend his sister's funeral, as his name does not appear on a list of attendees recorded in a letter sent by James Edward to his sister Anna.[35]

On 19th November 1852, Edward died unexpectedly, but peacefully. There was no indication on the previous day that there was anything wrong with him. Early in the morning of the 19th Edward asked his servant to leave him as he wanted to sleep longer. The servant returned later to find that he had died in his sleep. On hearing of his death, one of Edward's relations thought it 'a characteristic end of a prosperous and placid life ... he will certainly leave on the minds of all who knew him an image of Gentleness and quiet Cheerfulness of no ordinary degree.'[36]

Edward was buried beside his wife in the church of St Lawrence the Martyr, Godmersham. His children erected a tablet above his burial place bearing the following inscription:

> In the family vault beneath are deposited the remains of Edward Knight of Godmersham Park in this parish and of Chawton House

> in the county of Southampton, Esq., who departed this life Nov. 19th 1852, in the 86th year of his age. Mr Knight, whose paternal name was Austen, succeeded by will in 1794 to the estates of his cousin Thomas Knight Esq. and on the death of his widow in 1812, assumed the name and arms of Knight.

The inscription ends with some appropriate lines from Ecclesiastes: 'Living peaceably in his habitation he was honoured in his generation. A merciful man, whose righteousness shall not be forgotten.'

After her father's death, Marianne left Godmersham House and went to live firstly with her brother Charles at Chawton, and then with her brother Brook at Bentley in Hampshire. Godmersham House was sold by Edward's eldest son and heir in 1874.

5

# HENRY AUSTEN

Henry Thomas was born at Steventon Rectory on 8th June 1771. He was privately baptised on the day he was born and publicly baptised on 12th July. In a letter to Susannah Walter, written when Henry was eighteen months old, Mrs Austen wrote: 'My little boy is come home from Nurse, and a fine, stout little fellow he is, and can run anywhere…'[1] In another letter written three years later, his mother informed Susannah:

> Henry has been in Breeches some months, and thinks himself near as good a man as his Brother Neddy, indeed no-one would Judge by their looks that there was above three years and a half difference in their ages, one is so little and the other so great.[2]

Once he was able to read and write, Henry was taught by his father. Like James he was naturally academic, and in the opinion of his father was the most talented of his sons. Henry, like his older brothers, enjoyed outdoor pursuits and developed a love of field sports as a child.

When they were children, Henry was close to his sister Jane, whom he resembled physically and temperamentally, and he was her favourite brother. Their closeness continued into adult life; their niece Caroline described Henry as Jane's 'especial pride and delight'.[3]

Henry was an outgoing and happy child. He took an active part in the family theatricals organised by James and his cousin Eliza, who became close to Henry when she and her mother stayed at the rectory. At the age of seventeen Henry was taller than his father and was considered the most handsome of the Austen brothers. He had the same hazel-coloured eyes as his father and his sister Jane, and the same long sharp nose as his mother, which she described as 'aristocratic'.

In July 1788, Henry followed his brother James to St John's College, Oxford on a Founder's Kin Scholarship. Their cousin Eliza visited James and Henry soon after the latter's arrival at Oxford. In a letter to her cousin Philadelphia Walter, Eliza wrote: 'I do not think You would know Henry with his Hair powdered & dressed in a very ton-ish [fashionable] style; besides he is at present taller than his Father.'[4]

As well as studying for his Bachelor of Arts degree, Henry helped James by writing some amusing essays for *The Loiterer.* These included an essay warning readers of the dangers of indulging too much in romantic ideas and advising them not to copy the emotional heroines of the popular sentimental novels. This was a theme which Jane took up in *Love and Freindship* [sic], an early piece of writing, and her novel *Sense and Sensibility.*

The extrovert and happy disposition Henry displayed as a child continued into adulthood. According to his niece Anna:

> For the most part, he was greatly admired. Brilliant in conversation he was, and like his father, blessed with a hopefulness of temper which, in adapting itself to all circumstances, even the most adverse, served to create a perpetual sunshine.[5]

Henry was also very amusing. Jane described a letter she had received from him as 'most affectionate & kind as well as entertaining' and added 'there is no merit to him in that, he cannot help being amusing.'[6]

Despite these positive attributes Henry was the least stable of the Austen brothers. His nephew James Edward pointed out that 'He was a very entertaining companion, but had perhaps less steadiness of purpose, certainly less success in life, than his brothers.[7]

Other adjectives which could be used to describe this complex man include mercurial, erratic, impulsive, impetuous, and impatient. To illustrate the latter characteristic, Henry's great-nephew Lord Brabourne related the following story about him in the introduction to his edition of the letters of Jane Austen:

> He is said to have been driving on one occasion with a relation in one of the rough country lanes near Steventon, when the pace at which the post-chaise was advancing did not satisfy his eager temperament. Putting his head out of the window, he cried out to the postillion; 'Get on, boy! get on, will you.' The 'boy' turned round in his saddle, and replied: 'I do get on sir, where I can!' 'You stupid fellow!' was the rejoinder. 'Any fool can do that. I want you to get on where you can't![8]

In 1793 Henry joined the Oxfordshire Militia. He had originally intended to follow his father and brother into the church, but he was not yet old enough to be ordained. He decided instead to serve his country. France had recently declared war on Great Britain and many young men were joining up to fight. The role of the Militia, which only existed during wartime, was to defend the country when the regular army was abroad. Each county had to provide a certain number of officers and men to serve in it. The Oxfordshire Militia was based in East Anglia to protect the exposed eastern coastline of England. Henry, who joined as a Lieutenant, enjoyed the regimental social life. Henry combined this role with his Fellowship of St John's College. In 1796 he was awarded his M.A. and in the following year was promoted to Captain, Adjutant and Paymaster.

In 1795, Henry proposed to his widowed cousin Eliza. He had known Eliza, who was ten years his senior, since childhood when she and her mother often stayed at Steventon Rectory. In 1787 Henry visited his Aunt Philadelphia, Eliza, and her son Hastings when they were staying in London. The mutual attraction between Henry and Eliza dated back to this visit. At that time, Eliza was married to Jean-Francois, Comte de Feuillide, a wealthy French soldier with estates in south-west France. In 1794, the Comte was executed during la Terreur in France, leaving Eliza free to marry again.

Despite her attraction to and affection for Henry, Eliza turned down his proposal because she did not want to lose her freedom. Not long afterwards, on the rebound from Eliza's rejection, Henry became engaged to Mary Pearson. Mary was the daughter of Sir Richard Pearson, R.N., who was an officer of

Greenwich Hospital for Seamen. A miniature portrait of Mary, which Henry showed his parents, revealed that she was a 'very pretty' young lady.[9]

The engagement did not last long, however; Mary soon broke it off, as Eliza explained in a letter to her cousin Philadelphia.

> Our Cousin Henry Austen has been in Town, he looks thin & ill – I hear his late intended is a most intolerable Flirt, and reckoned to give herself great Airs – The person who mentioned this to me says She is a pretty wicked looking Girl with bright Black Eyes which pierce thro' & thro'. No wonder the poor young Man's heart could not withstand them.[10]

For the next two years Henry pursued Eliza until she finally agreed to marry him. Henry's parents were worried because of his instability, and they feared that marriage to his pleasure-loving cousin, who had in her youth enjoyed high society in Paris and London, would not remedy this.

On 28th December 1797 Eliza wrote a letter to her godfather Warren Hastings, the former Governor-General of Bengal, announcing her engagement:

> I have consented to an Union with my Cousin Captn. Austen who has the honour of being known to You. – He has been for some time in Possession of a comfortable Income, and the excellence of his Heart, Temper, & Understanding, together with his steady attachment to me, his Affection for my little Boy, and disinterested concurrence in the disposal of my Property, in favour of this latter, have at length induced me to an acquiescence which I have withheld for more than two years.[11]

Henry and Eliza were married three days after this letter was written, in Marylebone parish church. In another letter to her cousin Philadelphia, Eliza wrote:

> Unmixed Felicity is certainly not the Produce of this World, and like other People I shall probably meet with many unpleasant and untoward circumstances but all the Comfort which can result from the tender Affection and Society of a Being who is possessed of an excellent Heart, Understanding and Temper I have at least ensured – to say nothing of the pleasure of having my own way in everything, for Henry well knows that I have not been much accustomed to controul [sic] and should probably behave rather awkwardly under it, and therefore like a wise Man he has no will but mine, which to be sure some people would call spoiling me, but I know it is the best way of managing me.[12]

For the next four years Eliza and her son Hastings followed Henry around the country to wherever the Oxfordshire Militia took him. In January 1801, Henry resigned his army commission and started a new career as a banker and army agent for the sale and purchase of commissions. He set up a business with his army friend Henry Maunde, based in offices in Cleveland Court, close to St James's Palace. Another army friend, James Tilson, later joined them and they became Austen, Maunde and Tilson. Henry also became an associate of the banking firm Austen, Gray and Vincent in Alton, Hampshire. Eliza's son Hastings, who had never enjoyed good health, died in the autumn of 1801 at the age of fifteen.

That year Henry and Eliza moved into a house in Upper Berkeley Street, Portman Square where, according to their cousin

Philadelphia Walter, they lived comfortably with a French cook, a French housekeeper and a new carriage. They were financially well-off as Eliza had a £10,000 trust fund which had been given to her by her godfather, and Henry's businesses were doing well. They soon became part of a large social circle, which included refugees who had fled to London during the French Revolution, and Henry's business colleagues and their wives.

After the Peace of Amiens, which was signed in March 1802, hostilities between Great Britain and France came (temporarily) to an end. The following year Henry and Eliza travelled to France to try to reclaim the confiscated property of Eliza's first husband. They failed to do this because while they were in France Napoleon broke the terms of the peace treaty and hostilities were resumed. Orders were given that all British nationals should be arrested and detained. Henry and Eliza only managed to escape because Eliza's excellent French enabled them to pose as a French couple.

In 1804, Henry and Eliza moved home to 16, Michael's Place, Brompton. That summer they went on holiday to Lyme Regis with his parents and sisters. It is believed that they stayed at Pyne House in Broad Street. They enjoyed the seaside and walks in the countryside around Lyme. They may have visited the villages of Charmouth, Uplyme and Pinny, which appear in Jane's novel *Persuasion*. In September, Henry, Eliza and Cassandra moved on to Weymouth, which they found a dull and disappointing place.

When his father died in January 1805, Henry was at Godmersham visiting Edward and his family. On hearing the news of their father's death Henry hurried to Bath to be with his mother and sisters, and he was one of the brothers who offered their mother an annual sum of money to make up for her loss of income.

Henry and Eliza moved again in 1809 to fashionable Sloane Street, Chelsea, where Jane and Cassandra visited them frequently. They always went separately because their mother did not like both daughters to be away from home at the same time. Henry and Eliza enjoyed taking their guests to the theatre and art galleries, and for carriage rides around the streets of the capital, which Jane particularly enjoyed.

In 1811 Jane stayed with Henry and Eliza when she was checking the proofs of *Sense and Sensibility*, the first of her novels to be published. It was easier for her to do this in London, where her publishers were based. Henry conducted all the business negotiations for this and the other three of Jane's novels published in her lifetime. He also chased the publishers and printers when necessary.

During this visit Henry and Eliza held a party to which eighty guests were invited. Jane became involved in the preparations and in a letter written the day after the party, she described it to Cassandra:

> The rooms were dressed up with flowers &c, & looked very pretty... The Music was extremely good... Between the Songs were Lessons on the Harp, or Harp & Piano Forte together – & the Harp Player was Wiepart, whose name seems famous, tho' new to me. – There was one female singer, a short Miss Davis all in blue ... whose voice was said to be very fine indeed; & all the Performers gave great satisfaction by doing what they were paid for, & giving themselves no airs.[13]

Two days later a report of the party appeared in the *Morning Chronicle*.

Not long after the party Eliza became ill. It is thought that she may have had breast cancer, the disease which killed her mother. In a letter to a friend dated 16th February 1813 Jane wrote: 'We have no late account from Sloane Street, & therefore conclude that everything is going on in one regular progress, without any striking change.[14]

In April, Jane went to London to help nurse her sister-in-law in her final days. She died on 25th April at the age of fifty-one and was buried in the churchyard of Hampstead parish church, in the same grave as her mother and son. The inscription on her gravestone describes her as 'a woman of brilliant, generous and cultivated mind'.[15]

Jane returned to London the following month to help Henry wind up his wife's affairs. This was the last time she stayed at the house in Sloane Street, as Henry was about to move to rooms above his bank in Henrietta Street, Covent Garden.

Henry appeared to recover quickly from the loss of his wife. It was a relief to his family to see him getting on with his life. Jane wrote to her brother Frank in July 1813:

> Upon the whole his Spirits are very much recovered. – If I may so express myself, his Mind is not a Mind for affliction. He is too Busy, too active, too sanguine, – Sincerely as he was attached to poor Eliza moreover, & excellently as he behaved to her, he was always so used to be away from her at times, that her Loss is not felt as that of many a beloved Wife might be, especially when all the circumstances of her long & dreadful Illness are taken into the account. – He very long knew that she must die, & it was indeed a release at last.[16]

In the late summer of 1813, Henry went to Scotland accompanied by his young nephew Edward Knight. In a letter to her brother

Frank dated 25th September Jane wrote: 'I wish he had had more time & could have gone farther north, & deviated to the Lakes in his way back … & he met with Scenes of higher Beauty in Roxburghshire than I had supposed the South of Scotland possessed.'[17]

Edward did not enjoy the scenery as much as his uncle. According to Jane, he was 'no Enthusiast in the beauties of Nature. His Enthusiasm is for the Sports of the field only.'[18]

While he was in Scotland, Henry overheard a conversation between Lady Robert Kerr and another lady in which his sister's novel *Pride and Prejudice* was warmly praised. Due to what Jane described as his 'Brotherly vanity and Love'[19] Henry immediately told the ladies that his sister was the novel's author. At that time, only a few family members knew this and Jane had hoped to keep it that way. Although she forgave Henry, Jane was grateful to those who kept her secret.

Jane stayed at Henry's new home for the first time in September 1813. She wrote to Cassandra, 'This house looks very nice. It seems like Sloane Street moved here.[20]

Edward and three of his daughters were there, too. Henry, as usual, made sure his guests had a good time by taking them to the theatre and other places of interest.

In March 1814, Henry collected Jane from Chawton in his curricle to take her to London. On the long journey he read the proofs of *Mansfield Park* and delighted Jane with his praise and enthusiasm for it.

Three months later, Henry moved back to Chelsea. That summer, peace celebrations across the country marked the end of the war with France. Cassandra, Edward and his daughter Fanny joined Henry to take part in the celebrations in the capital. Henry clearly knew some influential people in London, as he was invited to a celebration ball at White's, the private gentleman's club in Burlington House, Piccadilly, on 21st June. Henry's fellow guests included the Prince Regent, the Emperor of Russia, and the King of Prussia. 'Henry at White's!' exclaimed Jane on hearing of this. 'Oh! What a Henry.'[21]

By the time of Jane's next visit Henry had moved to 26, Hans Place near his previous home in Sloane Street. On this visit Jane met two sisters, Eliza and Harriet Moore, who lived in Hanwell. Henry seemed to have a romantic interest in Harriet, whom Jane named 'the Hanwell favourite'.[22] He wanted Jane's approval, which was positive, but the relationship did not progress.

Henry was not always in the best of health, as there are several references in Jane's letters to him being unwell. He frequently suffered from what Jane described as 'bile'. In the autumn of 1815, Jane was staying with Henry in Hans Place when he came home early from work feeling unwell. At first Jane was not too worried, but when Henry took a turn for the worse, Mr Haden, an apothecary from Sloane Street, was summoned. In a letter to her sister dated 18th October Jane wrote:

> Mr H. calls it a general Inflammation. – He took twenty ounces of Blood from Henry last night – & nearly as much more this morning – & expects to have to bleed him again tomorrow, but he assures me that he found him quite as much better today as he expected. Henry is an excellent Patient, lies quietly in bed & is ready to swallow anything. He lives upon Medicine, Tea & Barley Water. – He has had a great deal of fever, but not much pain of any sort – & sleeps pretty well... You must fancy Henry in the back room upstairs – & I am generally there also, working [needlework] or writing.[23]

Over the next two days Henry seemed to be getting better, but he then had a relapse. On 22nd October Jane wrote summoning James, Edward, and Cassandra because she thought Henry was dying. Cassandra helped Jane to nurse their brother over the next week, when his life was in the balance. Mr Haden called an eminent London doctor to help him. He is thought to have been Dr Matthew Baillie, who had treated Henry in the past, and was one of the physicians who attended the Prince Regent. As a result of the doctor's treatment, Henry gradually got better, until a week later the crisis had passed. James and Edward then returned home, leaving Jane and Cassandra to nurse their brother back to full health.

While attending Henry, Dr Baillie discovered that Jane was the author of *Pride and Prejudice*. He told Jane that the Prince Regent was an admirer of her works and that he kept a set in every one of his residences. Dr Baillie told the prince that Miss Austen was staying in London and, as a result, Jane was invited by his librarian, the Reverend James Stanier Clarke, to visit Carlton House, the prince's London residence. The invitation was accepted, and on 13th November Jane was given a tour of Carlton House. During the tour the librarian said that he had been charged to say that Jane was at liberty to dedicate any forthcoming novel to the prince. Although Jane did not particularly like the prince because of the way he had treated his wife, she reluctantly dedicated *Emma* to him. So, as a result of Henry's illness, Jane received what her family referred to as her 'little gleam of court favour'.[24]

In March 1816, Henry was declared bankrupt. Due to the economic problems which followed the Napoleonic Wars, the Alton branch of his bank failed and led to the collapse of Austen,

Maunde and Tilson and the army agency. Henry's bankruptcy also led to the loss of his appointment as Receiver General for Oxfordshire, which he had held since 1813. Several family members, including Jane, lost money which they had invested in Henry's bank. Fortunately, Jane's loss was small, but others lost hundreds of pounds. Edward and Henry's uncle James Leigh-Perrot, who had stood surety when he was appointed Receiver General, lost considerable sums. Henry was left penniless – he had lost all his money, including Eliza's dowry. Being an optimistic and positive person, Henry soon bounced back, with what his niece Caroline described as 'all the energy of a sanguine elastic nature'.[25]

Following his bankruptcy, Henry decided to take Holy Orders, the profession or calling he had originally intended to enter after university. He also decided to leave London, which was a place he now hated. For the next few months Henry moved between Chawton, Steventon and Godmersham. Henry began to prepare for ordination. He studied the Greek testament in readiness for an examination by the Bishop of Winchester, which took place on 16th December 1816. Henry, who had hoped to show off his knowledge, was disappointed when the Bishop put his hand on a copy of a Greek testament and said, 'As for this book, Mr Austen, I dare say it is some years since either you or I looked into it.'[26] According to Jane, Henry wrote some 'very superior' sermons in preparation for conducting services.[27]

Henry was ordained Deacon by the Bishop of Salisbury and was appointed Curate of Chawton on a stipend of 52 guineas a year. The Rector of Chawton was the Reverend John Rawston Papillon, who had been incumbent there since 1801. Early the next year Henry was ordained priest in London. In a letter dated 24th January 1817 to her friend Alethea Bigg, Jane wrote:

> Our own new Clergyman is expected here very soon, perhaps in time to assist Mr Papillon on Sunday. I shall be very glad when the first hearing is over. It will be a nervous hour for our Pew, though we hear that he acquits himself with as much ease & collectedness, as if he had been used to it all his Life.[28]

Henry became a diligent and hardworking clergyman, like his father and brother. He was described by his niece Anna as a 'zealous Preacher of the Gospel, according to the religious views of the Calvinistic portion of the Evangelical Clergy, and so consistently remained to his life's end.'[29]

In 1816, Jane had begun to suffer from the first symptoms of the illness which led to her untimely death. It seems that the strain and anxiety of nursing Henry through his serious illness had taken its toll on her and left her susceptible to illness herself. Henry, who called regularly at Chawton Cottage, could see how rapidly Jane was deteriorating.

When, in May 1817, Jane and her sister travelled to Winchester to be near her doctor, Henry and his nephew William Knight rode all the way beside their carriage in the rain. When Jane was settled in lodgings in College Street, Henry visited her regularly to comfort her and administer Holy Communion.

When Jane died on 18th July, Henry went to Winchester to make the funeral arrangements and used his influence as a clergyman to have her buried in Winchester Cathedral. He attended the funeral with Edward, Frank, Charles, and their nephew James Edward. Henry then went to Chawton to be with his mother. Henry placed an obituary of Jane in a Winchester newspaper. Jane left her favourite brother a legacy of £50 in her will.

Soon after Jane died, Henry, as her literary executor, began to prepare her two unpublished novels for publication. The first novel that Jane wrote, which had originally been named *Susan* and then *Miss Catherine*, Henry renamed *Northanger Abbey*. He named her last untitled novel *Persuasion*. These were published together as a four-volume set by John Murray at the end of 1817. As with Jane's four other novels, her name did not appear on the title page, but Henry included a *Biographical Notice of the Author* in which he identified Jane as the author of all six novels. This, the first biographical information to be published about Jane, was written in a solemn, elegiac style, and using flowery language. It reads like an epitaph to Henry's lost sister. He portrays Jane, unrealistically, as a perfect human being, which Jane would not have been happy about. This *Notice* was later revised, extended, and republished as *A Memoir of Miss Austen*.

In 1818, while Curate of Chawton, Henry went to Berlin to be temporary chaplain to the British Embassy. Some sermons that he delivered there on the book of Genesis were later published. In January 1820 Henry succeeded his brother James as Rector of Steventon. This was a position which he held in trust for three years, until his nephew William Knight was old enough to take over. Henry's niece Caroline described leaving the rectory with her mother and brother for him to move in. 'We left Uncle Henry in possession. He seemed to have renewed his youth, if indeed he could be said ever to have lost it, in the prospect before him. A fresh life was in view.'[30]

Caroline remembered that Henry 'was always very affectionate in manner to us, and paid my mother every due attention,' but failed to suppress his excitement at becoming Rector of Steventon.

Caroline recalled that it was 'not pleasant to witness the elation of your successor in gaining what you have lost.'[31]

In April of that year Henry married again. His second wife was Eleanor Jackson, niece of the Reverend Papillon, for whom Henry had worked until recently as curate. Eleanor was considerably younger than Henry. The Reverend Papillon officiated at the marriage service, which took place on 11th April in Eleanor's local church, St Luke's, Chelsea. Henry had known Eleanor's family for some time, as they were neighbours when he lived in Sloane Street.

Cassandra thought so highly of Eleanor that she gave her Jane's turquoise ring when she became engaged to Henry. She went to stay with the newly married couple at Steventon Rectory and described her new sister-in-law as 'Henry's excellent wife', noting that she 'seems much pleased with her habitation and environs.'[32]

Henry and Eleanor were very happy together. In a letter to a nephew Henry described his wife as 'one dearer to me than life and for whose comfort I am solicitous beyond my own existence.'[33] Their only problem in the early years of their marriage was that Henry was troubled by debts. In order to pay these off he took in private pupils.

In August 1822, when William Knight took over as Rector of Steventon, Henry became Curate of St Andrew's Church in Farnham, Surrey, and, later, a teacher at Farnham Grammar School. He and Eleanor moved into The Old Vicarage, which was in the centre of this market town, close to the shops. Two years later Henry also became Perpetual Curate of St Mary's Church, Bentley, Hampshire. One of his achievements as curate of Bentley was to oversee the erection of a cage for the drunk and disorderly.

In 1827, Henry resigned from his post as Curate of Farnham and from his teaching post. That year his finances improved when he received an inheritance on the death of his mother. In 1836 he inherited a further £1,000 on the death of his aunt, Jane Leigh-Perrot, and Eleanor also came into several inheritances.[34] The couple moved into the newly refurbished eighteenth-century rectory at Bentley, where they remained until Henry retired in 1839. During these years they regularly joined family gatherings at Godmersham.

On his retirement, Henry and Eleanor moved to Colchester in Essex, where they stayed for three years, to be close to Eleanor's family.[35] In 1842, they moved again to Sion Place, Tunbridge Wells, Kent. It was here that Henry spent the final years of his life.

In March 1845 Cassandra Austen died of a stroke. When Henry attended the funeral at Chawton his nephew James Edward noticed that, despite his seventy-three years, he did not appear very old.[36] Cassandra, who was buried next to her mother at St Nicholas' Church, Chawton, left Henry £1,000 in her will.

Around this time both Henry and Eleanor suffered from ill health and went to Eastbourne for the benefit of sea air. Henry died of gastritis at home on 12th March 1850, at the age of seventy-nine. He was buried at Woodbury Park Cemetery, Tunbridge Wells. Inscribed on his gravestone are the following words:

*Beneath this stone*
*Are deposited the mortal remains*
*of the*
*Rev Henry Thomas Austen*
*Minister of Christ.*
*He was born in June 1771*
*and died*
*12th March 1850.*

There is also a scriptural text, which is difficult to read, but appears to be a statement of his hope in the afterlife.

After her husband's death, Eleanor was left with enough money to live comfortably. She moved to Bath to be near her sister and died there in 1864.[37]

# 6

# FRANCIS AUSTEN

Francis William, who was known in the family as Frank, was born on 23rd April 1774 and was privately baptised two days later. His public christening took place the following month. The first mention of Frank in family records was in a letter written in August 1775 by his mother to her sister-in-law Susannah Walter: 'My last boy is very stout [healthy], and has run alone these two months, and he is not yet sixteen months old.'[1]

Frank, who was small for his age, was full of energy and for this reason was nicknamed Fly by his family. At the age of seven, presumably with the permission and help of his father, Frank bought a chestnut-coloured pony which he named Squirrel, but which his brothers nicknamed Scug to tease him. Frank rode the pony when he joined his older brothers as they followed the local hunt. He wore a scarlet suit, which his mother made from a riding-habit she wore to travel in after her wedding. Squirrel was sold a year after he bought him for a guinea more than he paid for him.

Frank was a brave and bold child. His sister Jane remembered that the only thing which ever intimidated him was the bray of a donkey. Frank enjoyed a close relationship with his siblings and Jane, who was close to him in age, admired him greatly.

Like his brothers, Frank was educated by his father. As his education was coming to an end, Frank decided that he wanted to join the Navy. His parents accepted his decision and enrolled him at the Royal Naval Academy at Portsmouth, which he entered at the age of twelve. Frank left the Academy at the end of 1788, with the following excellent report from the headmaster to the Lords of the Admiralty:

> I beg leave to observe to their Lordships that this Young Gentleman has completed his plan of Mathematical learning in a considerably shorter time than usual, his assiduity indeed has been uncommon, and his conduct during the whole time he has been at the Academy, has been in all respects so properly correct, that I have never had a complaint or one unfavourable report of him from any Master or Usher altho' he has a lively and active disposition.[2]

Frank had made such a good impression that the Lords of the Admiralty marked him out as a candidate for early promotion.

After leaving the Academy Frank went to sea as a Volunteer on board HMS *Perseverence*. Volunteers experienced a sailor's life at sea under the supervision of the captain. Their participation introduced them to the privations and hardships they would later endure and enabled them to empathise with the sailors they would one day command. Frank, who later described himself as 'rather small of stature, of a vigorous constitution and possessing great activity of body',[3] had no difficulty in completing this practical training.

Frank's appointment as a Midshipman, the first rung on the naval career ladder, was to the same ship on which he had served as a Volunteer, bound for the East Indies. Before he left England in December 1788, Frank received a long letter from his father, under the heading: 'Memorandum for the Use of Mr Frank Austen, on his first going to the East Indies on board His Majesty's Ship Perseverence (Captain Smith)'. The following excerpt provides an insight into the moral values and duties Frank learned from his parents, and the behaviour they expected of him:

> Your behaviour, as a member of society, to the individuals around you may be also of great importance to your future well-doing, and certainly will to your present happiness and comfort. You may either by a contemptuous, unkind and selfish manner create disgust and dislike; or by affability, good humour and compliance, become the object of esteem and affection; which of these very opposite paths 'tis your interest to pursue I need not say.
>
> The little world of which you are going to become an inhabitant, will occasionally have it in their power to contribute no little share to your pleasure or pain; to conciliate therefore their goodwill, by every honourable method, will be the part of a prudent man. Your commander and officers will be most likely to become your friends by a respectful behaviour to themselves, and by an active and ready obedience to orders. Good humour, an inclination to oblige and the carefully avoiding every appearance of selfishness, will infallibly secure you the regards of your own mess and of all your equals. With your inferiors perhaps you will have but little intercourse, but when it does occur there is a sort of kindness they have a claim on you for, and which, you may believe me, will not be thrown away on them. Your conduct, as it

> respects yourself, chiefly comprehends sobriety and prudence. The former you know the importance of to your health, your morals and your fortune. I shall therefore say nothing more to enforce the observance of it. I thank God you have not at present the least disposition to deviate from it. Prudence extends to a variety of objects. Never any action of your life in which it will not be your interest to consider what she directs! She will teach you the proper disposal of your time and the careful management of your money, – two very important trusts for which you are accountable. She will teach you that the best chance of rising in life is to make yourself as useful as possible, by carefully studying everything that relates to your profession, and distinguishing yourself from those of your own rank by a superior proficiency in nautical acquirements.

The letter concluded with 'I have nothing to add but my blessing and best prayers for your health and prosperity, and to beg you would never forget you have not upon earth a more disinterested and warm friend than Your truly affectionate father, George Austen.'[4]

Frank treasured this letter so much that he kept it until the end of his very long life. It was found, clearly much read, among his papers after his death.

After serving for four years in the East Indies on the *Perseverence,* Frank was transferred, still in the East Indies, to HMS *Crown* under The Honourable W. Cornwallis. He then followed Cornwallis to HMS *Minerva.* Frank had taken notice of his father's advice and made excellent progress. In December 1792 he was promoted to Lieutenant and a year later he returned home, after an absence of five years, to await his next posting.

Frank returned as a mature and confident young man. His family were delighted to see him and to hear his tales of life at sea. Jane remembered her conversations with Frank about his adventures and later used the knowledge she gained about the navy when she wrote *Mansfield Park* and *Persuasion*.

Throughout his naval career Frank corresponded with his family, but letters often took a long time to arrive. It is clear from surviving letters how interested Frank's family were in his naval career and how eager they were to hear news of him. They must have been very anxious to hear from him when he was involved in the Napoleonic Wars.

Republican France declared war on Great Britain and Holland in February 1794. Frank was involved in this war from the beginning until it ended twenty-two years later. The many references to Frank's career in Jane's letters to her sister show how concerned his family were about him. Apart from the glory of being involved in the Wars, they provided opportunities for sailors to make money. When enemy vessels were captured, the spoils (known as 'prize money') were divided among the Commander, officers, and crew.

From 1793 to 1796, Frank worked on vessels attached to the home station. His duties were routine and mundane, but Frank was able to go ashore to visit his family.

Frank was a Senior Lieutenant on HMS *Lark* when, from 1794 to 1795, it was involved in evacuating British troops from Ostend to Nieuport in freezing weather. In 1795, the *Lark* accompanied a naval squadron which collected Princess Caroline of Brunswick from Cuxhaven in Germany to England, where she was to marry the Prince of Wales. That year Frank was briefly transferred to two other vessels before returning home.

During this period of leave Frank visited his brother Edward at his home in Kent. Jane was also staying there at that time. In a letter to her sister, she wrote of him: 'He enjoys himself here very much, for he has just learnt to turn (wood), & is so delighted with the employment, that he is at it all day long.'[5] He made a small butter churn for his niece Fanny.[6] Frank later made wooden toys for his own children. It is thought that Frank was the inspiration for Captain Harville in *Persuasion,* who was also good with his hands. While staying at Godmersham Frank also went hunting with Edward, although their hunting expeditions were not always fruitful.

When he returned from Kent, Frank was appointed to HMS *Triton,* a new 32-gun frigate, where he stayed for eighteen months. He then spent six months on HMS *Seahorse,* around the time that Spain joined the war as an ally of France. In 1798 Frank was transferred *to* HMS *London,* which was part of the squadron under the command of Earl St Vincent that blockaded the Spanish fleet at Cadiz. This happened at the same time as Napoleon's campaign in Egypt and Nelson's victory over the French fleet in the Battle of the Nile.

Despite being directly involved in the theatre of war Frank was restless and impatient for promotion and he also wanted to serve on a larger ship. Although the Navy was more meritocratic than the Army, knowing the right people was useful for promotion. Fortunately, George Austen knew someone who could help his son's progress. Admiral James Gambier was a family connection of General Mathew, the father of James Austen's first wife. The Admiral spoke on Frank's behalf to Lord Spencer, the First Lord of the Admiralty. As a result, Frank was promoted and given the opportunity to prove himself in a senior role. In a letter to her sister Jane excitedly wrote: 'Frank is made. – He was yesterday raised to the Rank of Commander, & appointed to the Petterel (sic) Sloop, now at Gibraltar.'[7]

While serving on the *Peterel* Frank participated in the blockade of Genoa before joining the squadron of Sir Sidney Smith on the coast of Egypt. The *Peterel* prevented a Turkish ship from being captured by the French, for which the Egyptian Pasha rewarded Frank with the gift of a sabre and pelisse.

In 1799, Frank was entrusted with conveying dispatches to Nelson at Palermo, informing him that Admiral Bruix had escaped from Brest with a large fleet and had entered the Mediterranean. The *Peterel* also cruised the Mediterranean in pursuit of enemy vessels.

In March 1800, Frank was responsible for the capture of three French vessels. He drove two of these onto rocks and captured the third in a fierce battle, without the loss of any men. In recognition of this, Frank was promoted to the rank of Post-Captain in May of that year. He did not find out about this promotion until October, when the *Peterel* reached Rhodes and command was passed to Captain Inglis, who was waiting there to succeed him. Frank's family knew of his promotion before he did. Jane wrote to Cassandra in January 1801:

> What a surprise to him it must have been on 20th October to be visited, collar'd & thrust out of the Petterell (sic) by Captn. Inglis! ...– What a pity it is that he should not be in England at the time of this promotion, because he certainly would have had an appointment![8]

After returning home, Frank did not have too long to wait for his next appointment. He became Flag-Captain to Admiral Gambier, whose influence had helped to get him his first promotion, on the 98-gun *Neptune*. In August of the following year, when the *Neptune* was anchored at Portsmouth, Frank's parents, James, and Mary had the opportunity of looking around the ship. Frank was serving on this ship when the Peace of Amiens was signed in March 1802.

In early 1803, Napoleon broke the terms of the treaty and hostilities recommenced. It was feared that France would attempt to invade England and Sea Fencibles, comprised of local volunteers, were set up to defend the east coast of England. Frank was put in charge of the North Foreland unit of Sea Fencibles and moved to Ramsgate in Kent.

Underpinning Frank's sense of duty and the way he treated others was his strong Christian faith. He was a regular churchgoer when living and working on shore. While he was in Ramsgate, Frank became known as 'the officer who knelt in church.'[9] It was in Ramsgate that Frank met his first wife, Mary Gibson, the daughter of John Gibson, a former Governor of Bermuda. Mary, who was ten years younger than Frank, was only seventeen when they became engaged. The couple had to wait for Frank to earn some more prize money before they could afford to get married.

In May 1804, Frank was appointed to HMS *Leopard*, the flagship of Rear-Admiral Thomas Louis, who was commanding a squadron tasked with blockading Napoleon's flotilla in Boulogne. This was a short posting, as Frank was back in England when his father died in January 1805. He was one of the sons who offered their newly widowed mother financial assistance.

Soon after his father's death, Frank was transferred with Rear-Admiral Louis to HMS *Canopus*. This was originally a French vessel captured during the Battle of the Nile and became part of the English squadron that sailed with Nelson's fleet, chasing the French Admiral Villeneuve to the West Indies and back. Just before Frank joined the *Canopus*, Lord Nelson, in a letter to Lord Moira, wrote:

> I hope to see [Captain Austen] alongside a French 80-gun ship, and he cannot be better placed than in the Canopus … Captain Austen I knew a little of before; he is an excellent young man.[10]

To be described in such glowing terms by Lord Nelson was quite an accolade.

Frank expected to be involved in the Battle of Trafalgar and his diary reveals his excitement leading up to the battle. However, on 21st October, the day of the battle, the *Canopus* was sent to Gibraltar to fetch supplies of water, so Frank did not take part in the final defeat of the French and Spanish. In a letter to Mary written on 27th October Frank reveals his great disappointment at missing the battle. The letter also provides a description of Lord Nelson by one of the sailors who served under him, showing how much he was revered.

> Alas! my dearest Mary, all my fears are but too fully justified. The fleets have met, and, after a very severe contest, a most decisive victory has been gained by the English twenty-seven over the enemy's thirty-three. Seventeen of the ships are taken and

> one is burnt; but I am truly sorry to add that this splendid affair has cost us many lives, and amongst them the most invaluable one to the nation, that of our gallant, and ever-to-be regretted, Commander-in-Chief, Lord Nelson, who was mortally wounded by a musket shot, and only lived long enough to know his fleet successful. In a public point of view, I consider his loss as the greatest which could have occurred; nor do I hesitate to say there is not an Admiral on the list so eminently calculated for the command of a fleet as he was. I never heard of his equal, nor do I expect again to see such a man. To the soundest judgment he united prompt decision and speedy execution of his plans; and he possessed in a superior degree the happy talent of making every class of persons pleased with their situation and eager to exert themselves in forwarding the public service ... by a fatal combination of unfortunate though unavoidable events, to lose all share in the glory of a day which surpasses all which ever went before, is what I cannot think of with any degree of patience.[11]

Frank had not only missed the glory of being part of the Battle of Trafalgar, but he had also missed out on valuable prize money. He hoped that 'time and reflection' would 'reconcile' him to his disappointment.[12] A few weeks later, Frank took part in the victory over the French at San Domingo, which helped to compensate for missing Trafalgar. He was rewarded with a gold medal and a silver vase, as well as the gratitude of both Houses of Parliament.

Following the Battle of San Domingo, Frank made enough prize money to enable him to marry Mary and to set up home. They were married in Ramsgate in July 1806, followed by a honeymoon spent at Godmersham. Frank's family were very fond of his new wife and she is frequently mentioned in Jane's letters. Jane much preferred this Mary to the other Mary, James' wife.

After their honeymoon, the young couple moved into temporary lodgings in Southampton while they looked for a permanent home. Southampton was chosen because of its proximity to Portsmouth for Frank. In autumn 1806, Mrs Austen, her daughters and their friend Martha Lloyd, who was part of their household, moved in with Frank and Mary.

A permanent home was soon found in Castle Square. This large old house, which had an excellent view of the Solent, belonged to John Henry Petty, the 2nd Marquis of Lansdowne. The garden was bounded on one side by the old city walls, which were wide enough to walk along. In a letter to Cassandra, who was at Godmersham when the move took place, Jane described Frank making a fringe for the drawing room curtains. She also told her about the 'alterations and improvements' being made to the house and that the garden 'was being put in order'.[13]

Nelson was correct in his assessment of Frank as 'an excellent young man'. According to his nephew James Edward,

> He possessed great firmness of character, with a strong sense of duty, whether due from himself to others, or from others to himself. He was consequently a strict disciplinarian; but, as he was a very religious man, it was remarked of him (for in those days, at least, it was remarkable) that he maintained this discipline without ever uttering an oath or permitting one in his presence.[14]

Like his father, Frank had strong principles. He was honest, considerate, dignified, self-reliant, bold and fearless. Frank was also a loving husband and father, who enjoyed being with his family when home on leave.

Soon after moving into Castle Square, Frank was appointed Commander of HMS *St Albans*. He spent a few weeks on board at Sheerness in Kent as she was being prepared for her next voyage. He was therefore absent when his first child, a daughter named Mary Jane, was born on 27th April 1807. Mrs Austen and her daughters helped Mary through a difficult confinement and a period of illness afterwards. Fortunately, Mary soon recovered.

The *St Albans* left Sheerness on 21st May and arrived at Spithead a few days later, in time for Frank's daughter's christening. He spent a month at home before the *St Albans* set off for the Cape of Good Hope at the end of June.

In summer 1808, the British entered the Peninsular War. The *St Albans* escorted a division of troopships to the Portuguese coast, and Frank watched the Battle of Vimeiro through a telescope while his ship was stood off at sea. This was the first British victory of the war. The *St Albans* then had the task of picking up the wounded and French prisoners and taking them to Portsmouth.

Frank's next mission was convoying East Indiamen to China. While there, he had to deal with disputes between English sailors and the local Chinese, and his success allowed a convoy of East Indiamen to leave China safely.

While Frank was at sea, Mary and Mary Jane moved into Rose Cottage in Alton, not far from the new home in Chawton of Mrs Austen, her daughters and Martha Lloyd. It was at Rose Cottage that Mary gave birth to their second child, a son named

Francis William, after his father. Jane wrote a humorous poem to mark the birth of her nephew. This poem looks back to Frank's childhood, gives an insight into his character, and refers to Jane's new home in Chawton:

My dearest Frank I wish you Joy
Of Mary's safety of a boy,
Whose birth has given little pain
Compared with that of Mary Jane. –
May he a growing Blessing prove,
And well deserve his Parents' Love! –
Endow'd with Art's and Nature's Good,
Thy name possessing with thy Blood;
In him, in all his ways, may we
Another Francis William see! –
Thy infant days may he inherit,
Thy warmth, nay insolence of spirit; -
We would not with one fault dispense
To weaken the resemblance.
May he revive thy Nursery sin,
Peeping as daringly within,
(His curley Locks but just descried)
With 'Bet, my be not come to bide.'
Fearless of danger, braving pain,
And threaten'd very oft in vain,
Still may one Terror daunt his soul,
One needful engine of controul
Be found in this sublime array,
A neighbouring Donkey's aweful Bray! -

So may his equal faults as Child,
Produce Maturity as mild,
His saucy words & fiery ways
In early Childhood's pettish days
In Manhood shew his Father's mind,
Like him, considerate & Kind;
All Gentleness to those around,
And eager only not to wound.
Then like his Father too, he must,
To his own former struggles just,
Feel his Deserts with honest Glow,
And all his Self-improvement know. -
A native fault may thus give birth
To the best blessing, conscious worth.

As for ourselves, we're very well,
As unaffected prose will tell.
Cassandra's pen will give our state
The many comforts that await
Our Chawton home – how much we find
Already in it to our mind,
And how convinced that when complete,
It will all other Houses beat,
That ever have been made or mended,
With rooms concise or rooms distended.
You'll find us very snug next year;
Perhaps with Charles & Fanny near –
For now it often does delight us
To fancy them just over-right us.[15]

Frank did not see his son until July 1810, when he returned home from China earlier than expected. Mary and the children hurried to Chatham to stay with Frank in his lodgings. Soon after his return, Frank received formal thanks from the Admiralty for the way he dealt with the problems between English sailors and the Chinese. The East India Company expressed their gratitude with a reward of 1,000 guineas and some silver plate. From December 1810 until the following May, Frank was Flag-Captain to Admiral Gambier on HMS *Caledonia*, which was involved in blockading the French coast.

In 1811, Frank and Mary moved from Alton to lodgings in Cowes on the Isle of Wight, awaiting Frank's next appointment. It was there that their second son, Henry Edgar, was born. Frank and Mary went on to have eight more children over the next twelve years. Frank was a devoted father.

In July of that year Frank took command of HMS *Elephant* and was once more involved in the Napoleonic Wars. The *Elephant* was stationed in the Baltic where, among other duties, it protected merchant convoys. Meanwhile, battles raged on the southern shores of the Baltic, which preceded the fall of Napoleon. Frank wrote letters home and two of Jane's replies have survived. In her letters Jane brought Frank up to date with family news. She told him that she was writing another novel (*Mansfield Park*) and asked 'shall you object to my mentioning the *Elephant* in it, & two or three other of your old Ships?'[16] Frank did not object.

In April 1814, Napoleon abdicated and was exiled to Elba. Hostilities ceased and Frank returned home. He left HMS *Elephant* at Spithead and went to live on shore with his wife and young children. He kept his naval rank and went onto half-pay. Frank did not return to sea for the next thirty years. One year after his return home, Frank was made a Companion of the Bath. For the first two years after his return Frank, Mary and their children borrowed Chawton Great House from Edward. They stayed there until new tenants moved in. The long war with France broke out again when Napoleon escaped from Elba and retook power in Paris. In June 1815 the war finally ended with the battle of Waterloo and Napoleon was exiled again, this time to the island of St Helena.

Frank was unable to visit Jane during the last few weeks of her life, as Mary had recently given birth and his mother needed one son nearby at this difficult time. He was beside Edward, Henry, and James Edward on 24th July when they followed Jane's coffin from College Street, Winchester, to the cathedral where she was buried.

In July 1823, Frank's wife Mary died while giving birth to their eleventh child, who survived but died a few months later. Mary was the fourth of Jane's sisters-in-law to die during or shortly after childbirth. Frank's eldest daughter, Mary Jane, took over the running of her father's household and caring for her younger siblings – as her cousin Fanny had done in similar circumstances.

In 1827, Frank's elderly mother died. The following year Frank married again. His second wife was Jane's and Cassandra's friend Martha Lloyd, sister of James's second wife Mary. Many years earlier the Austen sisters had wished that Frank would marry Martha and now it had happened. Frank's great-aunt Jane Leigh-Perrot had been talking of leaving her home in Berkshire to him, but for some unknown reason she did not approve of this marriage and changed her mind. She did, however, give Frank £10,000 as compensation. With this money he bought Portsdown Lodge, a large house on the north side of Portsdown Hill, near Portsmouth, which became the marital home of Frank and Martha. The couple had a happy marriage and according to Cassandra, who often visited them, Martha was an 'excellent mother' to Frank's younger children.[17]

Frank became a rear-admiral in 1830. His fine service in the navy was recognised when he was made a Knight Commander of the Bath at the last investiture of the reign of William IV. In the same year he became a vice-admiral.

In 1843, Martha died at the age of seventy-seven. Frank and his eldest two sons, Francis and Henry, were with her when she died. She was buried in Wymering churchyard, not far from Portsdown Lodge.

Frank's illustrious career was not yet over. His last naval appointment was as Commander of HMS *Vindictive* on the North American and West Indies Station. Cassandra visited Frank to say goodbye before he set off. While she was at Portsdown Lodge, Cassandra suffered a stroke. Frank could not delay his departure, so he summoned Henry, Charles and his niece Caroline to be with her. Cassandra did not recover and died five days later. In her will she left Frank £1000 and the second volume of Jane's *Juvenilia*.

Two anecdotes recorded by Fanny Knight's husband Lord Brabourne in his edition of Jane Austen's letters probably relate to Frank's time on the *Vindictive*. They show how meticulous Frank was:

> He was exceedingly precise, and spoke always with due deliberation, let the occasion be what it might, never having been known to hurry himself in his speech for any conceivable reason. It so fell out, then, that whilst in some foreign seas where sharks and similar unpleasant creatures abound, a friend, or sub-officer of his (I know not which), was bathing from the ship. Presently Sir Francis called out to him in his usual tone and manner, 'Mr Pakenham, you are in danger of a shark – a shark of the blue species! You had better return to the ship.' 'Oh! Sir Francis; you are joking, are you not?' 'Mr Pakenham, I am not given to joking. If you do not immediately return, soon will the shark eat you.' Whereupon Pakenham, becoming alive to his danger, acted upon the advice thus deliberately given and, says the story, saved himself 'by the skin of his teeth' from the shark.[18]
>
> ... On one occasion he is said to have visited a well-known watchmaker, one of whose chronometers he had taken with him during an absence of five years, and which was still in excellent order. After looking carefully at it, the watchmaker remarked, with conscious pride; 'Well, Sir Francis, it seems to have varied none at all.' Very slowly, and very gravely, came the answer: 'Yes, it *has* varied – *eight seconds*!'[19]

While he was serving on the *Vindictive,* Frank was promoted to a full admiral. He returned home from the West Indies in 1848. Frank lived for the rest of his life at Portsdown Lodge with his daughters and grandsons.

In the 1860s, Frank received much recognition for his naval services. In 1862 he became Rear-Admiral and then Vice- Admiral of the United Kingdom. Then in 1863 Frank received the following letter promoting him to the highest rank of all.

The Admiralty, April 27th, 1863

Sir,

I am happy to acquaint you that I have had the pleasure of bringing your name before the Queen for promotion to Admiral of the Fleet, and that Her Majesty has been graciously pleased to approve of the appointment 'as a well-deserved reward for your brilliant services.

I am Sir, your most obedient servant,

Somerset[20]

Frank outlived all his siblings. He died in August 1865 at the age of ninety-one. He was buried in Wymering Churchyard beside his second wife, Martha.

# 7

# CHARLES AUSTEN

Charles John, the youngest of the Austen siblings, was born at Steventon on 23rd June 1779 and was privately baptised the same day. His public christening took place at the end of July. From early childhood he was close to his sisters, who were very protective towards him and, in later life, referred to him affectionately as 'our own particular little brother', a misquotation taken from the novel *Camilla* by Fanny Burney.

Charles, like his brothers, was educated at home by his father. He then followed his brother Frank to the Royal Naval Academy in Portsmouth in July 1791, at the age of twelve. In September 1794, Charles left the Academy to embark on his naval career and from then until 1815 he was actively involved in the long war against France. His first appointment was as a midshipman on HMS *Daedalus* under the command of Captain Thomas Williams, the husband of his cousin Jane Cooper.

His family took a great interest in Charles' career from the beginning. They kept in touch by letter, although communication was difficult when he was at sea. It is clear from Jane's letters to Cassandra that Charles continued to enjoy an affectionate relationship with both his sisters. They eagerly awaited news of him and looked forward to his periods of home leave.

Charles second appointment was on HMS *Unicorn,* still as a midshipman and again under the command of Thomas Williams. On 8th June 1796 the *Unicorn* was engaged in a battle against the French frigate *La Tribune* off the Scilly Isles. After a ten-hour fight the *Unicorn* won. For this victory Thomas Williams was knighted, and from then on Jane referred to him as His Royal Highness Sir Thomas Williams.

In March 1797, Charles went with Williams when he transferred to HMS *Endymion.* At the end of that year the *Endymion* helped to drive the Dutch battleship *Brutus* into the harbour of Helvoesluys after the victory of Admiral Duncan over the Dutch at Camperdown. This was an important naval action in the war against France. For his part in this victory Charles was promoted to the rank of lieutenant and was moved to HMS *Scorpion,* a smaller vessel under the command of Captain John Tremayne Rodd. Jane used her knowledge of her brother's work as a midshipman and his promotion to lieutenant when writing about William Price's naval career in *Mansfield Park.*

Charles' duties on the *Scorpion* were less challenging than they had been on the *Endymion* and he soon became restless and bored. He longed to be on a larger vessel again, where there would be more action. His father learned of his son's dissatisfaction and mentioned it to Admiral Gambier when he wrote to him about Frank. The Admiral replied:

> As it is usual to keep young officers in small vessels, it being most proper on account of their inexperience, and it being also a

> situation where they are more in the way of learning their duty, your son has been continued in the Scorpion; but I have mentioned to the Board of Admiralty his wish to be in a frigate, and when a proper opportunity offers, and it is judged that he has taken his turn in a small ship, I hope he will be removed.[1]

Charles was too impatient to wait, however, and he wrote to Lord Spencer, First Lord of the Admiralty, asking to be moved. In less than two years he was promoted to Second Lieutenant. Before taking up his new appointment Charles was able to go home to see his family. It was around this time that Charles had his hair cut short and stopped powdering it to make it easier to manage when on board ship.

Charles's next appointment was as Second Lieutenant on HMS *Tamar,* which was in dock awaiting repairs at Deal in Kent. The Admiralty then decided not to refit the *Tamar* and Charles was re-appointed to the *Endymion* under Thomas Williams and his successor, Captain Philip Durham. At this time the *Endymion* was based in the western Mediterranean. She was engaged in attacking gunboats off Algeciras near Gibraltar, and capturing privateers. The officers and men involved in capturing these vessels received prize money from the sale of the vessels and their cargo.

Charles received £40 as his share of the prize money from the capture of the French privateer *La Furie.* He spent the money on gifts for his sisters. In a letter to Cassandra written in May 1801, Jane wrote: '... but of what avail is it to take prizes if he lays out the produce in presents to his Sisters. He has been buying Gold chains & Topaze [sic] Crosses for us; – he must be well scolded.'[2] These gifts inspired the episode in *Mansfield Park,* when Fanny Price's sailor brother William buys her an amber cross with some of his prize money. When Charles and four of his men held the captured vessel *Scipio* during a storm until reinforcements arrived, he received both prize money and a special commendation for bravery.

The *Endymion* was also engaged in convoying East Indiamen home from St Helena. This enabled Charles to pay quick visits to his family. In November 1800 he was again on leave and went with Jane to the annual ball held by Lord Lymington, their father's former pupil, at his home Hurstbourne Park. According to Jane, Charles 'danced the whole Evening, & today is no more tired than a gentleman ought to be.'[3]

Charles, who had grown up to be a tall and good-looking young man, made a good impression on those who met him. He was charming and good-humoured. According to his nephew James Edward, Charles had a 'sweet temper and affectionate disposition'[4] and, like his siblings, he had a strong Christian faith.

When Charles returned from leave, the *Endymion* was given the task of transporting Prince Augustus Frederick, the Duke of Sussex, to Lisbon. The duke, who suffered from asthma, was taken to Portugal so that he could benefit from the warmer climate.

In March 1802 the Treaty of Amiens was signed and the hostilities between Great Britain and France ended. Napoleon did not intend to honour the treaties, however, and set about re-equipping his armed forces. The crew of the *Endymion* were paid off and Charles went to Bath to stay with his parents and sisters. That summer they all went to Devon on holiday and, in the autumn, they went on a tour of Wales. This was followed by a visit to James and his family at Steventon. Charles then went with his sisters for a stay of several weeks at Godmersham.

In May 1803 war broke out again. Charles returned to the *Endymion* as First Lieutenant. He was promoted in October 1804 to Commander of the sloop *Indian* on the North American Station. This promotion was his reward for capturing three men-of-war and two privateers.

Charles's main task was searching ships to stop neutral countries from trading with France. He was still involved in capturing vessels, but there was no profit to be made on this in the North American Station. Charles was highly respected in his new appointment and Jane tongue in cheek claimed that he was 'looked up to by everybody in all America.'[5]

When his father died in January 1805 Charles was far away in Halifax, Nova Scotia, and it was many weeks before news of this reached him.

In April 1805 Jane and her mother found out how much Charles was esteemed by people he met during his career. They received a message from Lord and Lady Leven, the parents of Lord Balgonie who was a lieutenant in the navy and a friend of Charles. The Levens, who either lived or were staying in Bath, wanted to meet the Austens. Instead of waiting for the Levens to call, Jane and her mother decided to call on them. In an amusing passage in a letter to Cassandra, who was away from home, Jane described the visit:

> They seem very reasonable, good sort of people, very civil, & full of his [Charles's] praise. – We were shewn at first into an empty Drawing-room, & presently in came his Lordship, not knowing who we were, to apologise for the servant's mistake, & tell a lie himself, that Lady Leven was not within;... – after sitting with him ten minutes we walked away; but Lady L. coming out of the

> Dining parlour as we passed the door, we were obliged to attend her back to it, & pay our visit over again... By this means we had the pleasure of hearing Charles's praises twice over; – they think themselves excessively obliged to him, & estimate him so highly as to wish Ld. Balgonie [who had been unwell] when he is quite recovered, to go out to him.[6]

It is not clear what Charles had done to make them so obliged to him.

Charles visited Bermuda when he was working on the North American Station, and while there he met his first wife Fanny. She was the daughter of John Grove Palmer, a former Attorney General of Bermuda, and his wife Dorothy. On his retirement the Palmers had moved from Bermuda to Keppel Street in London. Charles and Fanny became engaged in the spring of 1806 and were married just over a year later, when Fanny was only seventeen. The Austen family did not meet her until 1811.

In December 1808, Fanny gave birth in Bermuda to their first child, Cassandra Esten. Charles informed his family of her arrival in a letter to his sister Cassandra, written on Christmas Day: 'I am sure you will be delighted to hear that my beloved Fanny was safely delivered of a fine girl on 22nd December and that they are both doing remarkably well.'[7]

He described his baby as 'the finest that ever was seen ... really good-looking [and] healthy.'[8] Charles also informed his sister that a small French vessel with twelve of his men on board had recently been lost at sea. Charles and Fanny's second daughter, Harriet Jane, was born in Bermuda in February 1810.

Charles remained as Commander of the *Indian* until in May 1810 he was promoted to the position of Post-Captain on HMS

*Swiftsure*, the flagship of Sir John Warren. He remained on this vessel for five months, then took command of HMS *Cleopatra* and brought her and his family home to England, after an absence of six-and-a-half years. Cassandra wrote about her brother's return in a letter to her cousin Philadelphia Walter:

> After an absence from England of almost seven years you may guess the pleasure which having him amongst us again occasion'd. He is grown a little older in all that time, but we had the pleasure of seeing him return in good health and unchanged in mind. His Bermudan wife is a very pleasing little woman, she is gentle and amiable in her manners and appears to make him very happy. They have two pretty little girls.[9]

Cassandra's only worry for Charles was that everything in England was so expensive that she was afraid they would find themselves 'very, very poor'.[10]

Charles' next appointment was as Flag-Captain on the guardship HMS *Namur*, anchored at the Nore Station off Sheerness. His family lived on board to economise on living expenses. This was not ideal, as their quarters were cramped and little Cassandra suffered from sea-sickness when the weather was rough. Their family were able to visit them on board the *Namur* and members of both sides of the family did so in 1812. In December of that year, a third daughter, Frances, was born to Charles and Fanny.

During the summer of 1813 Charles was on leave and the family took lodgings in Southend. During this time on shore, they visited Charles's mother and sisters at Chawton Cottage. When Charles and Fanny left to go to London their two elder daughters remained with their grandmother and aunts. Jane wrote to her brother Frank in July 1813: 'Charles's little girls were with us about a month, & had so endeared themselves that we were quite sorry to have them go.'[11] Jane described Harriet as a 'truely [sic] sweet-tempered little Darling'. She thought that her older sister Cassy needed parental guidance. 'She will really be a very pleasing Child, if they will only exert themselves a little.'[12]

Later that year Charles and Fanny visited James and Mary at Steventon Rectory. Caroline Austen recorded her impressions of her uncle and aunt during this visit in her *Reminiscences*: 'I was much charmed with both – but thought they looked very young for an uncle and aunt – tho' she must then have been the mother of two children. She was fair and pink, with very light hair, and I admired her greatly.'[13]

Charles and his family returned to the *Namur* on 20th September but left again in October to pay a brief visit to Godmersham, where Jane was also staying. In a letter to Cassandra she described how, after a difficult journey, they arrived 'just like their own nice selves, Fanny looking as neat & white this morning as possible & dear Charles all affectionate, placid, quiet, chearful [sic] good humour. They are both looking very well.'[14]

Jane was delighted to see her brother and sister-in-law again. She described to Cassandra how she and Edward 'sat snugly talking' to them in the library.[15] During his stay, which ended on 22nd October, Charles went shooting on his brother's estate with his nephew George and George Moore, the husband of Edward Austen's sister-in-law.

On 5th April 1814, Napoleon abdicated and was exiled to the island of Elba. It appeared that hostilities between Great Britain and France and her allies were finally over. Charles remained in his position as Commander of the *Namur.* He and his family enjoyed some more shore leave that year and returned to the ship in July.

It was there, on 31st August, that Fanny gave birth prematurely to another daughter, Elizabeth, during a violent storm. All appeared to be well at first, but then complications set in and Fanny died, at the age of just twenty-four. Edward Austen, who had lost his wife in similar circumstances, hurried to the *Namur* to comfort his brother. To add to the tragedy, baby Elizabeth died not long after.

Charles immediately resigned his command of the *Namur* so that he could arrange for the care of his three motherless daughters. It was decided that they would live at the Palmer family home at Keppel Street, Bloomsbury, under the care of their mother's older unmarried sister, Harriet. Fanny and her baby were commemorated on a marble plaque, decorated with a weeping willow tree and anchors, which was placed on the wall of St John the Baptist Church, Kentish Town, near the Palmers' home. The epitaph on the tablet reads: 'Sleep oh dear fair one, wait the Almighty's will/Then rise unchanged and be an angel still.'

Jane went to see her brother and nieces in November 1814, while she was staying at Henry's house in Hans Place. She described the visit in a letter to her niece Fanny Knight. 'I called in Keppel Street & saw them all,' she wrote 'including dear Uncle Charles, who is to come & dine with us quietly today.'[16] Jane described her niece Fanny as a 'fine stout [healthy] girl, talking incessantly' and Harriet as 'gentle and affectionate as ever'.[17] 'That puss Cassy', as Jane described their older sister, did not seem very pleased to see her aunt.

When Charles was ready to return to work, he was sent to the Mediterranean Station in command of HMS *Phoenix*. Charles's journal shows how greatly he was affected by the loss of his young wife: 'Very sad thinking of past happiness. Alas! Not to be recalled.'[18] He re-read his 'dear departed angel's' letters and was 'much struck by the exquisite tenderness and simplicity of her stile (sic).' His entry for 3rd December of that year reads: 'My dear departed angel's birthday on which she would have compleated [sic] her 26th year. Alas!'[19]

In March 1815 Napoleon escaped from the Island of Elba and hostilities resumed. The *Phoenix* and two other vessels under Charles's command were sent to the Adriatic to pursue a Neapolitan squadron. The city of Naples surrendered in May, but the port of Brindisi held out. The *Phoenix* and another of Charles' ships blockaded the port. He then induced the garrison in the castle and two enemy frigates to hoist the flag of the restored King of Naples. For this action Charles received a special commendation.

In June 1815 the long war between Great Britain and France finally ended with the Battle of Waterloo. In the aftermath of the war Charles was involved in suppressing piracy in the Greek archipelago.

Charles, who shared a love of literature with Jane, enjoyed reading her novels while at sea. When *Emma* was published in December 1815 Jane sent a copy to Charles, who was in the Mediterrean. In his letter of thanks Charles wrote: '*Emma* arrived in time to a moment. I am delighted with her, more so I think than even with my favourite Pride & *Prejudice*, & have read it three times in the Passage.'[20] Their mutual love of literature created a bond between them.

In February 1816 the *Phoenix* was wrecked in a hurricane off the coast of Turkey. Fortunately, no lives were lost and the ship's stores and guns were saved. Charles had to face a court-martial two months later. The local pilots who guided the vessel into port were found to be responsible and Charles was absolved of all blame. Until Charles was exonerated, this was a worrying time for his family. His niece Caroline recorded the ship's loss in her *Reminiscences.* She noted that although Charles was not to blame, 'such a misfortune is always a disparagement; and the war being over, he knew he was likely to wait long for another ship.'[21]

At the end of June Charles returned to England in a depressed state of mind, which continued while he awaited another command. While he waited, Charles stayed mostly with the Palmers and his daughters in Keppel Street, to keep in contact with the Admiralty. In November he visited his mother and sisters at Chawton. This visit, according to Jane, 'greatly improved his Health, Spirits and Appearance'.[22]

Charles was in England throughout the final months of Jane's life. Despite being unwell himself, he visited her in Winchester on 19th June and recorded in his diary that he had seen her 'for the last time in this world'.[23] Charles was unable to visit Jane again as his daughter Harriet was undergoing painful treatment for a serious medical condition described as 'water on the brain'.

Henry wrote to inform Charles of Jane's death. Charles did not attend his sister's funeral in Winchester Cathedral, probably because of his daughter's illness. He received copies of an announcement of Jane's death that Henry placed in a Winchester newspaper, the epitaph on her gravestone, and a poem entitled *Winchester Races,* written by Jane shortly before her death.

It appears that Charles did not work again until in February 1820 he was appointed to a position in the coastguard service based in Padstow, Cornwall. In a letter to her granddaughter Anna, Mrs Austen described his new duties:

> He will spend great part of his time on Horseback, fortunately he is very fond of that exercise, he is to ride along the Coast to a certain distance, 12 miles on one side the Town and 15 on the other, if any smuggling Vessels appear, he sends out his Boats & Men, but does not go himself.[24]

In August 1820, Charles married Harriet Palmer, his late wife's sister, who had cared for his daughters after their mother's death. Mrs Austen was not happy with Charles's choice of a second wife. She had once described Harriet as 'not agreeable' but conceded that she was 'very good and very useful' and that she had 'good principles and good sense'. Mrs Austen also considered that Harriet was 'a careful and attentive mother'[25] to Charles's daughters. Anna Austen also disliked Harriet, although she could not explain why.[26] Her brother James Edward described Harriet as 'plain and sour-countenanced'.[27]

The family may have had some misgivings because marriage to a deceased wife's sister, although not illegal, was not approved of by the Church. Despite the disapproval of some members of the Austen family, Charles and Harriet had a happy marriage. They had four children, two of whom died in infancy.

In 1822, Charles moved to Devon, holding the same position in the coastguard service. He wrote to his sister-in-law Mary on 5th May to tell her about the move:

Reverend George Austen.

Jane Austen, depicted in a watercolour painted by her sister.

Edward Austen, Jane's brother. This portrait was painted when he was on a Grand Tour of Europe between 1786 and 1788.

Henry Austen, Jane's brother. (Courtesy of Jane Austen House)

Frank Austen, Jane's brother.

Charles Austen, Jane's brother.

James Edward Austen-Leigh, Jane's nephew and the author of her first biography.

Francis Austen, George Austen's uncle.

*Above:* Steventon Church, where George Austen was rector for thirty years.

*Below:* Steventon Rectory.

Godmersham House, Kent, home of Edward Austen.

St John's College, Oxford, where George, James and Henry Austen studied for their degrees.

Exeter College, Oxford, where James Edward Austen (later Austen-Leigh) studied for his B.A. and M.A. degrees.

Abbey Church, Bath, 1788, from an aquatint by Thomas Malton. George Austen, his wife and daughters are believed to have worshipped here.

Dr Oliver and Mr Pierce examining patients in Bath. Edward Austen consulted Bath's physicians in 1799.

Holborne Museum, Bath. Originally the Sydney Hotel, near the home of George Austen, his wife and daughters in Sydney Place.

1, Paragon, Bath. Home of James Leigh-Perrot and his wife Jane.

Pulteney Bridge, Bath, 1805, from an aquatint by J.C.Nattes. This bridge is near Sydney Place where the Austens lived when they first moved to Bath.

The Pump Room, Bath, where James Leigh-Perrot went daily to drink the healing spa water.

Royal Crescent, Bath, 1788, from the original watercolour by Thomas Malton. This was the most famous and most exclusive residential street in Bath.

Queen's Square, Bath, from an aquatint by Thomas Malton. Edward Austen stayed here on a visit to Bath for a health cure in 1799.

*Above:* The Thames at Chelsea by John Varley. Henry Austen lived in Chelsea from 1804 to 1813. (Paul Mellon Collection, Yale Center for British Art)

*Below:* Covent Garden by Peter Angillis. Henry Austen lived in Henrietta Street, Covent Garden from 1813 to 1816. (Paul Mellon Collection, Yale Center for British Art)

Ramsgate by an unknown artist. Frank Austen lived in Ramsgate when he was Commander of the Sea Fencibles. (Paul Mellon Collection, Yale Center for British Art)

Chawton Cottage, now a museum, where Jane Austen lived for the last eight years of her life.

Chawton House, Edward Austen's Hampshire residence.

St Nicholas Church, Chawton, where Henry Austen was curate from 1816 to 1820.

*Above:* Action between the English frigate *Unicorn* and the French frigate *La Tribune,* by Francis Chesham. Charles Austen took part in this sea battle in June 1796.

*Below: The Battle of Trafalgar*, by John Christian Schetky. Francis Austen was deeply disappointed not to have taken part in this famous battle.

8, College Street, Winchester, where James, Henry and Charles Austen visited Jane in the last weeks of her life and where she died in July 1817.

Memorial to Jane Austen in Winchester Cathedral, paid for with the profits of her nephew's biography of her.

*Right:* 'He cut off a long lock of her hair.' An illustration from *Sense and Sensibility*.

*Below right:* 'Now, be sincere; did you admire me for my impertinence?' An illustration from *Pride and Prejudice*.

*Below left:* 'My father is come!' An illustration from *Mansfield Park*.

*Above left:* 'He stopped to look the question.' An illustration from *Emma*.

*Above right:* 'Off they went, without a plunge or a caper.' An illustration from *Northanger Abbey*.

*Left:* 'Looking on her with a face as pallid as her own.' An illustration from *Persuasion*.

> The neighbourhood we are going to holds out the prospect of many advantages – a fine country, an excellent and cheap market at Plymouth, and Instruction for the Girls which was not to be obtained here. The Roads too are much better than the Cornish ones, and my district not above half as long. We shall however leave our nice cottage here with a certain amount of regret – we have passed near two years in it with great comfort, and have made some friends amongst our neighbours whom we shall be sorry to part from.[28]

Charles told Mary that his wife and children had 'certainly benefited by their stay in Cornwall'. One disadvantage of the move was the reduction in Charles's salary.

Despite his successful career in the navy, Charles was never very well-off financially. His sister Cassandra, who had previously expressed concern about this, mentioned it in a letter to their cousin Philadelphia Walter: 'He is the fond father of three daughters and two little boys. I wish he were richer, but fortune has not yet smiled on him.'[29]

In 1826 Charles returned to sea as Commander of the frigate *Aurora* on the West Indies Station. The *Aurora* was mainly engaged in suppressing the slave trade. During his two years in this posting no crew members were lost through sickness or any other cause. Charles's men presented him with a silver snuff box and a silver salver in gratitude. He performed so well that in 1828 Charles was promoted to the position of flag captain to Admiral Colpoys on the *Winchester*, also based on the West Indies Station. By then Charles had been away from his family for more than two years, during which time his mother had died.

Charles returned home in December 1830 after being severely injured when he fell from a mast during a gale. He settled with his wife and family at Anglesey, near Gosport in Hampshire, where his sister Cassandra frequently visited him. Charles made a full recovery from his injuries.

In 1838 Charles was appointed Captain of HMS *Bellerophon* based in the Mediterranean. He took part in the joint English and French campaign against Mehemet Ali, Viceroy of Egypt. Charles was also involved in the bombardment of St Jean d'Acre in 1840, for which he was made a Companion of the Bath. He was also awarded a good service pension.

In March 1845, Charles was present with Henry and Caroline when Cassandra died at Frank's house in Portsmouth. He and Henry led the mourners at her funeral in Chawton. James Edward, who was one of the mourners, informed his sister Anna that their uncle was 'kind, grave and thoughtful'[30] at the funeral. Charles was executor of Cassandra's will, under the terms of which he inherited £1000, volume one of Jane's *Juvenilia,* and all of Cassandra's personal effects.

In 1846, Charles became a Rear-Admiral and four years later he became Commander-in-Chief of the East India and China Station, which had its headquarters at Trincomalee, Ceylon. In April 1852 he commanded the naval forces that captured Rangoon. During this campaign he contracted cholera and was moved to Calcutta to recover.

On his return to Rangoon, Charles transferred from the *Hastings* to the steam sloop *Pluto* and led a combined military and naval force up the Irrawaddy River to Prome, on reconnaissance. On this mission Charles became ill again, but this time he did not recover. He died on 7th October 1852, at the age of seventy-three. A great-nephew of Charles, an officer in the navy who had seen action in the Burma War, wrote about his uncle's death in a letter to his brother:

> You will have heard of our great loss in the death of our dear and gallant old Admiral Uncle Charles Austen. He died near Prome of cholera, very suddenly the day before I arrived there ... he was beloved by everybody that knew him and he had so endeared himself to such of the army as came in contact with him that I saw several officers shed tears when they heard of his death. He was without exception the kindest-hearted and the most perfectly gentleman-like man I ever knew.[31]

An officer who was with Charles when he died wrote:

> Our good Admiral won the hearts of all by his gentleness and kindness while he was struggling with disease, and endeavouring to do his duty as Commander-in-Chief of the British naval forces in these waters. His death was a great grief to the whole fleet. I know that I cried bitterly when I found he was dead.[32]

Some time after his uncle's death, James Edward wrote of him:

> His sweet temper and affectionate disposition, in which he resembled his sister Jane, had secured to him an unusual portion of attachment, not only from his own family, but from all the officers and common sailors who served under him.[33]

Charles was buried at Trincomalee. His wife Harriet died in 1869.

# 8

# JAMES LEIGH-PERROT

James Leigh-Perrot was the brother of Jane Austen's mother. Born in 1735, he was the eldest of the four surviving children of the Reverend Thomas Leigh, Rector of Harpsden, near Henley-on-Thames in Oxfordshire, and his wife Jane. In 1751, James added the name of Perrot to his surname in order to inherit the estate of his maternal great-uncle Thomas Perrot. Included in the inheritance was Northleigh, the Perrot family home in Oxfordshire.

When he was old enough to take up his inheritance James moved to Northleigh, but two years later he sold the house and estate to the Duke of Marlborough. He then bought Scarlets, a property situated in the village of Hare Hatch in Berkshire. This house, which had once belonged to James's mother, had been in the possession of the Perrot family and their maternal ancestors since the thirteenth century.

In October 1764, James married Jane Cholmeley, who belonged to an old Lincolnshire family. The couple were very wealthy, as in addition to James' inherited wealth, his wife had inherited her late father's estate in Barbados. They spent some of their money enlarging and improving Scarlets, which became their main home. Here they lived in style and comfort. Their large circle of friends included Richard Lovell Edgeworth, father of the novelist Maria Edgeworth. The Leigh-Perrots did not have any children, but they were very happy and devoted to each other. James called his wife Jenny, and she called him Perrot.

The Leigh-Perrots and the Austens kept in contact by letter and by exchanging visits. Mrs Austen was very close to her brother. Jane got to know her uncle and aunt while a child. She later referred to the Leigh-Perrots as 'my Uncle' and 'my Aunt' in her letters.

From around 1770 the Leigh-Perrots rented a house in Bath. James was suffering from gout and rheumatism, and he wanted to make use of the medical facilities and doctors there. From then on, the Leigh-Perrots lived for part of the year in Bath. Their house, 1, Paragon, was in the upper part of the city, near the Upper Assembly Rooms and the fashionable shops in Milsom Street. It had an extensive view of the city.

The Leigh-Perrots soon got into the well-established daily routine of residents and visitors in Bath. Those who wished to bathe in the waters went to the open-air baths in the early morning. Drinking the spa-water in the Pump Room, accompanied by music and conversation, followed. Next came breakfast and a morning service at the Abbey for those who wished to attend. Afternoon diversions which included walking, riding, driving out, shopping, and visiting the circulating library, went on until dinner, eaten between two o'clock and three-thirty in the afternoon. Afterwards the fashionable crowd paraded in their finery until teatime. In the evening there were plays, concerts, balls and parties to attend.

It is not difficult to see why Jane preferred her uncle to her aunt. James Leigh-Perrot was a kind, affectionate, amiable and generous man. He was also a cultured man who, in the words of his great-nephew James Edward Austen-Leigh, was 'a man of considerable natural power, with much of the wit of his uncle [Theophilus Leigh], the Master of Balliol.'[1]

Jane Leigh-Perrot, although highly respected, was not an amiable person. She was a forceful, opinionated and domineering woman, although she could also be kind. Jane noticed her snobbishness and, despite her wealth, her meanness.[2]

Rather like James Austen, who continually deferred to his wife, James Leigh-Perrot always agreed with his, and allowed himself to be dominated by her. He gave her everything she wanted, but she always seemed discontented. Her letters to the Austens were full of complaints about her and her husband's ailments, some of which in her case were imaginary. Jane described these negative aspects of her aunt's character as her 'sad' nature.[3]Jane Leigh-Perrot seemed to be aware of these faults as she once said: 'I cannot dissemble with anyone... If I am angry all must know it – if I am miserable, I cannot hide it.'[4]

Although Jane Austen did not describe any real people when she created her characters, she may have used some of her aunt's negative traits when she drew the character of the selfish Mrs Churchill in *Emma*, who 'governed her husband entirely'.

In November 1797, Mrs Austen, who had been in poor health for some time, went to Bath accompanied by her daughters in the hope that taking the waters would be beneficial to her. They stayed with the Leigh-Perrots.

Mrs Austen enjoyed a good relationship with her brother and sister-in-law. Jane and Cassandra got on well with their uncle but, unsurprisingly, not so well with their aunt. It is not known if Mrs Austen bathed in the hot baths or just drank the healing spa-water, but she did benefit from the visit. Before the Austen ladies returned home some time in December, James Leigh-Perrot, who shared Jane's interest in history and literature, gave his niece a copy of Hume's *History of England* from his own library. He later gave her more volumes from his library including Oliver Goldsmith's *An History of the Earth* and James Thomson's poetical works.

In May 1799, as described in Chapter 4, Edward Austen, who was in poor health, went to Bath to take the waters. He was accompanied by his wife, their two eldest children, Fanny and Edward, Mrs Austen, and Jane. It was wet and gloomy when they arrived. They stopped briefly at the Leigh-Perrot's home, where they were told by a manservant that James was unwell, so they did not stay long.[5] Their lodgings were in Queen Square, near the famous Royal Crescent and not far from the Leigh-Perrot's home. The Austens saw the Leigh-Perrots several times during their stay and noticed an improvement in James. On 16th June they had tea with them and Jane was able to inform Cassandra that their uncle was getting better.[6] The Austens left Bath the following week.

Jane next saw her uncle and aunt when she moved to Bath with her parents and sister in 1801. She arrived with her mother in May and her father and sister joined them in June. The Austens stayed with the Leigh-Perrots while they looked for suitable, reasonably priced accommodation to rent.

James Leigh-Perrot went to the Pump Room every day to drink the spa-water, and Jane usually accompanied him. They also went together to look for accommodation for the Austens. In a letter to Cassandra dated 5th-6th May Jane wrote: 'When my Uncle went to take his second glass of water, I walked with him, & in our morning's circuit we looked at two Houses in Green Park Buildings, one of which pleased me very well.'[7] Jane, who was a fast walker, found it frustrating to accompany her uncle, who walked slowly with the aid of a stick.

While staying with her uncle and aunt, Jane often went with them on social calls and to the Assembly Rooms. She was rather irritated by some of the people in their social circle. She wrote to Cassandra: 'Another stupid party last night; perhaps if larger they might be less intolerable, but here there were only just enough to make one card table, with six people to look over, & talk nonsense to each other.'[8] Although she found some of his friends dull, Jane enjoyed the company of her uncle. Later, when she was a published novelist, her uncle and his wife were among the few people who were trusted with the secret of her authorship.

Despite James's ill-health, the Leigh-Perrots led happy and uneventful lives in Bath until August 1799, when their peace was shattered. The story passed down in the Austen family is that on the eighth of that month Jane Leigh-Perrot bought some black lace from a haberdashery shop known as Smith's, on the corner of Bath Street and Stall Street, where she was a regular customer. The owner of this shop was a Miss Elizabeth Gregory, who had recently taken the business over when the previous owner was declared bankrupt. She ran the shop with her lover, a man called Filby, a disreputable character who had himself been made bankrupt twice.[9]

Mrs Leigh-Perrot selected her lace and Filby took it to the back of the shop to wrap it up. Having completed her purchase Mrs Leigh-Perrot went outside to meet her husband. As they passed the shop again half-an-hour later, the couple were stopped by Elizabeth Gregory, who demanded to know if there was a card of white lace in Mrs Leigh-Perrot's package. This was opened and, on finding the white lace, Gregory removed it. Thinking a mistake had been made by the shopkeeper, the Leigh-Perrots walked on. Filby then ran after them asking for their name and address, declaring that he had not put the white lace in the package. This alarmed Mrs Leigh-Perrot, as she had neither asked for white lace nor seen any in the shop. Mrs Leigh-Perrot was subsequently charged by the Bath magistrate with stealing lace valued at 20 shillings. The value of the lace made it a great larceny punishable by death, which was usually commuted to transportation to Botany Bay for fourteen years.

The family believed that this was a bogus charge on the part of Filby in an attempt to extort hush money from Mrs Leigh-Perrot's wealthy husband, who was well known in Bath. James Leigh-Perrot refused to pay up so his wife was committed to Ilchester Jail to await trial at the Spring Assizes the following March, with no bail permitted. James was able to pay for special treatment for his wife, and she was allowed to stay under house arrest in the jailer's house, instead of being put in a prison cell. Showing the strength of his devotion to his wife, James asked and was allowed to stay there with her.

The jailer, a man named Edward Scadding, treated the Leigh-Perrots well, but the conditions in his home were unpleasant to say the least, as revealed in a letter Jane wrote to her cousin Montague Cholmeley:

> One of my greatest Miseries here (indeed my very first) is the seeing what my dearest Husband is daily going through – Vulgarity, Dirt,

> Noise from Morning till Night. The People, not conscious that this can be Objectionable to anybody, fancy we are very happy, and to do them justice they mean to make us quite so.[10]

The worst thing they had to endure was the dirt, which was particularly objectionable to the fastidious James: 'Cleanliness has ever been his greatest delight and yet he sees the greasy toast laid by the dirty Children on his Knees, and feels the small Beer trickle down his sleeves on its way across the table unmoved.'[11]

James suffered a severe attack of gout while staying there but was unable to get the medical help he needed.[12]

Jane Leigh-Perrot's family and friends never doubted her innocence and she received many sympathetic letters while awaiting her trial. Mrs Austen, not knowing how she could best help her sister-in-law, suggested, presumably with their permission, that one or both of her daughters stay with their aunt during her house arrest and be with her during her trial. Fortunately for Cassandra and Jane, Mrs Leigh-Perrot declined the offer. She said that she could not allow 'those elegant young women' to stay in such conditions and suffer the 'inconvenience' she had to put up with there. 'To have two Young Creatures gazed at in a public Court would,' she added 'cut one to the very heart.'[13]

While they were staying in the jailer's house, James Leigh-Perrot received the following letter from a former servant, which shows what a kind and honourable man he was. Treating your social inferiors respectfully was one of the characteristics of a true gentleman.

> White Hart, Bath. Honored Sir – You may have forgot your old postillion Ben Dunford but I shall never forget yours & my

> Mistresses great Goodness to me when I was taken with the small pox in your sarvice. You sent me very careful to Mothers and paid a Nurse & my Doctor, & my Board for a long time as I was bad, & when I was too bad with biles all over my Head so as I could not go to sarvice for a many weeks you maintaned me. The Famaly as I lives with be going thro Bath into Devonshire & we stops 2 days at the Inn and there I heard of the bad trick as those bad Shopkeepers has sarved my Mistress and I took the libarty of going to your House to enquire how you both do and the Housekeeper said She sent a pasel to you every Week and if I had anything to say She coud send a letter. I hope Honored Sir you will forgive my taking such libarty to write but I wish any body could tell me how to do you & Mistress any good. I woud travel Night & Day to sarve you both. I be at all times with my humble Duty to Mistress & you Honored Sir your dutyfull Sarvant Ben Dunford.[14]

The trial was held on 29th March 1800 in the Great Hall of Taunton Castle. The case had attracted so much public attention that the courtroom was packed, and crowds also gathered outside. Mrs Leigh-Perrot, who pleaded not guilty, was represented by a top London barrister and she also made a statement herself. James, who had never left his wife's side, wept when her voice faltered.[15] A number of witnesses testified to Mrs Leigh-Perrot's honesty and good character. The defence also called as witnesses other people whom Gregory and Filby had attempted to blackmail in the same way.[16]

The trial lasted seven hours. It took the jury just ten minutes to return a not guilty verdict, which was met with spontaneous applause in the courtroom. The Leigh-Perrots returned to their Bath home after the trial. To add pecuniary insult to injury, they had to pay heavy costs of £2,000.[17] James Leigh-Perrot's devotion to his wife was increased by her ordeal, and he did all he could to make up for what she had suffered. He told his relations that if she had been transported, he would have sold his property and gone with her.[18]

In 1808, the Leigh-Perrots more than recouped the costs they had incurred eight years earlier as a result of the attempted blackmail. Two years before, the Honourable Mary Leigh of Stoneleigh Abbey in Warwickshire, died. The estate then reverted to the nearest male relative of Rowland Leigh of Longborough and Adlestrop. Under this reversion the Reverend Thomas Leigh inherited it, James Leigh-Perrot was second in line, and James Henry Leigh was third.[19]

James Leigh-Perrot agreed to relinquish his claim to James Henry Leigh, in exchange for a capital sum of £24,000 and an annual allowance of £2,000 for himself and, if his wife survived him, to her for the rest of her life.[20] As Jane Leigh-Perrot outlived her husband, the couple did very well out of the settlement.

In 1810, the Leigh-Perrots stopped renting 1, Paragon and bought their own house in Great Pulteney Street. This was made possible by the Stoneleigh inheritance.[21] They also bought a smart new carriage and horses. Sadly, as Mrs Leigh-Perrot later told her great-nephew James Edward, their increasingly poor health prevented them from enjoying their wealth. They could no longer socialise as they had previously and had to lead quiet lives.[22] They did, however, still occasionally visit Mrs Austen and her daughters at Chawton. These visits continued until 1812, when travelling that far became too much for them.

Even though the Leigh-Perrots no longer saw their niece Jane, when her novels were published, beginning with *Sense and Sensibility* in 1811, they became very interested in her writing career. They particularly admired *Pride and Prejudice* and considered that none of her other novels were its equal.[23]

When Henry Austen was made bankrupt in 1816, James lost £10,000, as he had stood surety for this sum when his nephew was appointed Receiver General for Oxfordshire. Despite his wealth, this was a considerable sum of money to lose.

On 28th March 1817 James died peacefully at Scarlets at the age of eighty-two, having been unwell for some time. Cassandra Austen hurried to Berkshire to comfort her aunt. Her brother James, who was sole trustee of his uncle's estate, and his wife Mary soon followed.

When the will was read, Mrs Austen was shocked to discover that no mention was made of her or her daughters. Her brother's estate was left to his wife for her lifetime, with a reversionary interest to her son James. Those of Mrs Austen's children who outlived Jane Leigh-Perrot were left £1,000 each, but they received no immediate benefit. Mrs Austen, whose financial position had been precarious since the death of her husband had, not unreasonably, expected to benefit from her brother's will, as he had always been good to her. She and her daughters seem to have been counting on receiving something.[24] Mrs Austen soon got over her disappointment but Jane, who was then terminally ill, was very upset, and the distress caused a relapse in her illness.[25] It seems that James Leigh-Perrot's love for his wife and his determination to compensate for the ordeal she had undergone at the hands of blackmailers outweighed any consideration of the financial needs of his sister and her family. Jane Leigh-Perrot, naturally devastated at the loss of her husband, spoke of how happy they had made each other and stated that he was the 'whole world' to her.[26]

After her husband's death, it was envisaged that James Austen would inherit his uncle's estate, of which he was sole trustee, on the death of his wife. James Austen, however, died less than three years after the death of his uncle. Jane Leigh-Perrot then had to decide who would inherit her property and money.[27] On James's death in 1819, knowing that he contributed to his mother's income, Jane generously paid Mrs Austen an allowance of £100 a year.[28]

As previously mentioned, at first it seemed that Frank Austen would inherit the vast Leigh-Perrot wealth, but Jane Leigh-Perrot objected to his marriage in 1828 to Martha Lloyd. Frank was given £10,000 by way of compensation.[29] James Edward Austen, who had for some years been receiving an allowance of £300 a year from his great-aunt, was then expected to be her heir.[30] When James Edward decided to become a clergyman, the capricious Mrs Leigh-Perrot threatened to change her mind again. James Edward refused to change his career plans and in the end she relented when he married Emma Smith, who met with her approval, in 1828.[31]

Jane Leigh-Perrot died in November 1836, at the advanced age of ninety-two. She was buried beside her husband in the churchyard of Wargrave parish church in Berkshire. Her heir had a memorial placed inside the church with the following inscription.

Jane, Daughter Of Robert Cholmeley
Esq. And Widow Of James Leigh Perrot
Esq. Died At Scarlets In This Parish
Nov. 13th 1836 Aged 92
In Humble Hope That Through The Merits

Of Her Redeemer She Shall Rejoin In
Heaven, Him Who Had Been The Object
Of Her Constant And Undiminished
Affection Upon Earth Through Fifty
Years Of Wedlock And Twenty Years Of Widowhood.

On the death of his great-aunt, James Edward Austen added the surname of Leigh to his own, which was a condition of his inheritance. Mrs Austen's six surviving children each inherited £1,000, according to the wishes of their late great-uncle.

# 9

# TWO NEPHEWS

George Thomas Austen, later Knight, the third child of Edward and Elizabeth Austen, was born at Rowling, their home in Kent, on 22nd November 1795. He enjoyed a close and affectionate relationship with his Aunt Jane, who was nearly twenty years old when he was born.

George was ten months old when Jane first met him on a visit to her brother and his family. In a letter to her sister Jane wrote: 'I have taken little George once in my arms since I have been here, which I thought very kind.'[1]

The next time she saw George was on her first visit to Godmersham House with her parents and sister in August 1798. George, or Itty Dordy as he called himself, was by then a lively toddler. Jane was captivated by him and this was the start of their close relationship. Cassandra remained at Godmersham when Jane and her parents returned home. In a letter to her sister, written on her journey back to Hampshire, Jane boasted that 'I flatter myself that itty Dordy will not forget me at least under a week. Kiss him for me.'[2]

From then on Jane and Cassandra visited Godmersham separately. Cassandra's letters to her sister from Godmersham have not survived, but we gather from Jane's replies that they frequently mentioned George. Jane was delighted that her little nephew continued to remember her. In a letter dated $27^{th}$-$28^{th}$ October 1808, she wrote: My dear itty Dordy's remembrance of me is very pleasing to me; foolishly pleasing, because I know it will be over so soon. My attachment to him will be more durable.'[3] She recalled his 'beautiful and smiling countenance and interesting Manners'.[4]

Jane drew pictures for George in her letters and he was allowed to choose the wafer (seal) for her sister's replies. On Jane's birthday in 1798, George was allowed to drink tea as a special treat. Her comment on hearing this was, 'I am sincerely rejoiced however that I ever was <u>born</u>, since it has been the means of procuring him a dish of Tea.[5]

In another letter Jane wrote that she was delighted to hear that 'sweet little George' had 'such an inventive Genius as to face-making.'[6] She was very pleased to hear that he was good at skipping.

On a visit to Godmersham in 1805, when George was nearly ten years old, Jane described him as a 'fine boy, and well-behaved.' He amused his elders with his fun and high spirits. She told Cassandra that 'George's enquiries were endless & his eagerness in everything reminds me often of his Uncle Henry'[7]

Early biographies of Jane claim that she did not like children. This myth seems to have derived from her description of the spoilt and disagreeable Middleton children in *Sense and Sensibility*. Jane liked children immensely, as demonstrated by her close relationship with George and her enjoyment of the company of all her young nephews and nieces. It was only badly behaved children that she disliked.

At the age of twelve George followed his older brother Edward to Winchester College. He had not been there long when his mother died in October 1808. The brothers were granted compassionate leave and were taken to Steventon Rectory to be with their Uncle James and Aunt Mary. After a few days they travelled by coach to Southampton to be comforted by their grandmother and Aunt Jane. Cassandra was at Godmersham supporting her brother and his other children.

Jane occupied and distracted Edward and George from their grief by playing games with them, taking them for walks and on a boat trip. She also took them to a tailor to be fitted out with mourning clothes. The brothers showed 'quite as much feeling as one wishes to see on the death of their mother.' George sobbed at the description of his mother's funeral in a letter from their father. However, with the resilience of the young, they enjoyed the distractions their aunt provided for them. Jane noticed the return of their natural high spirits and, in a letter to Cassandra, described George 'industriously making and naming paper ships', which he then 'bombarded with horse chestnuts'. Edward was quieter and preferred to read.[8]

The next reference to George in Jane's letters was when he was seventeen and had grown more like his brother Edward. He remained at Winchester College for four years and then, a year later, followed Edward to St John's College, Oxford. In the holidays George and his brothers enjoyed shooting and hunting at Godmersham, using the 'best guns' bought for them by their father. Their Aunt Jane could not understand their passion for field sports or their 'sporting mania' as she called it. Although Jane did not approve of her nephews' obsession with sport, she was pleased with their pleasant manners and good behaviour.

George did not read *Sense and Sensibility* when it was published, but he did read *Pride and Prejudice* and *Mansfield*

*Park,* of which he preferred the former. He disliked the quiet, well-behaved, principled heroine of *Mansfield Park,* and was not interested in any of the characters in this novel except the witty, sophisticated, but unprincipled Mary Crawford.

Jane must have been pleased with her nephew's sense of humour. Being fond of parody herself, she would have enjoyed George's parody of the following poem, written by his Uncle Henry in praise of Godmersham.

Godmersham The Temple of Delight

Gentle Pilgrim, rest thy feet,
Open is the gate to thee;
Do not doubt that thou shalt meet
Mirth & Hospitality,
Elegance & grace shall charm thee,
Reason shall with wit unite –
Sterling sense shall here inform thee
How domestic love can find
All the blessings, which combined
Make the temple of Delight.[9]

The following is George's version:

*George Knight to his Dog Pincher*

*Gentle Pincher, cock thy tail,*
*Open is the door to thee;*
*Enter, and there ne'er shall fail*
*Mirth and Hospitality –*

*Partridge bones, & Pork shall charm thee*
*Mutton shall with Veal unite;*
*Sterling Beef shall then inform thee*
*How domestic Dogs can find*
*All the savings, which combined*
*Make the Temple of Delight.*[10]

It is not known what Henry thought of his nephew's parody of his poem!

Little is known about George's adult life. According to his brother-in-law, Lord Brabourne, 'He was one of those men who are clever enough to do almost anything, but live to their lives' end very comfortably doing nothing.'[11]

In 1837 George married Hilaire, Lady Nelson, the widow of William Nelson, brother of Horatio. All that is known of the marriage is that they did not have any children, and they enjoyed travelling on the Continent. George died in 1867 at the age of seventy-two.

James Edward Austen-Leigh, the son of James Austen and his second wife Mary, was born at Deane Rectory on 17th November 1798. Jane announced her nephew's arrival in a letter to her sister, who was at Godmersham at the time.

Sunday (18th November)
I have just received a note from James to say that Mary was brought to bed last night, at eleven o'clock, of a fine little boy, and that everything is going on very well.[1]

It was this 'fine little boy', said to be Jane's favourite nephew, who would many years after her death write the first biography of her, which has been used as a source by every biographer since. Although he was christened James Edward, the baby was always known in the family as Edward, to distinguish him from his father. When he was born, James Edward's half-sister Anna was five-and-a-half years old.

Jane met her new nephew a few days after his birth. She saw him briefly as he lay sleeping in his cradle. His mother's friend, who had helped at the birth, told Jane that the baby's eyes were 'large' and 'dark'. Mary was very proud of her son and described him as 'handsome'.[2]

In April 1801, James Edward moved with his parents and Anna to Steventon Rectory when his grandfather retired. James Edward was a kind, affectionate and much-loved boy. His favourite pastimes as a child were writing poetry and riding horses, both of which he continued to enjoy as an adult. Writing poetry was a tradition in the Austen family. James Edward's grandmother wrote clever epigrammatic verses and his father wrote religious and pastoral poetry. The following is the first poem written by James Edward, when he was six years old. It is an early example of his wit.

The Neck of Veal

Poor neck of Veal, don't pity me
For pity more belongs to thee,
Though I've not tasted of thy meat
I've had the pleasure of seeing my Father eat.[3]

James Edward's sister Caroline, who was five years younger than him, remembered that he had a pony which died in January

1811 and was buried in the corner of a meadow near the rectory. This loss was the cause of much grief to James Edward, who was delighted when he was given a new pony a few months later. Caroline recalled that this pony, which was called Sutton, lived with them for many years and 'was a most useful animal, carrying anybody on the road, and taking his young master with the hounds.'[4] James Edward enjoyed accompanying his father when he went riding around the surrounding countryside with the Vyne Hunt.

James and Mary Austen took their children to visit relatives in other parts of the country, as described in Chapter 2. In the summer of 1808, they took James Edward and Caroline to Godmersham to visit their Uncle Edward, Aunt Elizabeth, and their family. It was the children's first visit there and, to add to the novelty, their Aunt Jane went with them. They stayed at Godmersham for three weeks, during which time James Edward played happily with his cousins Lizzy and Charles, and slept in the attic with his boy cousins. A highlight of the holiday for James Edward was when he went on horseback with his father and uncle to see a pond being drained on the Godmersham estate. Jane noticed how well he got on with his uncle. 'His Uncle Edward,' she informed Cassandra, 'talks nonsense to him delightfully – more than he can always understand.'[5]

In September of the same year, James Edward went to Southampton with his family to visit his grandmother and his aunts Jane, Cassandra, and Martha. He remembered their large house in a corner of Castle Square which belonged to the 2nd Marquis of Lansdowne. James Edward particularly remembered an unusual building in the centre of the square. He described it in his *Memoir* of his aunt, written nearly fifty years later:

> At that time Castle Square was occupied by a fantastic edifice, too large for the space in which it stood, though too small to accord well with its castellated style, erected by the 2nd Marquis of Lansdowne... The Marchioness had a light phaeton, drawn by six, and sometimes by eight little ponies, each pair decreasing in size, and becoming lighter in colour, through all the grades of dark brown, light brown, bay, and chestnut, as it was placed farther away from the carriage. The two leading pairs were managed by two boyish postilions, the two pairs nearest to the carriage were driven in hand. It was a delight to me to look down from the window and see this fairy equipage put together; for the premises of this castle were so contracted that the whole process went on in the little space that remained of the open square.[6]

James Edward also remembered that his grandmother's garden was 'bounded on one side by the old city walls.'[7] The top of the wall, which was wide enough to walk along, overlooked the Solent – no doubt another pleasure enjoyed by visiting children.

During childhood visits to his grandmother's homes in Southampton, and later in Chawton, James Edward developed a close and affectionate relationship with his Aunt Jane. On one visit to her brother and his family, Jane gave her nephew a book entitled *The British Navigator, or, A Collection of Voyages made in different parts of the world*, indicating that he shared his aunt's interest in history.[8]

James Edward also had close, affectionate relationships with his sisters from childhood, and was kind and considerate towards them. Caroline remembered her brother's kindness to her and recalled one instance of it in her *Reminiscences*. It happened in 1809, when they went with their parents to stay with their great-uncle and aunt at Stoneleigh Abbey in Warwickshire. Day trips were made to places of interest, to which ten-year-old James Edward was invited, but his four-year-old sister was not.

> I never forgot, my brother's great good nature to his little sister. He made one in all these parties, therefore I saw but little of him, and at last when I heard he was going off again that morning to Kenilworth, I burst out crying, and complained, I believe, that he was always away from me; and he instantly said, he would stay at home, and play with me instead, and this he did.[9]

In July 1809 Mrs Austen, her daughters and Martha moved to Chawton in Hampshire. As their new home was just a short journey from Steventon, James Austen and his family became regular visitors. James Edward recalled those visits and, later realised that writing at Chawton Cottage could not have been easy for his Aunt Jane because 'she had no separate study to retire to, and most of the work must have been done in the general sitting-room, subject to all kinds of casual interruptions.'[10] Jane wanted to keep her writing a secret so 'She wrote upon small sheets of paper which could easily be put away, or covered with a piece of blotting paper.'[11]

James Edward recalled that near where she worked there was a swing door which creaked when it was opened, but Jane would not allow this to be remedied, because it gave her notice of anyone approaching.

Jane did not see so much of her nephew after he started at Winchester College in 1814, but they clearly remained close, as there are frequent references to him in Jane's letters. These show him as a warm-hearted, affectionate, and much-loved nephew. Despite James Edward's closeness to his aunt, he did not discover that she was a published author until he was fifteen years old. He had read both *Sense and Sensibility* and *Pride and Prejudice* and enjoyed them. He was so surprised to find out that they were written by his aunt that he wrote the following delightful poem:

No words can express, my dear Aunt, my surprise
Or make you conceive how I opened my eyes,
Like a pig Butcher Pile has just struck with his knife,
When I heard for the very first time in my life
That I had the honour to have a relation
Whose works were dispersed through the whole of the nation.
I assure you, however, I'm terribly glad;
Oh dear! just to think (and the thought drives me mad)
That dear Mrs Jennings' good-natured strain
Was really the produce of your witty brain,
That you made the Middletons, Dashwoods, and all,
And that you (not young Ferrars) found out that a ball
May be given in cottages, never so small.
And that though Mr Collins, so grateful for all,
Will Lady de Bourgh his dear Patroness call,
'Tis to your ingenuity really he owed
His living, his wife, and his humble abode.
Now if you will take your poor nephew's advice,
Your works to Sir William pray send in a trice,
If he'll undertake to some grandees to show it,
By whose means at last the Prince Regent might know it,
For I'm sure if he did, in reward for your tale,
He'd make you a countess at least, without fail,
And indeed if the Princess should lose her dear life
You might have a good chance of becoming his wife.[12]

In August 1816 Cassandra Austen accompanied her sister-in-law Mary to Cheltenham. James Edward stayed at Chawton Cottage with Jane, who had been unwell since the beginning of the year. Jane enjoyed having Edward with her in Cassandra's absence, as in a letter to her dated 4th September, she wrote: 'We go on very well here. [James] Edward is a great pleasure to me; – he drove me to Alton yesterday…'[13] In the same letter Jane informed Cassandra that James Edward was writing a novel: 'It is extremely clever; written with great ease & spirit; – if he can carry it on in the same way, it will be a first-rate work, & in a style, I think, to be popular.'[14]

Jane encouraged her nephew to keep writing. When she discovered that he had mislaid part of his novel, she expressed her concern in a letter and made an interesting comparison of their different writing styles.

> By the bye, my dear Edward, I am quite concerned for the loss your Mother mentions in her Letter; two Chapters & a half to be missing is monstrous! It is well that I have not been at Steventon lately, & therefore cannot be suspected of purloining them; – two strong twigs & a half towards a Nest of my own, would have been something. – I do not think however that any theft of that sort would be really very useful to me. What should I do with your strong, manly, spirited Sketches, full of Variety & Glow? – How could I possibly join them on to the little bit (two Inches wide) of Ivory on which I work with so fine a Brush, as produces little effect after much labour?[15]

As well as writing a novel, James Edward continued to write poetry. He wrote poems about the countryside around Steventon, about events of the day, and poems for family members, such as *To Anna. A Riddle* and *To Caroline on her Birthday*.

At the end of 1816, James Edward left Winchester College, where he had been a diligent and well-behaved pupil. His father received a letter from his headmaster saying: 'To the very favourable reports which I have had the pleasure of making to you from time to time on the conduct of your excellent son, I can add nothing.'[16]

Jane sent her nephew an affectionate and humorous letter in which she congratulated him on leaving the college, and she teased him about his time there. The letter began:

> One reason for my writing to you now, is that I may have the pleasure of directing to you Esq.– I give you Joy of having left Winchester. – Now you may own, how miserable you were there; now, it will gradually all come out – your Crimes & your Miseries – how often you went up by the Mail to London & threw away Fifty Guineas at a Tavern, & how often you were on the point of hanging yourself – restrained only, as some ill-natured aspersion upon poor old Winton [Winchester] has it, by the want of a Tree within some miles of the City.[17]

Shortly after receiving this letter, James Edward went to Exeter College, Oxford, on a Craven Founder's Kin Scholarship, for which he was eligible as his mother was a descendant of a founder of the college.

At the beginning of 1817, James Edward stayed at Chawton Cottage again. It was a great help to Cassandra to have him there, as he could keep Jane company and take her out when Cassandra was busy running the household, a responsibility she had taken over from her elderly mother. Jane told James Edward's sister

Caroline that it was an unexpected pleasure to have him there. She also paid tribute to him in a letter to her friend Alethea Bigg dated 24th January 1817.

> He grows still, & still improves in appearance, at least in the estimation of his Aunts, who love him better & better, as they see the sweet temper and warm affections of the Boy confirmed in the young Man...[18]

James Edward was at Chawton again in March, when Jane felt strong enough to ride out for a short distance on a donkey, led by Cassandra and her nephew. By May, however, Jane's health had deteriorated, and Cassandra took her to Winchester to be near her doctor, who was a surgeon at Winchester Hospital. Three days after her arrival in Winchester, Jane wrote a cheerful letter to James Edward which began: 'I know no better way my dearest [James] Edward, of thanking you for your most affectionate concern for me during my illness, than by telling you myself as soon as possible that I continue to get better.'[19] She told him that her doctor 'says he will cure me, & if he fails, I shall draw up a Memorial & lay it before the Dean and Chapter, & have no doubt of redress from that Pious, Learned & disinterested Body.'[20] This was the last letter James Edward received from his aunt.

On 12th June James Austen wrote to his son to tell him that Jane was dying.

> I grieve to write what you will grieve to read; but I must tell you that we can no longer flatter ourselves with the least hope of having your dear valuable Aunt Jane restored to us... Mr Lyford [her doctor] has candidly told us that her case is desperate.[21]

A few weeks later, on 18th July, Jane died at her lodgings in Winchester, with her sister by her side. James Edward attended her funeral as his father's representative, because he was unwell. He walked with his uncles Henry, Edward, and Frank, beside her coffin as it was carried from her lodgings in College Street to the cathedral, where she was laid to rest in the north aisle.

Shortly after his aunt's death, James Edward wrote a long, formal poem entitled *To the Memory of Miss Jane Austen,* in which he refers to her 'Piety' and Genius' and how dear she was to her family.[22] In her will Jane left her nephew a volume of her early writing.

Throughout 1819, James Austen's health deteriorated and by the autumn it was clear that he was dying. A week before his father died, James Edward arrived from Oxford to be with him. He attended his funeral on 18th December and then stayed with his mother and sister until they vacated the rectory, a few weeks later, for Henry Austen, the new rector, to move in. According to Caroline Austen, they left their home 'with sad hearts, we did not desire to linger in it any longer.' They went to Bath to stay with Mary's friend Mrs Hulbert, who offered them 'a quiet retreat for a little while'.[23] After this short break James Edward returned to Oxford to finish his studies. His mother and sister went to Berkshire. There they lived in a series of borrowed and rented homes in the Newbury area. After his father's death James Edward became the heir of Jane Leigh-Perrot's estate, but it would be many years before he came into his inheritance.

James Edward visited his grandmother and aunts Cassandra and Martha at Chawton Cottage whenever he could. Mrs Austen, despite frequent bouts of ill-health over many years, lived to an advanced age. On one of his visits James Edward remembered his grandmother saying to him: 'Ah, my dear, you find me just where you left me – on the sofa. I sometimes think that God Almighty must have forgotten me; but I daresay He will come for me in His own good time!'[24] Mrs Austen eventually died in 1827 at the age of eighty-seven and was buried in the churchyard of St Nicholas Church, Chawton.

When he had completed his studies at Oxford, James Edward decided to take Holy Orders, despite Jane Leigh-Perrot threatening to disinherit him if he did so. He was ordained on 1st June 1823 by the Bishop of Winchester, and became curate of a church in Newtown, near Newbury. His clerical duties do not appear to have been very onerous because James Edward enjoyed a busy social life, which included attending balls and hunting two or three times a week. In 1825 Mrs Austen and Caroline moved to Newtown to be near James Edward, who was always concerned for their welfare.

As a child and youth James Edward and his father had hunted together with the Vyne Hunt. It was through hunting that James had befriended William Chute, M.P. for Hampshire, and his wife. The Chutes lived at the Vyne, a large centuries-old house near Basingstoke. James Edward maintained his friendship with the Chute family after his father's death, and it was at their home that he met his future wife, Emma Smith. Emma was a niece of Mrs Chute, who approved of James Edward and wrote of him:

> He certainly is a very agreeable companion, cheerful, lively, animated, ready to converse, willing to read out loud, never in the way and just enough of poetry and romance to please me and yet not to overlook sober reason.[25]

James Edward and Emma married in December 1828 at Tring, Hertfordshire. They lived at Tring Park, Emma's family home, for the first five years of their marriage. James Edward gave up his curacy of Newtown to become curate of Tring. Jane Leigh-Perrot approved of his marriage to Emma, which outweighed her disapproval of his chosen career. She informed him that he would inherit her estate after all, and also promised the young couple an allowance of £600 a year.

In November 1833, James Edward, his wife and three children left Tring Park and moved into a house in Speen, Buckinghamshire. While he was there James Edward developed a throat condition which made it difficult for him to talk, and he was no longer able to officiate in church. This illness lasted for several years and enforced a period of inactivity. To keep himself occupied James Edward took up the new pastime of cutting out silhouettes. Some of his pictures were put on screens or cabinets and then varnished, but most were collected together in a book.

Jane Leigh-Perrot died in 1836 and James Edward, who had recovered from his illness, finally inherited her house Scarlets and the bulk of her money. In January 1837, he and his family moved to Scarlets and he added the name of Leigh to his own, which was a condition of his inheritance. The house at Speen was taken over by James Edward's mother and sister, to whom he now paid a generous allowance, enabling them to live in comfort.

The Austen-Leighs lived at Scarlets for fifteen years, during which time renovations were carried out to the house and gardens. While he lived there James Edward was vicar of Knowl Hill, were he built a school for local children at his own expense.

As his grandfather had done, James Edward educated his sons himself. He enjoyed spending time with his ten children, and in the Austen family tradition he read aloud to them in the evenings, wrote poems to amuse them, and they played charades and word games together.

On 3rd August 1843 James Edward's mother died following a seizure. Caroline remained in the house in Speen until July of the following year. She did not settle anywhere for a while, but making her 'headquarters',[26] as she described it, at Scarlets, she spent the next few months visiting various relations and friends. She then rented a house at Knowl Hill, before buying 'Wargrave Lodge' near Scarlets in 1851.[27] Like her Aunt Jane, Caroline was a loving aunt to her brother's children.

In 1853 James Edward was offered the post of vicar of St Michael's Church in Bray, in Berkshire – the church memorialised in the eighteenth-century satirical song *The Vicar of Bray*. In April of that year the Austen-Leighs moved to Bray. Scarlets was at first let to a tenant and then sold to him.

While he was at Bray, James Edward wrote *Recollections of the Early Days of the Vine* [sic] *Hunt*, which contained some fascinating stories about the men who hunted in the north Hampshire countryside when he was a young man and later. It included sketches of some of his grandparents' old friends and neighbours. Like his aunt, who did not want to reveal her authorship, the title page stated that it was written by 'a Sexagenarian'.

A few years later James Edward wrote another, much more significant book – the first biography of his famous aunt. Jane was only a moderately successful novelist in her own lifetime. Her fame and literary reputation did not begin to grow until the 1860s. Soon her readers wanted to know more about Jane's life and character. People began to flock to her grave in Winchester

Cathedral, which led to a puzzled verger enquiring 'Is there anything particular about that lady?'[28]

The only biographical information about her was a brief sketch written by Henry Austen, which was published with *Northanger Abbey* and *Persuasion* in 1818. There was so much interest in his Aunt Jane that James Edward decided it was time to record family memories of her, before it was too late. As his sister Caroline pointed out, 'The generation who knew her is passing away – but those who are succeeding us must feel an interest in the personal character of their Great Aunt, who has made the family name in some small degree, illustrious.'[29]

James Edward was also concerned that, if he did not write a biography of Jane, someone from outside the family, with less knowledge of her, might attempt to write one.

As well as his own memories of Jane and the letters she had sent him, James Edward had his sisters' recollections from which to draw material for his memoir. His cousin Cassy, daughter of Charles Austen, offered the use of some letters of Jane's which she had inherited from Cassandra, and two watercolour portraits of Jane by her sister. It took James Edward less than six months to complete his biography. It was published under the title of *A Memoir of Jane Austen and Other Family Recollections* in December 1869.

As well as a biography, the *Memoir* traced Jane's development as a novelist, a history of the publication of her novels, and it outlined the growth of her literary fame and reputation. It contained four illustrations and a portrait of Jane, which was a prettified version of a portrait painted by her sister.

The *Memoir* portrayed Jane as a much-loved daughter, sister, aunt and friend, as well as a talented writer. There were a few shortcomings in the *Memoir,* however, including a tendency to digress at great length and an inaccurate depiction of Jane's life as sheltered and uneventful. This was because James Edward only knew his aunt well when she was leading a quiet, sedate life in Chawton. He did not know her as a young woman when she had a busy social life, travelled around the country to visit relations, and went on holiday in the west country and Wales. James Edward painted a rather unrealistic and idealised picture of his aunt.

Despite these limitations, the *Memoir* was well received by the Austen family and the reading public. It also received good reviews. James Edward was surprised and pleased by the public's reaction and was delighted to receive letters of praise from readers in England and America. He had not realised how many people had read Jane's novels. In the words of his sister Caroline, 'Perhaps never before has so small a volume attracted so much attention.'[30]

The success of the *Memoir* led to further editions of Jane's novels and the publication of new articles and reviews. There was also a demand for more information about Jane's life and for the publication of her unpublished works. To satisfy these demands, a second edition of the *Memoir* was published in 1871. In a preface to this edition, James Edward wrote:

> The Memoir of my Aunt, Jane Austen, has been received with more favour than I had ventured to expect. The notices taken of it in the periodical press, as well as letters addressed to me by many with whom I am not personally acquainted, show that an unabated interest is still taken in every particular that can be told about her.[31]

This second edition contained additional material, including the cancelled chapter of *Persuasion* and the unpublished short story *Lady Susan*.

The profits from the *Memoir* were used to pay for a brass memorial tablet to Jane, which was placed near her grave in Winchester Cathedral in 1872. The inscription on the tablet reads:

> Jane Austen known to many by her writings, endeared to her family by the varied charms of her Character and ennobled by her Christian faith and piety, was born at Steventon in the County of Hants. Dec. xvi, mdcclxxv and buried in this Cathedral July xxiv, mdcccxvii. She openeth her mouth with wisdom and in her tongue is the law of kindness. Provs. xxii v. xxvi

The reference to Jane's writing is significant, as there is no mention of it on her gravestone. This was because when she died Jane had not yet been recognised as a great writer – or indeed a writer – and her name had not been linked with her published novels.

James Edward continued to enjoy outdoor activities, such as following the hunt, until he began to suffer from some sort of rheumatic complaint which made it difficult for him to get about. From time to time, James Edward visited Caroline, who lived in Sussex from 1860 with his bachelor sons Charles and Spencer, for whom she acted as housekeeper. The last time he visited her was in October 1872.

On 14th April 1874, Caroline went with her brother, Emma and two of their daughters to see the Crystal Palace in Norwood, where it had been rebuilt after the Great Exhibition of 1851. Caroline noted in her diary that this was 'the last time I was ever to see my dear brother'.[32] James Edward died in September 1874 at Bray Vicarage. According to Caroline,

> His illness was very short. He kept his room but a few days, and although his family, considering his age, were in some degree anxious about him, there was no real cause for alarm till the night before. He breathed his last about ten o'clock Tues. morning the 8th.[33]

He had remained Vicar of Bray until the end of his life although, for some time, his son Arthur had helped him with his clerical duties.

James Edward was buried in Bray churchyard on 14th September. A memorial to him was placed in the church by his 'Parishioners and other Friends,' to record 'their affection for his memory; their admiration for his character and their recognition of his work.' He will also always be remembered as the author of the first biography of Jane Austen.

*Tom Lefroy, with whom Jane Austen had a brief romance over Christmas and New Year 1795-6.*

10

# COULD JANE HAVE MARRIED?

Jane Austen and her sister Cassandra both expected and wanted to marry, but their chances were limited because their father could not afford to give them a dowry. Cassandra, nevertheless, became engaged to a clergyman who unfortunately died before they could marry. She was so grief-stricken at his death that she never considered marriage again.

Jane met two men whom she could have married, if circumstances had been different. One other man proposed to her and a fourth was interested in her, but his interest was not returned.

## *Tom Lefroy*

Jane's first romantic attachment was with a young man she met in December 1795, when she was twenty. She had already attracted the attention of a few local men but had shown no interest in them. Tom Lefroy was different. This shy, fair-haired young man was the nephew of the Austen family's friend George Lefroy, rector of Ashe, near Steventon. Tom, who lived in Northern

Ireland, had recently been awarded a degree in law by Trinity College, Dublin. He was living in London with his wealthy uncle Benjamin Langlois, who was paying for him to train at Lincoln's Inn to become a barrister.

Tom was invited to spend Christmas and New Year with his uncle, aunt and their family at Ashe Rectory. He met and danced with Jane at several balls over the Christmas period. It soon became obvious that Tom and Jane had developed an affection for each other.

Jane's sister Cassandra, who was staying in Berkshire with her fiancé's family, was alarmed to learn of this budding romance. She was worried that if Jane was not careful people would gossip about her. It was essential to observe the strict rules that governed the behaviour of young people of marriageable age. Two important rules were not to dance more than two dances with the same partner, or spend too much time together between dances. If these rules were flouted, it could be assumed that an 'agreement' (engagement) had been reached. This sort of behaviour, which Jane and Tom were clearly indulging in, could stain the reputation of an unmarried woman and harm her chances of finding a husband. Cassandra was also worried that her sister might get hurt and told Jane off in a letter. Jane's reply shows that she was aware of her inappropriate behaviour.

> You scold me so much in the nice long letter which I have this moment received from you, that I am almost afraid to tell you how my Irish friend and I behaved. Imagine to yourself everything most profligate and shocking in the way of dancing and sitting down together. I can expose myself, however, only once more, because he leaves the country soon after next Friday, on which day we are

> to have a dance at Ashe after all. He is a very gentlemanlike, good-looking, pleasant young man, I assure you. But as to our having ever met, except at the last three balls, I cannot say much; for he is so excessively laughed at about me at Ashe, that he is ashamed of coming to Steventon, and ran away when we called on Mrs Lefroy a few days ago.[1]

In a letter Jane told Cassandra that she would be meeting Tom at a dance the following night and suggested that she was expecting him to propose to her during the evening. Jane was looking forward to the dance 'with great impatience'. The following day she added to the letter: 'At length the Day is come on which I am to flirt my last with Tom Lefroy, & when you receive this it will be over – My tears flow as I write, at the melancholy idea.'[2]

Cassandra was not the only one to have been worried about Jane and Tom. The Lefroys had also noticed their flirtatious behaviour. They were concerned that if Tom became engaged to the daughter of an impecunious clergyman, who could not afford to give her a dowry, he would lose the financial support of his uncle and not realise his ambition of becoming a barrister. It is also possible that the Lefroys were aware that before leaving Ireland, Tom had met and formed an attachment with a young lady named Mary Paul who, in the words of Jane's niece Caroline, 'had the convenience of money'.[3] The Lefroys acted quickly to end the romance. Tom left Ashe earlier than expected and returned to his uncle's house in London.

Cassandra was relieved to hear that Tom had gone. Jane's light-hearted letters to her suggest that she did not really expect a proposal from Tom, but there is a hint of sadness in her final letter. Maybe she really did shed tears when Tom left Ashe.

In 1797 Tom Lefroy became engaged to Mary Paul and married her two years later. They enjoyed a happy marriage and had seven children. Tom went on to have a glittering legal career, which culminated in his appointment as Lord Chief Justice of Ireland in 1852. He was also elected Member of Parliament for Dublin University in 1830. Many years later, Tom's nephew was recorded as saying that his uncle had been in love with Jane but that it was a 'boyish love'.[4]

Jane may have been thinking of Tom when, in November 1814, her niece Fanny sought her advice over a romance she had recently ended. What Jane wrote to her could have been applied to herself: 'He was the <u>first</u> young Man who attached himself to you. That was the charm, & most powerful it is.'[5]

### *Samuel Blackall*

In December 1797, another young man stayed with the Lefroys over Christmas and New Year. Samuel Blackall, a friend of the family, was a clergyman and a fellow of Emmanuel College, Cambridge. Anne Lefroy introduced him to Jane, thinking he would make her a good husband. She was possibly trying to make up for ending Jane's romance two years earlier.

Jane took an instant dislike to Samuel. She thought he was pompous and self-centred, and had too high an opinion of himself.[6] He was clearly attracted to Jane and told her that he hoped to be given a lucrative college living, maybe to enhance his eligibility as a potential husband. Jane was relieved when he returned to Cambridge.

The following Christmas Samuel was again invited to Ashe and his letter of acceptance, which Mrs Lefroy showed to Jane, revealed that he thought she would make him a good wife.

He wrote: 'It would give me particular pleasure to have an opportunity of improving my acquaintance with that family [the Austens] – with a hope of creating to myself a nearer interest. But at present I cannot indulge any expectation of it.'[7] That was because he was not in a position to marry and support a wife. Jane commented on this in a letter to her sister:

> This is rational enough; there is less love and more sense in it than sometimes appeared before, and I am very well satisfied. It will all go on exceedingly well, and decline away in a very reasonable manner. There seems no likelihood of his coming into Hampshire this Christmas, and it is therefore most probable that our indifference will soon be mutual, unless his regard, which appeared to spring from knowing nothing of me at first, is best supported by never seeing me.[8]

It is not known if Blackall did visit the Lefroys that Christmas, or if he ever met Jane again. If he attempted to make himself a 'nearer interest' he would not have succeeded. This episode was no more than a source of amusement to Jane.

In 1812 Samuel Blackall was given the college living he had been hoping for. He became the rector of North Cadbury in Somerset and the following year he married a Miss Susannah Lewis of Clifton near Bristol. On hearing of this, Jane wrote in a letter to her brother Frank: 'I should very much like to know what sort of a Woman she is. He was a piece of Perfection, noisy Perfection himself…'[9]

Jane may have used some of the characteristics of Samuel Blackall when creating the characters of Mr Collins in *Pride and Prejudice* and Mr Elton in *Emma*. Both were pompous clergymen with a high opinion of themselves. Mr Collins also fits the description of 'a piece of Perfection, a noisy piece of Perfection'.

### *The Mystery Suitor*

On one of their seaside holidays between 1801 and 1804 Jane met a man, believed to have been a clergyman, with whom she had a brief romance. The name of this man and where he met Jane are unknown. This romance remained a secret until, many years after Jane's death, Cassandra spoke about it to her niece Caroline. According to James Edward Austen-Leigh,

> She [Cassandra] said that, while staying at some seaside place, they became acquainted with a gentleman, whose charm of person, mind, and manners was such that Cassandra thought him worthy to possess and likely to win her sister's love. When they parted, he expressed his intention of soon seeing them again; and Cassandra felt no doubt as to his motives. But they never again met. Within a short time they heard of his sudden death. I believe that, if Jane ever loved, it was this unnamed gentleman; but the acquaintance had been short, and I am unable to say whether her feelings were of such a nature as to affect her happiness.[10]

It is thought that Jane may have used this experience when writing *Persuasion*. Anne Elliot, the heroine of this novel, suffers for years after breaking off her engagement to Frederick Wentworth, but she never forgets him. When Anne says, 'All the privilege I claim for my own sex (it is not a very enviable one, you need not covet it), is that of loving longest, when existence or when hope is gone,'[11] is she expressing the author's own pain? The use of the word 'existence' suggests when parted by death.

Jane was aware, however, of how marriage and bearing children would have curtailed her freedom, not least the freedom to write. This may be why, according to her niece Catherine Hubback, 'she always said her books were her children, and supplied her sufficient interest for her happiness.'[12]

### *Harris Bigg-Wither*

In the autumn 1802 Jane and her sister paid a brief visit to James and Mary Austen at Steventon, followed by a longer one to Godmersham. After returning to Steventon, Jane and Cassandra went to stay with their friends Catherine and Alethea Bigg at Manydown Park, near Basingstoke. A few days after their arrival, on 2nd December, Jane received an unexpected proposal of marriage from her friends' brother. Harris Bigg-Wither, who was eight years younger than her.

Jane, who had met Harris on previous visits but did not know him well, accepted his proposal. She changed her mind overnight, however, and retracted her acceptance the following morning. Jane was so embarrassed and distressed that she and Cassandra left Manydown immediately. They were accompanied back to Steventon by their friends. Mary Austen was surprised to see the Bigg-Wither family coach draw up outside the rectory and Jane, Cassandra and their two friends get out. After a tearful farewell, Catherine and Alethea got back into the carriage and left. Jane, who was very agitated, told Mary that they needed James to accompany them back to Bath immediately, but she would not say why. Mary tried to persuade them to wait as the next day was Sunday and James, who had no curate, would have to find someone to cover for him. Jane and Cassandra refused to wait so James had to do as they asked. They could not have travelled unaccompanied on a public coach. When the reason for their hasty departure was discovered, Mary expressed her disapproval that Jane had turned down an offer of marriage from such an eligible young man.

After accepting the proposal, Jane had quickly realised that she could not marry a man she did not love. Her niece Catherine described her acceptance as 'a momentary fit of self-delusion'.[13] Jane had been briefly tempted by the material and other advantages which marriage to Harris Bigg-Wither would have brought her. He was heir to his father's considerable estate and she would have been mistress of Manydown House. She would also have been able to look after her mother and sister, who would be poor and possibly homeless on her father's death. Another consideration may have been that at the age of twenty-seven Jane was already regarded as an 'old maid', and she was aware that she might not receive another offer of marriage.

Fortunately, Jane's refusal of their brother's proposal did not spoil her relationship with her friends. Harris married a young lady named Anne Howe-Frith two years later and lived with her at Wymering, near Portsmouth. He did not return to Manydown until his father died in 1813 and he inherited his estate.

Jane's novels demonstrate her firmly held belief that a woman's best chance of happiness was to be found in a happy marriage to a man she loved and respected, and who loved and respected her in return. She also believed that a couple should know each other well before marrying. Jane never regretted her decision to withdraw her acceptance of Harris Bigg-Wither's offer of marriage. This is reflected in another piece of advice to her niece Fanny. She advised that 'nothing can be compared to the misery of being bound without Love, bound to one, & preferring another. That is a Punishment which you do not deserve.'[14]

In *Pride and Prejudice* Jane portrays the dilemma faced by single women without a dowry. Elizabeth Bennet is worried about her friend Charlotte Lucas's willingness to marry the awful Mr Collins, following her own rejection of him. Although a 'sensible, intelligent woman', Charlotte was plain and already deemed an 'old maid' at the age of twenty-seven – the same age Jane was when she rejected Harris Bigg-Wither. Knowing that with these disadvantages she was unlikely to receive another proposal of marriage, Charlotte is prepared to accept Mr Collins to obtain her own 'establishment' (home) and the other advantages of being a married woman, and to avoid the stigma of being a spinster. Elizabeth, although no better off financially than her friend, believes, like her creator, that love is important in marriage and is prepared to wait until a man she loves and respects comes along.

# PART 2

# THE MALE CHARACTERS IN JANE AUSTEN'S NOVELS

*Frontispiece of the 1833 edition of* Sense and Sensibility.

I

# *SENSE AND SENSIBILITY*

*Summary*

Mrs Dashwood and her three daughters live at Norland Park in Sussex. On the death of her husband his heir John Dashwood, a son by a previous marriage, arrives to take possession of their home. John, who is controlled by his mean wife Fanny, fails to keep a promise to his father to look after his widow and their daughters. Mrs Dashwood is left with very little to live on.

The heroines of the novel are Mrs Dashwood's two elder daughters Elinor and Marianne. Elinor, who is sensible, prudent, and always in control of her emotions, represents the 'Sense' in the title; while Marianne, who is passionate, emotional, and impetuous, represents 'Sensibility'. The novel shows that the ideal personality is a combination of both these qualities.

Mrs Dashwood and her daughters go to live in Barton Cottage on the Devonshire estate of her distant cousin Sir John Middleton. They become part of Sir John's social circle, which includes his mother-in-law Mrs Jennings and his friend Colonel Brandon. Brandon is immediately attracted to Marianne, as she reminds him of a woman he once loved and lost. Marianne considers the Colonel to be too old and too dull for her.

When Marianne sprains her ankle while out walking one day, she is carried home by a handsome stranger named John Willoughby, who appears to have a lot in common with her, and they fall in love. They do not attempt to hide their feelings for one another, which leads people to suspect that they are engaged. Willoughby has to leave suddenly for London and does not know when, or if, he will return. Marianne cannot hide her grief at his departure, which causes her mother and sisters much anxiety.

Elinor does her best to comfort Marianne, but she is also suffering because of her separation from Edward Ferrars, the brother of Fanny Dashwood, with whom she has formed an attachment. There appears to be no future for their relationship as Elinor would not be an acceptable partner for Edward, whose mother expects him to marry a woman with money. Elinor has to control her own emotions so that she can help Marianne. Edward Ferrars visits Barton Cottage but he is cold and distant, leaving Elinor 'mortified'. When she notices that Edward is wearing a ring containing a lock of hair, he tells her that it belongs to his sister.

Lucy and Anne Steele, cousins of Mrs Jennings, arrive at Barton Park. When Lucy hears about Edward's attachment to Elinor, she tells her that she has been secretly engaged to Edward for four years and that the lock of hair in his ring is hers. They cannot announce their engagement because Edward's mother would not approve of the match and would probably disinherit him. Elinor is upset but keeps her feelings to herself.

Elinor and Marianne are invited to spend the winter with Mrs Jennings at her London town house. Marianne hopes to see Willoughby in London. She waits for him to call but he does not do so. When Colonel Brandon visits, he is upset to hear about Willoughby's treatment of Marianne and tells Elinor that he loves her sister.

The sisters attend a party in London where they see Willoughby with a young lady. He refuses to speak to Marianne, who is so distressed that they leave the party early. Marianne receives a letter in Willoughby's handwriting informing her that he is soon to marry another woman. Marianne is devastated. Elinor discovers that Willoughby is marrying for money and is shocked to hear that he and Marianne have never been engaged. Elinor learns from Colonel Brandon that Willoughby had seduced his young ward Eliza Williams, leaving her pregnant. He hopes that this knowledge will help Marianne. As soon as he is married Willoughby leaves London.

The Steele sisters arrive to stay with John and Fanny Dashwood in Harley Street, but their visit is cut short when Anne Steele reveals her sister's secret engagement to Fanny's brother Edward. His mother is furious, but he refuses to break the engagement and is disinherited by his mother, who settles her property on his younger brother Robert instead. Edward and Lucy cannot marry until he has taken holy orders and found a living. Colonel Brandon, with Elinor's unselfish encouragement, offers Edward the living of Delaford on his estate.

When Marianne hears of this, she realises that Elinor has ignored her own pain to help her. Marianne sees how strong Elinor has been and how self-indulgent she herself has been. Marianne resolves to control her emotions better and to be less selfish in future.

The Dashwood sisters, Colonel Brandon and Mrs Jennings go to Cleveland in Somerset, the home of Mrs Jennings' daughter and son-in-law. Marianne catches a cold when out walking in a storm. This turns to pneumonia and she nearly dies. The Colonel leaves for Devon to collect Mrs Dashwood. Willoughby, having heard that Marianne is dangerously ill, arrives at Cleveland unexpectedly. He tells Elinor that he is unhappily married and that this is his own fault for getting so heavily in debt that he had to abandon Marianne to marry a rich woman. He is sorry for hurting Marianne whom he has never stopped loving. When Marianne recovers, she hears about Willoughby's confession. She realises that her illness was the result of her own foolishness.

Elinor and Marianne return to Devon where Edward Ferrars visits them and reveals that Lucy Steele has married his brother Robert. This leaves Edward free to marry Elinor and they start their married life at Delaford Parsonage. Marianne, meanwhile, has fallen in love with Colonel Brandon and, having learned some important lessons, she marries him.

### *John Willoughby*

John Willoughby belongs to Sir John Middleton's social circle. He is the nephew and heir of Mrs Smith, the wealthy owner of Allenham Court, and he also has his own estate in Somerset. Willoughby enters the novel as the stranger who helps Marianne when she falls and sprains her ankle while out walking and carries her home. He is a very handsome young man with 'more than common gracefulness' and plenty of charm. He has the appearance, manners, and social status of a gentleman. To the romantic Marianne, Willoughby's 'person and air were equal to what her fancy had ever drawn for the hero of a favourite story.'[ch 9]

Like Marianne, Willoughby represents sensibility. They share an interest in music and poetry and Willoughby, as expected of a gentleman, is a good dancer. He and Marianne also share the same negative character traits of impulsiveness, self-indulgence, and selfishness. Elinor also notices that, like Marianne, Willoughby has a 'propensity' for 'saying too much what he thought on every occasion, without attention to persons or circumstances.'[ch 10]

Despite his apparent charm, a less pleasant side to Willoughby's character emerges early in the novel when he speaks unkindly of Colonel Brandon, who is a much better and more honourable man than he is himself. Willoughby dismisses the Colonel as 'just the kind of man, whom every body speaks well of, and nobody cares about; whom all are delighted to see, and nobody remembers to talk to.' [ch 10]

Willoughby later admits that, at first, he had no other intention when he became acquainted with Marianne 'than to pass my time pleasantly with her.' He was 'careless of her happiness' thinking only of his own 'amusement' and had no intention of returning her affection.

Instead of protecting Marianne, as a gentleman should have done, Willoughby leads her astray. He surreptitiously cuts off a lock of her hair in the presence of her sister and later claims that Marianne gave it to him. Willoughby takes her unaccompanied to Allenham Court. These actions break the important rules governing the behaviour of young people who are unmarried and add to suspicions that they are engaged. Willoughby also, inappropriately, offers to buy Marianne a horse, but Elinor, showing her usual good sense, persuades her not to accept such an expensive present from a man she has not known very long.

His lack of caution leads Willoughby 'by insensible degrees' to become 'sincerely fond' of Marianne. He fully intends to pay his 'addresses' to her and Marianne feels herself to be 'as solemnly engaged to him, as if the strictest legal covenant' [ch 29] bound them together. When his circumstances change, he has to give Marianne up, breaking her heart.

This change is due to his wealthy aunt discovering that he has callously seduced and abandoned Colonel Brandon's ward Eliza Williams. According to the Colonel, Willoughby has been 'expensive [extravagant], dissipated' and 'had left the girl whose youth and innocence he had seduced, in a situation of the utmost distress, with no creditable home, no help, no friends, ignorant of his address.' [ch 31] Willoughby's aunt insisted that he marry the unfortunate Eliza, but he refused and fled to London in pursuit of the wealthy heiress Maria Grey. In serious debt, he is forced to marry for money.

Willoughby does his best to avoid Marianne in London. When he sees her at the party he refuses to acknowledge or speak to her, causing her great distress. He then sends her a cruel letter saying that he had never given her reason to think he loved her and that he is about to marry another woman. He returns Marianne's letters and the lock of her hair. It is later discovered that this cruel letter was dictated by Willoughby's wife. His rejection of Marianne, without an explanation, devastates her and, because of her inability to control her grief, also distresses her family. It particularly affects Elinor who has to suppress her own pain on learning of Edward's secret engagement, so that she can comfort her distraught sister.

When a drunk Willoughby visits Cleveland on hearing of Marianne's illness, it is clear from his conversation with Elinor that he does love Marianne. Willoughby admits his wrongdoing and declares that he now realises that Marianne is 'infinitely dearer to me than any other woman in the world.' He admits that he is unhappily married and that it is his own fault for getting so heavily in debt that he had to abandon Marianne to marry a rich woman. He asks Elinor to tell Marianne that his 'heart was never inconstant to her,' and that she is 'dearer' to him than ever.' [ch 44]

When Marianne later reflects on the way Willoughby treated her she says 'cruel, cruel – nothing can acquit you.' She describes his behaviour as being 'far from the common decorum of a gentleman.'[ch 29] Willoughby is justly punished for hurting Marianne and for failing to behave like a gentleman, by having to spend the rest of his life with a woman he does not love.

### *Edward Ferrars*

Edward is the elder son and heir of a wealthy widow. His mother and sister, Fanny Dashwood, want him to be 'distinguished' in some field, but his ambition is to become a clergyman and enjoy a quiet domestic life. His mother expects him to marry well.

Edward is described, rather negatively, as 'not handsome and his manners required intimacy to make them pleasing.' Underneath his 'natural shyness' Edward possesses an 'open affectionate heart.'[ch 3] He has the status, appearance and bearing of a gentleman.

When Edward forms an attachment with Elinor Dashwood while staying at Norland he does not inform her of his secret engagement to Lucy Steele. This is unfair to both Elinor and Lucy. He knows that he is behaving dishonourably. Elinor becomes concerned when Edward visits her at Barton Cottage and is unhappy and distracted. He lies to her about the lock of Lucy's hair in his ring by claiming that it is his sister's. This is not how a gentleman should behave. Secret engagements are not permitted in the rules governing courtship as they lead to misunderstandings, subterfuge, and deceit.

When Lucy Steele hears about Edward's attachment to Elinor, she takes great pleasure in revealing the secret engagement. This causes Elinor much distress, which she has to suppress as her mother and sisters are all fond of Edward and expect him to marry her. She also has to hide her pain from Marianne.

Edward now regrets his engagement to Lucy, who is a silly, uneducated young woman. Edward was foolish to get engaged to Lucy because he knew his mother would not accept her and would probably disinherit him. The £2,000 he owns is not enough to marry and set up home.

Elinor suspects that Edward is weary of the engagement. She can see that he and Lucy are not well suited and is worried that their marriage would not make Edward happy. Although he was very young when he proposed to Lucy, he was very unwise to do so.

When Anne Steele reveals the secret to Edward's family and he is banished from his mother's home and disinherited Edward, like a true gentleman, is willing to keep his promise to Lucy, despite the consequences. Fortunately, Lucy transfers her affections to Robert Ferrars when he becomes his mother's heir. This releases Edward and, no longer being answerable to his mother, he now has the freedom to choose his own wife. Ironically, Mrs Ferrars states that Elinor would have been a much more acceptable choice of wife than Lucy.

Edward proposes to Elinor, declaring 'an affection as tender, as constant as she had ever supposed it to be.'[ch 49] She points out that his behaviour 'was certainly very wrong because – to say nothing of my own conviction, our relations were all led away by it to fancy and expect what, as you were then situated, could never be.'ch 49 The living of Delaford and Edward's £2,000 enable him to marry Elinor. He is eventually reconciled with his mother who also offers him some financial help.

Despite his secret engagement and the confusion and distress it causes, Edward is fundamentally a decent man. By the end of the novel, having gained maturity and independence, he marries Elinor.

### *Colonel Brandon*

Colonel Brandon has been 'loved and respected' for a long time by his friends Sir John Middleton and Mrs Jennings. He is a gentleman in both social rank and behaviour. Although the Colonel is not handsome 'his countenance was sensible, and his address was particularly gentlemanlike.' He is well-read, has a 'thinking mind' and has a grave and reserved manner, due to depression caused by losing the woman he loved.ch 7

The Colonel is attracted to Marianne Dashwood from their first meeting. Marianne dismisses him as an old and infirm bachelor, although he is only thirty-five. In any case, Marianne only has eyes for Willoughby. Elinor Dashwood likes Colonel Brandon and describes him as a 'sensible man, well-bred, well-informed, of gentle address, and, I believe, possessing an amiable heart.'ch 10

Despite his own worries about his young ward Eliza Williams, the Colonel is very concerned about Marianne's emotional suffering resulting from the cruel treatment she has received from Willoughby. He tells Elinor that he loves Marianne, and in the hope that the knowledge may help Marianne, he tells her what has happened to Eliza. This shows what a good, kind, and caring man the Colonel is, in contrast to the selfish, callous, and heartless Willoughby.

Colonel Brandon is a great comfort and support to Elinor when Marianne is dangerously ill and collects their mother from

Devon to be with her. When Edward Ferrars is disinherited by his mother, the Colonel offers him the living of Delaford so that he and Lucy Steele can marry. Edward is touched by this kindness from a man he hardly knows. He describes his benefactor as a 'man of great worth and respectability… I have always heard him spoken of as such,' he tells Elinor, 'and your brother I know esteems him highly. He is undoubtedly a sensible man, and in his manners perfectly the gentleman.'[ch 40] Like Elinor, the Colonel demonstrates the importance of sense.

As she recovers, Marianne sees Colonel Brandon's worth for herself and they become friends. In time she falls in love with him. Mrs Dashwood knows that the Colonel will make her daughter much happier than Willoughby would have done. She describes him as 'the worthiest of men' and says to Elinor, 'The Colonel's manners are not only more pleasing to me than Willoughby's ever were, but they are of a kind I well know to be more solidly attaching to Marianne. Their gentleness, their genuine attention to other people, and their manly unstudied simplicity is much more accordant with her real disposition, than the liveliness – often artificial and often ill-timed – of the other.'[ch 45]

Colonel Brandon is a true hero who has always behaved like a gentleman. His faithfulness to Marianne, and his unwavering love for her despite her obsession with Willoughby, are rewarded by him winning her hand in marriage.

### *Robert Ferrars*

Robert Ferrars is Edward's younger brother and their mother's favourite son. He is a conceited dandy and a snob. Robert's unpleasant characteristics are shown up by his brother's good ones.

When Edward is rejected by his mother because he decides to honour his promise to Lucy Steele, Robert looks down on him with contempt. 'Poor Edward,' he says, 'he has done for himself completely – shut himself out for ever from all decent society!'[ch 41] Robert also looks down on Edward when he becomes the clergyman of a small country parish. Robert declares that this 'diverted' him 'beyond measure,' and that he 'could conceive nothing more ridiculous.'[ch 41]

Robert and the unpleasant Lucy Steele deserve each other. Edward, a fundamentally honourable man, is rewarded with marriage to the woman he loves.

*Frontispiece of the 1833 edition of* Pride and Prejudice.

2

# *PRIDE AND PREJUDICE*

*Summary*

Elizabeth Bennet, the heroine of *Pride and Prejudice*, is the second of the five Bennet sisters. Their mother's main goal in life is to see her daughters well married. The Bennets live at Longbourn, Mr Bennet's small estate near the town of Meryton in Hertfordshire. As they do not have a son, Longbourn is entailed to a distant cousin of Mr Bennet's.

Nearby Netherfield Park has recently been let to Charles Bingley, an eligible, wealthy bachelor. Mrs Bennet is determined that he will marry one of her daughters. Elizabeth and her older sister Jane meet Mr Bingley, his two sisters and his friend Fitzwilliam Darcy at Meryton Assembly Rooms.

Bingley and Jane, who are immediately attracted to each other, dance together. Darcy refuses to dance with Elizabeth, who does not have a partner, because she is not handsome enough for him. Elizabeth overhears Darcy saying this and immediately dislikes him. This is the beginning of her prejudice against him. Other people at the ball also take a dislike to Darcy and decide that he is proud and disagreeable.

When Darcy and Elizabeth meet again at the Lucas family's party he begins to find her attractive. He notices the ignorance and embarrassing behaviour of Mrs Bennet and her younger daughters.

Jane Bennet is befriended by Bingley's sisters, who invite her to Netherfield. She is detained there because she develops a bad cold from riding to Netherfield in the rain. Elizabeth visits Jane and enjoys lively discussions with Darcy. He is becoming increasingly attracted to Elizabeth, despite her social inferiority and his misgivings about members of her family.

Mr Collins, the cousin who will one day inherit Longbourn, comes to stay. This unpleasant young man holds the living of Hunsford, which was given to him by Lady Catherine de Bourgh. Collins constantly boasts of his connection to the great lady. He has come to Longbourn in the hope of marrying one of the Bennet sisters.

Elizabeth meets George Wickham, an officer in the militia encamped nearby. She discovers that he and Darcy have known each other since childhood, as Wickham's father had worked as steward for Darcy's late father, and that Lady Catherine de Bourgh is Darcy's aunt. Wickham tells Elizabeth that Darcy had deprived him of a living which he had been promised by Darcy's late father. Elizabeth, who is taken in by Wickham's charm, believes him.

When Wickham does not attend a ball at Netherfield Elizabeth is disappointed, but she dances with Darcy, who is not pleased when she mentions Wickham. She also dances with Mr Collins, who is not a good dancer.

Elizabeth is horrified when, shortly after the ball, Mr Collins proposes to her. When she rejects him he transfers his affection to her friend Charlotte Lucas, who is desperate to marry.

Jane Bennet, being reserved, does not reveal her feelings for Bingley. Elizabeth suspects that Darcy has influenced Bingley against Jane.

Elizabeth visits the newly married Mr and Mrs Collins at Hunsford Parsonage and meets the formidable Lady Catherine de Bourgh at her grand house, Rosings. Darcy and his cousin Colonel Fitzwilliam arrive. Elizabeth is astonished to receive a proposal of marriage from Darcy who tells her that, although put off by her family, he cannot control his feelings for her. Darcy is shocked and angry when Elizabeth rejects his offer, accuses him of ruining Jane's happiness and repeats what Wickham has told her.

Shortly after his rejection, Darcy sends Elizabeth a letter telling her that Wickham's story is a lie motivated by revenge because Darcy prevented him from eloping with his sister for her money. He also explains why it appeared that he had come between Bingley and Jane. Elizabeth realises that she has badly misjudged Darcy.

The regiment of militia move to Brighton. Mr Bennet allows his youngest daughter Lydia, who has been wasting her time flirting with the officers, to go with the regiment, despite Elizabeth's warning of the moral danger to which this would expose her.

Elizabeth goes with her uncle and aunt Gardiner to Derbyshire where they visit Pemberley, Darcy's estate, after Elizabeth has been assured that Darcy is not at home. Elizabeth learns from Darcy's housekeeper that her initial view of him was incorrect – that he is in fact a good and kind man. Much to her embarrassment, Darcy appears and seems to be a changed man. He is kind and courteous to his visitors and Elizabeth realises that now, 'when all love must be vain,' she could love Darcy.

When Darcy goes to see Elizabeth at her inn, he finds her in tears as she has received the news that Lydia has eloped with Wickham. The reputation of the Bennet family is in danger, as it is the height of impropriety for a woman to live with a man to whom she is not married.

Elizabeth and the Gardiners set off home so that Mr Gardiner can help Mr Bennet search for Lydia. Unknown to them, Darcy also leaves for London, where the runaways were last seen. Motivated by guilt for not revealing Wickham's true character, he wants to help. Darcy finds them and, as Lydia refuses to leave Wickham, he pays him to marry her.

Jane and Bingley are reconciled and she accepts his proposal of marriage.

Elizabeth is astonished when Lady Catherine de Bourgh suddenly turns up at Longbourn to ask her about a 'most alarming' report that she and Darcy are to marry. She states that Darcy is engaged to her daughter and demands that Elizabeth promises not to marry him. Elizabeth stands up to the intimidating Lady Catherine and refuses to make such a promise.

When Darcy hears of this, he realises that Elizabeth may not be lost to him after all. Elizabeth happily accepts his second proposal of marriage. They have both changed and admit their faults – his of pride and hers of prejudice. Elizabeth and Jane marry in a double ceremony and Elizabeth becomes mistress of Pemberley.

### *Fitzwilliam Darcy*

Fitzwilliam Darcy is a 'fine, tall person' with 'handsome features' and a 'noble mien.'[ch 3] He is twenty-eight years old at the start of the novel. Darcy is a gentleman by birth who, on the death of his father, inherited Pemberley, a large country house and estate in

Derbyshire and an income of £10,000 a year. Darcy and Bingley are close friends.

Darcy has many of the qualities expected of a gentleman, including being a good dancer and conversing with ease, but he does not always behave like a gentleman. Darcy's worst ungentlemanly trait is his pride. At Meryton Assembly Rooms he haughtily rejects Bingley's suggestion that he ask Elizabeth, who does not have a partner, to dance. Darcy describes her as 'tolerable; but not handsome enough to tempt me…'[ch 3] Darcy is either not aware or does not care that Elizabeth hears this. It leaves her with 'no very cordial feelings' for him and is the start of her prejudice against him. At the ball, Darcy

> … was looked at with great admiration for about half the evening, till his manners gave a disgust which turned the tide of his popularity; for he was discovered to be proud, to be above his company, and above being pleased.[ch 3]

Mrs Bennet takes a strong dislike to Darcy for slighting her daughter, describing him as a 'most disagreeable, horrid man.'[ch 3]

Darcy's pride and haughtiness are on display again at the Lucas family's party. When Mr Collins speaks to Darcy he breaks the rule of not addressing a person of higher social rank before being formally introduced. Darcy replies with an 'air of distant civility'.[ch 18] When Mr Collins continues speaking to him Darcy's contempt increases. He makes a slight bow and moves away. Although Mr Collins is behaving inappropriately, Darcy responds in an ungentlemanly way by not concealing his contempt. It is at this party that Darcy notices the embarrassing behaviour of all members of the Bennet family apart from Elizabeth and Jane.

At the Lucas family's party, Darcy begins to change his initial assessment of Elizabeth's looks and is attracted by her lively personality and wit. Although he tries to resist it, his attraction deepens. When Elizabeth visits Netherfield she and Darcy enjoy lively discussions and he admires her intellectual quickness.

Elizabeth's opinion of Darcy does not change, and she is still prejudiced against him when he makes his first proposal of marriage to her. Darcy, in a most ungentlemanly way, tactlessly reveals his contempt for Elizabeth's family. Without thought for her feelings he tells her that he would be lowering himself by marrying her. Elizabeth is deeply offended.

Darcy clearly expects Elizabeth to accept his proposal and is shocked when she does not. She tells him that he is the 'last man' she would marry. She then criticises Darcy's behaviour towards Wickham and blames him for separating Jane and his friend Bingley. Darcy is humiliated and angry.

Following their next meeting Elizabeth begins to see another side of him. He appears when she is out walking and hands her a letter containing an answer to her accusations. He explains that he knew Bingley was in love with Jane but could see no evidence of her affection for him. He was also not happy about his friend marrying into the Bennet family because of the improper behaviour of all but her and Jane. Darcy admits that he did keep them apart. He apologises for any hurt he has caused Jane.

Darcy explains that Wickham's story was all lies told out of revenge for Darcy preventing him from eloping with his sister. He tells her about Wickham's profligacy and bad character.

It becomes clear that Darcy has learned from Elizabeth's rejection of his offer of marriage. He acknowledges that he proposed without a doubt of being accepted and tells her she showed him 'how insufficient were all my pretensions to please a woman worthy of being pleased.'[ch 58]

Darcy also admits his vanity in believing Elizabeth was 'wishing, expecting my addresses.' Darcy's ready admission of his failings makes Elizabeth aware of her own and leads her to reassess her behaviour. She realises that she had been too ready to believe Wickham because of her prejudice against Darcy, that she has misjudged him and has been 'blind, prejudiced and absurd'. [ch 36]

Darcy's letter concludes with the words 'I can only add God bless you.' It 'began in bitterness' but 'did not end so.'[ch 58] A different side to Darcy's character is emerging.

Elizabeth finds out how badly she has misjudged Darcy when she and the Gardiners are being shown around Pemberley. She is surprised to hear from the housekeeper that Darcy is 'the best landlord, and the best master that ever lived,' that he does much good among the poor, is held in 'much estimation' by local people and is a loyal and protective brother to his younger sister. When the housekeeper says, 'I have never had a cross word from him in my life.' Elizabeth wonders 'in what amiable light does that place him?'[ch 43] When he is described as quiet and reserved, Elizabeth questions whether she has sometimes mistaken Darcy's reserve for pride.

Elizabeth, who was under the impression that Darcy was not at home, is shocked when he appears and is worried about the 'impropriety' of her being there. She is surprised when Darcy kindly asks about her family. Elizabeth has 'never seen his manners so little dignified, never had he spoken with such gentleness.' His behaviour is 'so strikingly altered.'[ch 43]

Darcy is polite and kind to the Gardiners and there is no sign of his pride and haughtiness. Elizabeth wonders why he is 'so altered ... it cannot be for my sake.' She is astonished and 'gratified' to see such a change in Darcy. Elizabeth and the Gardiners are invited to dine at Pemberley, where they meet Darcy's sister Georgiana.

Darcy continues to behave like a gentleman when he saves the reputation of the Bennet family by locating Lydia and Wickham after they have eloped and paying Wickham to marry her. He lets Mr Gardiner take the credit for what he has done.

When Elizabeth hears that 'they owed the restoration of Lydia, her character, every thing'[ch 52] to Darcy, she begins to realise that he is 'exactly the man who, in disposition and talents, would most suit her.'[ch 50] She realises that their union would benefit them both as they complement each other but doubts that Darcy would want to marry into a family of which Wickham is a member.

It is only when Darcy hears of Elizabeth's refusal to promise Lady Catherine that she would not marry him that Darcy realises that she may not be lost to him after all. Elizabeth accepts Darcy's second proposal. They both apologise for their past behaviour. Darcy says that it was Elizabeth's accusation that he had not behaved like a gentleman which had most affected him – showing how important this was. They both admit their faults – his of pride and hers of prejudice.

### *Mr Bingley*

Charles Bingley was not born a gentleman. His wealth was inherited from his father, who made a fortune in the north of England through trade. Bingley's annual income is the £4,000 interest on his £100,000 inheritance. Like other members of the nouveaux riches, who liked to emulate the landed gentry and aristocracy, Bingley aspires to buy a large country house and estate, but he is happy, for now, to rent Netherfield and enjoy the benefits of being the Lord of the Manor.

Bingley is described as 'quite young, wonderfully handsome, extremely agreeable' with 'a pleasant countenance, and easy, unaffected manners.'[ch 3]

When Bingley meets Jane Bennet at the Meryton Assembly Rooms they are immediately attracted to each other. They dance together twice and Jane notices his 'happy manners' and 'perfect good breeding'. [ch 4]

Unlike his sisters and Darcy, Bingley is not a snob and mingles happily with everyone at the Assembly Rooms, including his social inferiors. He is not, unlike Darcy, put off by the lower social status of Jane's family and is not bothered by the embarrassing behaviour of some of them.

Although not born a gentleman, Bingley has all the gentlemanly qualities that his friend Darcy, who is a gentleman by birth, appears to lack. He is a good match for the beautiful, warm, and cheerful Jane Bennet, who never thinks ill of anyone, and has the same easy manners that he has.

Bingley and Darcy are close friends but, not trusting his own judgement, Bingley relies too much on Darcy's opinion. As a result, Bingley allows his friend to come between himself and Jane by believing Darcy's claims that Jane is not interested in him. Darcy takes Bingley to London to get him away from Jane and fails to tell him that she is also in London. By allowing himself to be influenced by Darcy, Bingley nearly loses Jane and causes her, and probably himself, much unhappiness. Once Darcy withdraws his objection to Bingley marrying Jane he immediately proposes and is accepted. Bingley shows the importance of behaving like a gentleman, regardless of your family background.

### *Mr Bennet*

A gentleman by birth, Mr Bennet is described as being an 'odd a mixture of quick parts, sarcastic humour, reserve, and caprice'.[ch 1] His wife, as the daughter of a lawyer, is his social inferior. He had been captivated by her 'youth and beauty, and that appearance of good humour, which youth and beauty generally give.'[ch 42]

The silly, foolish, shallow, and not very intelligent Mrs Bennet constantly complains about her nerves. She lost her husband's affection and respect early in their marriage. Mr Bennet has paid ever since for marrying a beautiful woman without knowing her true character. This probably explains why Elizabeth is determined to marry a man she loves and respects.

Mr Bennet's predicament illustrates how important it was in Georgian England to be careful when choosing a marriage partner. Divorce was impossible for most people, as it was expensive and had to be granted by an individual Act of Parliament. Mr Bennet has to live with the unhappy consequences of having been captivated by his wife's beauty and not getting to know her well before marrying her.

To escape his wife, Mr Bennet spends most of his time in his library. His only pleasures in life are the countryside and books, and his main source of amusement is the ignorance and folly of his wife and their youngest daughters, Kitty and Lydia. He leaves his wife in charge of their daughters, with the result that they are not properly disciplined, and Kitty and Lydia are out of control. Elizabeth, who shares her father's wit and intelligence, is his favourite daughter. She is aware of the 'impropriety of her father's behaviour as a husband' and 'the disadvantages'[ch 42] which the children of such an ill-matched marriage were likely to suffer.

Foolishly, Mr Bennet pinned his hopes on having a son to inherit his property, but this did not happen, and his estate is entailed to his distant cousin, Mr Collins. Mr Bennet has also failed to put aside enough money for good dowries for his daughters. This places them at a considerable disadvantage in the competitive marriage market and makes it difficult for their mother to achieve her ambition of seeing all her daughters well married.

Mr Bennet's worst failure is ignoring Elizabeth's advice not to let Lydia go with the militia regiment to Brighton. She can see the dangers of exposing her silly sister to the temptations of such a place. Lydia has 'never been taught to think on serious subjects' and has been allowed to waste her time 'in the most idle and frivolous manner'.[ch 47]

When Elizabeth's fears are realised and Lydia elopes with Wickham, she blames her father for 'his indolence and the little attention he has ever seemed to give to what was going forward in his family.'[ch 47] Mr Bennet admits his faults and says to Elizabeth, 'Let me once in my life feel how much I have been to blame... I bear you no ill-will for being justified in your advice to me last May, which, considering the event, shows some greatness of mind.'[ch 48] Unaware of Darcy's involvement in finding Lydia and Wickham, Mr Bennet is determined to repay his brother-in-law for paying off Wickham and saving the reputation of his family.

Finally, when it is too late, Mr Bennet shows some firmness and bans Lydia and Wickham from Longbourn. Elizabeth and Jane persuade him to change his mind.

After the worry and anxiety caused by Lydia is resolved, Mr Bennet's wit returns when he tells Elizabeth 'I admire all my three sons-in-law highly... Wickham, perhaps, is my favourite; but I think I shall like *your* husband quite as well as Jane's.'[ch 59]

When Elizabeth moves to Pemberley, her father misses her greatly and 'his affection for her drew him oftener from home than anything else could do.' He enjoys going to Pemberley, 'especially when he was least expected.'[ch 61]

### *George Wickham*

George Wickham, as the son of Darcy's late father's steward, has known him since childhood. Wickham is described as having 'all the best part of beauty, a fine countenance, a good figure, and very pleasing address'.[ch 15] He has plenty of charm and he uses this and his pleasing manners to deceive people. Wickham has the qualities of a gentleman and a hero, but he is neither.

Elizabeth Bennet, like many other people, is initially taken in by Wickham's charm and thinks that he is the 'most agreeable man' she has ever seen. She has clearly not heard that Wickham is in debt to every tradesman in Meryton.

At their second meeting Wickham tells Elizabeth a plausible story about Darcy, which reinforces her prejudice against him. Wickham tells her that Darcy has cheated him out of a clerical living which Darcy's late father had promised him. As a result, he claims that he has been forced to join the militia and is now living in poverty. Wickham tells Elizabeth that this mistreatment is due to Darcy's jealousy of him, as he was a favourite of the late Mr Darcy, who was his godfather. He tells her that Darcy's behaviour towards him has been 'scandalous' and he speaks of Darcy's pride. Wickham does, however, concede that Darcy possesses some good qualities such as being a good brother. Elizabeth believes Wickham because 'there was truth in his looks.'[ch 17]

Elizabeth appears to be falling in love with Wickham, but she assures her concerned aunt that she is not. It is not long before Wickham drops Elizabeth to pursue a wealthy heiress.

Wickham's true character is revealed to Elizabeth in the letter she receives from Darcy after her rejection of his first proposal of marriage. The truth is that Wickham accepted money in lieu of the clerical living so that he could pursue a career in law. Instead of using the money for this purpose, Wickham had used it to live a 'life of idleness and dissipation'.[ch 35] Having squandered the money, he then asked Darcy for the living when it became vacant but was refused. Wickham then attempted to elope with Darcy's fifteen-year-old sister Georgiana as revenge on him, and to try to get his hands on her fortune. According to Darcy, Wickham is 'profligate' and 'as false and deceitful as he is insinuating.'[ch 47]

Elizabeth sees that she and everyone else have been taken in by Wickham. As she realises the truth of Darcy's version of events Elizabeth is 'absolutely ashamed of herself.'[ch 36]

Confirmation of Darcy's revelation about Wickham comes when he elopes with Lydia, who is just sixteen. Wickham, whose attempt to snare an heiress failed, flees Brighton because he has run up gaming debts. He decides that he may as well have a companion and takes Lydia with him. Wickham does not love Lydia and has no intention of marrying her. He has no thought for the anxiety and distress his selfish behaviour will cause the Bennet family. Nor is he concerned that Lydia's elopement will destroy their reputation and jeopardise her sisters' chances of finding a husband, for who, in the words of Lady Catherine de Bourgh, 'will connect themselves with such a family'.[ch 48]

When Darcy finds the runaways and pays Wickham to marry Lydia, Wickham shows no gratitude or repentance. Immediately after their marriage, Wickham and Lydia turn up at Longbourn as if nothing has happened.

Elizabeth sees that Wickham is the opposite of her initial opinion of him. She concludes that Darcy possesses all the good qualities that Wickham only appears to possess. Unlike Darcy, Wickham does not become a better person. He is as selfish, immoral, and unscrupulous at the end of the novel as when he made his first appearance. Although Wickham appears to have got away with his appalling and ungentlemanly behaviour, he is punished by having to marry a woman he does not love.

### *Mr Collins*

The Reverend William Collins is Jane Austen's greatest comic creation. He is twenty-five, has a 'grave and stately' air and very formal manners. He is 'a mixture of pride and obsequiousness, self-importance and humility'[ch 15] and is given to making long-winded, pompous speeches. Mr Bennet soon sums him up as 'absurd'. It is possible that some of Mr Collins' characteristics were inspired by Jane Austen's clergyman cousin Edward Cooper, whom she found irritating.

Mr Collins arrives at Longbourn to choose a wife from among the Bennet sisters. His wealthy patroness, Lady Catherine de Bourgh, has told him to get married and he has decided to marry one of his cousin's daughters to compensate for the fact that he will inherit the Longbourn estate on the death of Mr Bennet.

Social rank is very important to Mr Collins, and he is impressed by wealth. He constantly boasts of his connection to Lady Catherine and praises her excessively. He believes that, as a clergyman, he is 'equal in point of dignity with the highest rank in the kingdom'.[ch 18] Due to this mistaken belief, Mr Collins makes a fool of himself at the Lucas family's party by speaking to Mr Darcy without being formally introduced to him. As Darcy's social inferior this is impertinent. When Darcy shows his contempt for him, Mr Collins is so thick-skinned that he thinks Darcy 'seemed much pleased with the attention.'[ch 18]

Mr Collins does not possess any of the characteristics of a gentleman, including the ability to dance well. When he dances with Elizabeth he is 'awkward and solemn' and often makes the wrong moves without knowing it and gives Elizabeth 'all the shame and misery which a disagreeable partner for a couple of dances can give.'[ch 18] Mr Collins also breaks another rule governing the conduct of a gentleman by constantly speaking about himself and boasting about his own merits.

When he proposes to Elizabeth, Mr Collins show how self-centred he is and what a high regard he has for himself. He cannot understand why Elizabeth rejects his proposal and she repeats her refusal many times before he will accept it. He then, unkindly, points out that she may never receive another offer of marriage because of her family's poor financial situation. Due to his hurt, Mr Collins hardly speaks to Elizabeth, which is ungentlemanly and not the way a supposed Christian should behave. In fact, he is not a true Christian with a genuine faith and vocation, but an example of the many clergymen in Jane Austen's time for whom the church was just a job.

Despite what he describes as the 'violence' of his affection for Elizabeth, Mr Collins soon transfers his affection to her friend Charlotte Lucas, who is desperate to marry and is prepared to put up with him in order to get a home of her own.

Not long after Charlotte's marriage, Elizabeth goes with her friend's father and sister to stay with the newly married couple at Hunsford Parsonage. Mr Collins greets his guests with his customary formal civility. Some of his unpleasant character traits are on display. When he shows his guests around the parsonage, he addresses Elizabeth in particular to make her realise what she has lost in turning down his proposal. Elizabeth feels sorry for Charlotte, who she notices has arranged the house in such a way that she will see as little as possible of her husband. She encourages his interest in gardening to keep him outdoors and out of her way.

When the Collinses and their guests are invited to dinner at Rosings, Mr Collins tells Elizabeth not to worry about what to wear. He unkindly reminds her of her social inferiority by telling her that Lady Catherine 'will not think the worse of you for being simply dressed.' Lady Catherine, he says, likes 'the distinction of rank'[ch 29] to be preserved. He seems to delight, in a most ungentlemanly manner, in trying to belittle Elizabeth.

Mr Collins' letters reveal as much about his unpleasant character as the way he behaves. Following Lydia's elopement with Wickham, Mr Collins sends her father a cruel and unforgiving letter, which shows his complete lack of empathy for the feelings of others. He pretends to be sympathetic but then says that Lydia's death 'would have been a blessing in comparison of this'. He blames Mr Bennet, not unfairly, for the 'faulty degree of indulgence' which has led to Lydia's behaviour. He seems to delight in pointing out that Lydia's actions will damage the marital prospects of her sisters and advises Mr Bennet to disown Lydia and 'leave her to reap the fruits of her own heinous offence.'[ch 48] This is not the sort of letter a gentleman or someone who purports to be a Christian ought to write. He clearly does not practise what he preaches.

Mr Bennet receives another interfering letter from his cousin which is sent ostensibly to congratulate him on Jane's forthcoming marriage to Mr Bingley. He then proceeds to offer what he calls a 'short hint' regarding Elizabeth's engagement to Darcy, whom he describes as 'one of the most illustrious personages in this land.'[ch 57] He informs Mr Bennet that Lady Catherine would never give her consent to 'so disgraceful a match'. He concludes his letter by saying 'You ought certainly to forgive them as a Christian, but never to admit them in your sight, or allow their names to be mentioned in your hearing.'[ch 48] Once again, he hypocritically fails to practise what he pompously preaches.

Mr Collins is a character who does not change. He is unbearable and lacking in self-awareness throughout. He never fails, however, to amuse Mr Bennet, who tells Elizabeth that he would 'not give up Mr Collins' correspondence for any consideration.'[ch 61]

*Frontispiece of the 1833 edition of* Mansfield Park.

3

# *MANSFIELD PARK*

*Summary*

Fanny Price is the ten-year-old daughter of a poor lieutenant in the Marines and his wife. She is given a home at Mansfield Park by her maternal aunt and uncle, Sir Thomas and Lady Bertram, to help her mother, who is struggling with a large family.

The timid and nervous Fanny becomes a companion to her aunt. She is mistreated by Mrs Norris, another, rather nasty, maternal aunt, who has been allowed too much control in the running of Mansfield Park. Fanny is frightened of her stern uncle, a wealthy baronet with estates in Antigua. As he is distracted by business, his duties as a Member of Parliament and frequent absences abroad, Sir Thomas has lost touch with what is happening in his home.

Only her cousin Edmund shows Fanny any kindness, in return for which she loves him dearly. Over several years Fanny grows to love her new home. The peace and harmony of Mansfield Park is broken when Henry and Mary Crawford arrive to stay at Mansfield Parsonage and befriend the young Bertrams. Henry

Crawford, who owns an estate in Norfolk, is an unprincipled womaniser. His sister Mary, with a fortune of £20,000, flirts with Tom Bertram, heir to Mansfield Park. When he shows no interest, she transfers her attentions to Edmund. Fanny alone perceives that the Crawfords are shallow and not to be trusted.

Maria Bertram, who is engaged to Mr Rushworth whom she does not love, and her sister Julia, are attracted to Henry Crawford, who causes jealousy by paying attention to both of them.

When Sir Thomas Bertram is away in Antigua, the young people and Tom's friend Mr Yates amuse themselves by putting on private theatricals. They choose an unsuitable play that involves Maria acting love scenes opposite Henry Crawford, with whom she is falling in love. Edmund, despite reservations about the propriety of the theatricals, plays opposite Mary Crawford.

Fanny, who has turned into a strong-minded young lady, knowing her uncle would not approve, refuses to take part. She is alarmed at the way Henry Crawford trifles with the feelings of her cousins and Mr Rushworth. Sir Thomas returns early and puts an end to the theatricals.

The relationship between Edmund and Mary worries Fanny. He is blind to Mary's faults and Mary is not happy that Edmund, whom she is clearly considering as a future husband, is planning to become a lowly clergyman.

Matters between Maria and Henry Crawford come to a head when she does not receive a declaration of love from him. Despite not loving him, Maria marries the wealthy Mr Rushworth for 'fortune and consequence'.

To amuse himself, Henry Crawford sets out to make Fanny fall in love with him. He proposes to her and is astonished when Fanny rejects him because she disapproves of his unprincipled behaviour, and more importantly, because her heart belongs to Edmund. No-one can understand Fanny's rejection of such a good offer, but she cannot explain why she has done so without incriminating Maria and Julia.

Fanny's much-loved brother William, who is a midshipman in the navy, comes to stay at Mansfield Park. In an unsuccessful attempt to ingratiate himself with Fanny, Henry Crawford obtains promotion for William through the influence of his admiral uncle.

An angry Sir Thomas sends Fanny back to her parents' chaotic home in Portsmouth to make her think again about rejecting such a wealthy suitor as Henry Crawford. While she is away Fanny dreads receiving news of an engagement between Edmund and Mary.

Tom Bertram becomes dangerously ill and Fanny is shocked to find out in a letter from Mary Crawford that if Edmund becomes heir of Mansfield Park, she would overlook him being a clergyman.

Henry Crawford, upset by Fanny's rejection of his offer of marriage, scandalously elopes with Maria and at the same time, Julia elopes with Mr Yates. Edmund collects Fanny from Portsmouth, as her distressed aunt needs her. Fanny's sister Susan goes with them.

Sir Thomas finally realises what a bad character Henry Crawford is and Fanny's refusal to marry him is now justified. Mr Rushworth divorces Maria, whose character is destroyed by her elopement. As punishment she is banished from society and sent away with her Aunt Norris to live in a 'remote and private' place. [ch 48] Henry Crawford, showing the double standards of the time, receives no punishment. He does, however, regret losing Fanny, the woman he loves.

Regretting how he has neglected his daughters and left them to the malign influence of their Aunt Norris, Sir Thomas realises what a negligent father he has been.

When Mary Crawford condones her brother's behaviour, Edmund finally sees her faults. He realises how dear Fanny is to him and that she will make an excellent wife. They marry and Edmund becomes Rector of Mansfield. Fanny's sister Susan takes her place as companion to Lady Bertram.

### *Edmund Bertram*

Edmund, the second son of Sir Thomas and Lady Bertram, is the hero of the novel. Unlike his older brother, he has all the characteristics of a gentleman. He is kind, polite, considerate, and shows concern for others, but his natural good nature is sometimes hidden due to his feelings for Mary Crawford.

Soon after Fanny Price's arrival at Mansfield Park, Edmund finds her alone and in tears. He becomes her friend, supporter, protector, and teacher. Realising that she is clever, Edmund encourages Fanny to read and develop her mind. In return for Edmund's many kindnesses to her, Fanny loves him devotedly.

When the Crawfords arrive at Mansfield Parsonage, Edmund becomes infatuated with Mary. He fails to see the faults in her character which are so evident to Fanny. Mary changes Edmund. He lets her, for example, take over Fanny's horse, which not only deprives Fanny of exercise but also distresses her.

Edmund makes sure that Fanny is not excluded from the visit to Sotherton Court, Mr Rushworth's grand country house, but seems to forget about her when they are there. He goes off alone with Mary, which is against the rules governing the behaviour of young unmarried people. They leave Fanny sitting alone on a bench, feeling unwanted.

Unlike his brother and sisters, Edmund does possess moral awareness. He tells Tom that it is not right to be building a theatre as 'it would be taking liberties' with their father's house. Edmund also considers it 'would show great want of feeling' towards their father who was absent in Antigua and 'in some degree of constant danger.'[ch 13] Then Edmund, against his better judgement, puts aside his reservations and agrees to take part. Fanny blames Mary for Edmund changing his mind.

Edmund cannot see what Fanny sees – that Mary is selfish, shallow, and unprincipled. His ambition is to be a clergyman, but he does not refute Mary's assertion that clergymen are 'nothing' or stand up for himself when she says, 'You really are fit for something better.' Edmund describes the faults in Mary's character as her 'little errors' and a 'tinge of wrong'.[ch 9]

Not being aware of Fanny's love for him, Edmund hurts her when he confides in her about his feelings for Mary. When she is in Portsmouth, Edmund sends Fanny a letter praising Mary and saying that she is 'the only woman in the world whom I could ever think of as a wife.'[ch 44] Not only does this hurt Fanny, but it also concerns her, as she can see how unsuitable Mary is for Edmund. Fanny considers it 'such an unworthy attachment'. She can see that Mary 'loves nobody but herself and her brother' and that Edmund is 'blind'.[ch 43]

Eventually, Edmund realises the truth about Mary when she dismisses her brother's elopement with Maria as 'mere folly' and only regrets that they were caught. Edmund considers it a 'perversion of mind which made it natural to her to treat the subject as she did.' He can finally say 'my eyes are opened' and talks of Mary's 'corrupted, vitiated mind'.[ch 47]

Edmund soon realises that Fanny has been 'growing as dear, as important to him in all her smiles, all her ways, as Mary Crawford had ever been.'[ch 48] Fanny has become the daughter Sir Thomas had always wanted and he consents to her marrying Edmund.

The young couple start married life in the rectory of Thornton Lacey, where Edmund is the incumbent and, not long after, he takes over the living of Mansfield.

### *Sir Thomas Bertram*

Sir Thomas Bertram, the owner of Mansfield Park, has risen into the upper-middle-class through making a fortune in Antigua. His niece Fanny finds him fierce and intimidating when she first arrives at his house. Sir Thomas is a distant father to his four children and does not show them any affection.

Lady Bertram, a foolish and indolent woman, has been allowed by Sir Thomas to hand over her duties in running Mansfield Park to her unpleasant sister Mrs Norris. They also allow her to have too much influence over their daughters.

Sir Thomas is, however, a charitable and generous man. As well as giving Fanny a home, he pays for the education of her brothers and sets them up in work. He also pays an allowance to Fanny's favourite brother William and takes an interest in his career. When Mrs Norris goes back on her promise to share the responsibility of Fanny and finds excuses for not letting her live with her, Sir Thomas generously responds by saying 'Let her home be in this house.'[ch 1]

When he returns home earlier than expected from Antigua and discovers that his rooms have been rearranged to make a theatre, Sir Thomas shows wisdom in the way he reacts. He does not remonstrate with his children or get angry. Instead, he shows his disapproval by dismantling the theatre and burning all the copies of *Lovers' Vows*, the play they have been rehearsing.

Unlike Fanny, her uncle is not a good judge of character and cannot see through the superficial charm and good manners of Henry Crawford. He describes Crawford as 'a young man of sense, of character, of temper, of manners and of fortune'.[ch 32]

When Fanny rejects Henry Crawford's offer of marriage her uncle's reaction is harsh and cruel. He unfairly accuses her of being 'self-willed, obstinate, selfish and ungrateful'. Fanny is deeply distressed when Sir Thomas tells her that she has 'disappointed every expectation' he had for her and that she has proved herself 'of a character the very reverse of what I had supposed.'[ch 32] He only stops berating Fanny when she starts crying. After her firm rejection of Crawford's proposal, Sir Thomas allows him to continue harassing her.

When Henry Crawford elopes with Maria Bertram, Sir Thomas finally discovers his true character. He blames himself for the behaviour of both his daughters and realises the damage caused by the 'excessive indulgence and flattery'[ch 48] of their Aunt Norris, which was inconsistent with his own severity.

Sir Thomas recognises far too late that his daughters, despite their expensive education, have not received any moral instruction, which would have protected them against the unprincipled and immoral Henry Crawford. He realises that they had never learned about 'duty, discipline or decorum' or the necessity of 'self-denial and humility'.[ch 48] Fanny, in contrast, possesses moral awareness and concern for others.

Sir Thomas puts this moral superiority down to the hardships of her early life.

At least Sir Thomas is big enough to acknowledge the 'errors in his own conduct as a parent'.[ch 48] He realises that he was culpable in authorising Maria's marriage to Mr Rushworth, when he knew that she did not love him. Sir Thomas readily consents to Edmund and Fanny's marriage as he has had enough of 'ambitious and mercenary connections, prizing more and more the sterling good of principle and temper.'[ch 48] The anguish he suffers from his faults as a parent never entirely leave him.

### *Tom Bertram*

Tom Bertram, the heir of Mansfield Park, should conduct himself like a gentleman, but he fails to do so. A selfish and extravagant young man, Tom wastes his life in drinking and partying with his friends. His debts force his father to sell the church living intended for his brother Edmund.

Tom's character flaws highlight his brother's good character. Unlike Edmund, Tom does not see, or does not care about, the impropriety of acting *Lovers' Vows* and browbeats his brother, against his better judgement, into taking part.

Following a drunken fall Tom becomes dangerously ill, which gives him time to think. Like his father, Tom repents of his bad behaviour and becomes 'what he ought to be, useful to his father, steady and quiet, and not living merely for himself.'[ch 48]

### *Henry Crawford*

Henry Crawford and his sister Mary are the half-siblings of Mrs Grant, wife of the Rector of Mansfield. When they arrive for a long visit to the Grants, the Crawfords become friendly with the young Bertrams. The worldly Crawfords have come from London, which was regarded as an immoral and decadent place.

Henry Crawford, the villain of the novel, is a wealthy young man with an estate in Norfolk. He is charming, witty, polite, and intelligent, and, as all gentlemen should be, he is a good dancer. Although not handsome, Henry uses his charm to seduce women and is used to a lot of female attention. His charm, however, is superficial and hides a selfish, vain, and immoral character. Henry has no plans to marry and flirts with women only to amuse himself. Despite the many negative aspects of his character, Henry is not all bad. One of his good points is his devotion to his sister Mary, who describes him as 'exactly what a brother should be, who loves me, consults me, confides in me, and will talk to me by the hour together.'[ch 6]

Henry starts a flirtation with both Maria and Julia Bertram. He is aware of Maria's engagement to Mr Rushworth, but this does not stop him, as 'an engaged woman is always more agreeable than a disengaged.'[ch 5] On the day of the visit to Sotherton Court, Henry flirts with both sisters, causing jealousy between them. By disappearing alone with Maria at Sotherton he breaks the code of conduct regarding the conduct of single young people. He is not concerned how others view his behaviour.

Fanny is shocked at Henry's improper behaviour and that he does not seem 'to care how he exposed or hurt'[ch 35] Mr Rushworth. He appears to be 'never happier than when behaving so dishonestly and unfeelingly.'[ch 35] Fanny develops a deep distrust of Henry Crawford, who then turns his attentions to her.

Henry embarrasses and confuses Fanny by indirectly giving her a gold chain to wear with her amber cross at her coming-out ball. He tells his sister that, to amuse himself, he intends to make Fanny fall in love with him, unaware that she loves Edmund. He tells Mary that he 'cannot be satisfied ... without making a small hole in Fanny Price's heart.'

Matters do not go as planned because Henry, unintentionally, falls in love with Fanny. He describes himself as 'fairly caught' and is determined that Fanny will marry him. Fanny will not change her mind, however, despite her uncle's anger.

Henry is indifferent to the pain he causes when he persists in courting Fanny. She is angry at his 'gross want of feeling and humanity where his own pleasure was concerned.'[ch 33] Henry even follows Fanny to Portsmouth where he seems 'gentler' and 'more obliging', but he reverts to type when Fanny stands firm in her determination not to marry him.

Henry's immoral character is evident when, having been rejected by Fanny, he sets about seducing the newly married Maria. Their elopement brings shame on her family and ends her marriage. Henry then breaks Maria's heart by deserting her.

Maria is punished for the 'sin' of her elopement by social ostracism, whereas Henry is allowed back into society, free to sin again. Women were punished more harshly for sexual misbehaviour than men.

Henry does not escape punishment altogether, as he suffers the loss of Fanny, whom he 'passionately loved'. His vain, selfish, and ungentlemanly behaviour results in 'no small portion of vexation and regret: vexation that must rise sometimes to self-reproach, and wretchedness.'[ch 48]

### *William Price*

William, the beloved elder brother of Fanny, is a midshipman in the navy. The siblings have a very close and affectionate relationship. It is to William that, with Edmund's help, Fanny writes when she finds it difficult to settle in at Mansfield Park.

Despite the hardship he experienced growing up in a poor home with the bad example of an alcoholic and uncouth father, William has grown up to become a happy, well-adjusted, and affable young man. He is liked by everyone at Mansfield Park and has an excellent relationship with his uncle Sir Thomas, who has supported him in his career in the navy.

The naval characters in Jane Austen's novels are, with one exception, good people. This reflects their creator's high esteem for the navy, based on her admiration for her sailor brothers, from whom she acquired her intimate knowledge of the navy. It is thought that Jane used elements of her brother Charles's character when creating William Price. The amber cross which William gives Fanny was inspired by the gift of topaz crosses made by Charles to his sisters.

Fanny's great pride in William, especially when he is promoted, reflects Jane's pride in her brothers. When Henry Crawford informs Fanny that William 'has been made', he uses the exact words Jane used in a letter telling her sister Cassandra of their brother Frank's promotion.

William cannot understand how Fanny could be so cold towards Henry Crawford, who has gone to such trouble to secure his promotion. He demonstrates his good character when, unlike others, he does not upset Fanny by making the 'slightest allusion' to the matter. William's fine character shows that it is not necessary to be born a gentleman to behave like one.

*Frontispiece of the 1833 edition of* Emma.

# 4

# *EMMA*

*Summary*

Emma, the eponymous heroine of the novel, is nearly twenty-one years old. She lives with her elderly, widowed and wealthy father in their large house, Hartfield, near Highbury. They are the 'first family' in Highbury, a 'large and prosperous village, almost amounting to a town',[ch 1] in Surrey. Emma is mistress of her father's house and looks after him as he is frail, nervous and needy.

Mr Woodhouse is unhappy because Miss Taylor, Emma's former governess, has left the household following her marriage to Mr Weston. The Westons live at Randalls, a large house bought with the fortune Mr Weston made through business. Mr Weston has a son from a previous marriage who, following the death of his mother, was brought up by a wealthy uncle and aunt, the Churchills. Frank has promised numerous times to visit his father but has failed to do so. He did not even attend his father's wedding but sent a letter instead.

Emma has been used to getting her own way and thinks 'too well of herself'.[ch 1] The only person who criticises her is

Mr Knightley, a close family friend, who is the wealthy owner of Donwell Abbey.

Although Emma does not want to marry herself, she enjoys making matches for other people and claims to have promoted the match of Miss Taylor and Mr Weston.

Emma befriends Harriet Smith, a parlour boarder at a boarding school for young ladies who appears to have no family. She decides to 'improve' Harriet and introduce her to good society. Emma disapproves of Harriet's friendship with the Martin family. She encourages her to reject a proposal of marriage from Robert Martin, a tenant farmer on Mr Knightley's estate, because he is too poor and lowly for her. Instead, she encourages Harriet to think she would be a good match for Mr Elton, the vicar of Highbury.

Mr Knightley disapproves of Emma's friendship with Harriet. He is also angry that she encouraged Harriet to reject Robert Martin's proposal, as he has a high regard for Robert. Mr Knightley tells Emma that Mr Elton would never consider Harriet as a potential wife. Emma ignores Mr Knightley and brings Harriet and Mr Elton together in the hope that he will propose to her. Although this does not happen, Emma believes her plan will succeed.

Emma's sister Isabella is married to Mr Knightley's younger brother John. They arrive with their children to stay at Hartfield. Emma is alarmed when her brother-in-law warns her that Mr Elton is interested in her, not Harriet.

At the Westons' Christmas Eve party Emma is annoyed that Mr Elton is paying her a lot of attention. Frank Churchill is a topic of conversation. The Westons think he would be a good match for Emma who thinks that, if she were to marry, from all she has heard of Frank Churchill, that he would be the ideal husband for her.

On leaving the party, Emma finds herself alone in a carriage with Mr Elton. She is horrified and distressed when he proposes to her and reveals that he feels nothing for Harriet. When Emma repeatedly repulses Mr Elton, he accuses her of leading him on. Both are very angry.

Emma realises that she was wrong to try and bring two people together. Having talked Harriet into loving Mr Elton, she must now 'destroy' her hopes. Emma vows never to matchmake again, but she still thinks she was right to encourage Harriet to reject Robert Martin. Emma is relieved when Mr Elton leaves for a visit to Bath.

Two of Mr Woodhouses's good friends are Mrs Bates, widow of a previous vicar of Highbury, and her unmarried daughter. Jane Fairfax, Mrs Bates' orphaned grand-daughter, arrives for a three month stay. Jane has been brought up by her father's army friend Colonel Campbell and his wife. They have a daughter of their own, now Mrs Dixon. Jane has been well-educated and is a good piano-player and singer. Mr Knightley suggests that Emma befriends Jane, but Emma dislikes her because she is distant and shy. Emma, ever the schemer, wonders whether Jane is in love with Mr Dixon, the Campbells' son-in-law. The Campbells cannot continue to support Jane and she is destined to become a governess.

Emma learns that Mr Elton is going to marry a woman he met in Bath. Although Harriet Smith is still obsessed with Mr Elton, she is pleased to meet Robert Martin and his sister Elizabeth in a shop. When Elizabeth visits Harriet she has to return the visit, which Emma ensures is brief and formal.

Frank Churchill finally arrives in Highbury. Emma's first impressions of him are good, and she hears from the Westons that Frank admires her. Frank visits Jane Fairfax, whom he recently met in Weymouth.

When Emma attends a party at the Coles's house, Frank pays her a lot of attention. Everyone is talking about a piano that has been delivered to Jane Fairfax with no indication of who has sent it. There is much speculation as to the identity of the donor. Frank criticises Jane to Emma, who tells him that she suspects Jane is in love with Mr Dixon.

Frank suggests that a dance is held at the Crown Inn, but before it takes place he is called away because his adoptive mother is ill. Emma believes that Frank loves her but has decided not to accept if he proposes.

Mr Elton returns with his new wife who is a vain, vulgar, opinionated and self-satisfied woman. Frank returns and the Crown ball takes place. Mr Knightley dances with Harriet when she is snubbed by Mr Elton. Harriet turns her affections to him, but when she tells Emma that she is in love, Emma thinks she is referring to Frank.

Mrs Elton takes it upon herself to find a governess position for Jane. Emma's suspicions about her and Mr Dixon are increased when she hears that Jane collects her own mail from the Post Office.

When Frank Churchill rescues Harriet from some gypsies who are harassing her in the woods near Highbury, Emma thinks they will make a good match. She cannot keep to her vow of not matchmaking. Mr Knightley concludes that there is an attachment between Frank and Jane, but Emma disagrees.

On a group outing to Box Hill Frank again flirts openly with Emma. Emma learns the importance of respecting her social inferiors when Mr Knightley scolds her for being rude to Miss Bates.

Not long after the picnic, Jane Fairfax accepts a governess position found for her by the officious Mrs Elton. This leads to Frank revealing that he and Jane are secretly engaged and that he had ordered the piano for her on a trip to London, ostensibly to get his hair cut. Everyone except Mr Knightley is astonished at the revelation.

Emma's next shock is the discovery that Harriet has fallen in love with Mr Knightley, not Frank Churchill as she thought. Emma is mortified by the harm caused by her matchmaking and that this is the result of her encouraging Harriet to think she could marry above her rank. Emma realises that she is responsible for what would be a very 'unequal' connection by trying to improve Harriet and encouraging her to reject Robert Martin. This leads to some painful reflection. Emma realises that she has never loved Frank and the thought that Mr Knightley may return Harriet's affection makes her see that he is the man she loves.

The death of Frank Churchill's controlling aunt, who was the reason for the secret engagement, frees him to marry Jane. Emma, having gained self-knowledge, marries Mr Knightley, who has always loved her and feared she was in love with Frank. Robert Martin, who has 'thoroughly supplanted' Mr Knightley in Harriet's affections, proposes to her again and is accepted. The complicated plot is tied up by the marriages of these three couples.

### *Mr Knightley*

George Knightley is the wealthy owner of Donwell Abbey, near Highbury. He has been a friend of the Woodhouse family for a long time. Mr Knightley, who, in recognition of his high social status, is never referred to by his Christian name, is highly respected in the local community and serves as a magistrate.

Introduced as a 'sensible man about seven-or-eight and thirty',[ch 1] Mr Knightley comes from a family described by Emma as 'of such true gentility, untainted in blood and understanding.'[ch 39] He always conducts himself as a gentleman should.

Mr Knightley has looked out for Emma since she was a child and has been a better guide to her than her own father. Emma is clever and he encourages her, unsuccessfully, to better herself by reading. Emma complains that Mr Knightley loves to find fault with her, but she does not realise that, despite her faults, he loves her.

When Emma encourages Harriet Smith to reject Robert Martin's proposal of marriage, Mr Knightley is not pleased. He is a good judge of character who thinks highly of Robert and considers that he would make a good husband for Harriet.

Mr Knightley shows wisdom by recognising the dangers of Emma lifting Harriet out of her social class. It will make her used to being with people of a higher social rank and result in her not wanting to mix with her natural friends, like the Martin family. He wisely warns Emma not to try and match Harriet with Mr Elton, who he knows would not marry anyone of Harriet's social rank.

People from the higher social classes are expected to be courteous and respectful to those lower down the social scale, as Mr Knightley unfailingly is. He is particularly kind and attentive to Mrs Bates and her daughter, for whom he has a 'great regard'. He is careful not to overdo his kindness, however, because he does not want to embarrass them. Mr Knightley also encourages Emma to visit the Bateses, with little success.

When he receives an invitation to the Cole family's party, Mr Knightley happily accepts, despite the fact that they are not true members of the gentry, having accrued their wealth from trade. He arranges for his carriage to take Jane Fairfax to the party because she has been unwell, which leads Mrs Weston to say 'Such a very kind attention – and so thoughtful an attention! – the sort of thing that so few men would think of.' To which Emma adds:

> I know no man more likely than Mr Knightley to do the sort of thing – to do anything really good-natured, useful, considerate or benevolent … and for an act of unostentatious kindness there is nobody whom I would fix on more than on Mr Knightley.[ch 26]

When Emma mocks Miss Bates during the trip to Box Hill, Mr Knightley upbraids her. 'How could you be so unfeeling to Miss Bates?' he asks, 'How could you be so intolerant in your wit to a woman of her character, age and situation?'[ch 43] He points out that Miss Bates was poor, having fallen down the social ranks since the death of her father and, as a poor spinster, she was likely to sink further. Emma is mortified and repentant.

Mr Knightley is always aware of the people around him and their needs. He is attentive to Mr Woodhouse and is very patient with him. He notices that no-one, apart from Mrs Elton, pays much attention to Jane Fairfax and encourages Emma to befriend her. Mr Knightley is aware that due to her lowly social status Jane has no choice but to put up with Mrs Elton's patronising attitude towards her.

A strong sense of right and wrong guides Mr Knightley. He is very angry at the way the Eltons snub Harriet Smith at the Crown

Inn ball. He describes it as 'unpardonable rudeness' and shames Mr Elton by dancing with Harriet himself. Being a good judge of character, Mr Knightley can see that Harriet has 'some first-rate qualities' and is 'infinitely to be preferred by any man of sense and taste to such a woman as Mrs Elton.'[ch 38]

Mr Knightley is also critical of Frank Churchill's failure to visit his father, after many promises to do so. He believes that Frank thinks only of 'his own pleasure'[ch 18] and that he is guilty of a dereliction of duty towards his father.

Even before he meets Frank, Mr Knightley distrusts him and, correctly, suspects him of having an 'understanding' with Jane Fairfax while openly flirting with Emma. At the end of the novel, when Frank's secret engagement to Jane is revealed, Mr Knightley says to Emma, 'Does not everything serve to prove more and more the beauty of truth and sincerity in all our dealings with each other.'[ch 50]

All the attributes of a true gentleman, including the important ability to dance well, can be found in Mr Knightley. As Emma says of him 'You might not see one in a hundred with "gentleman" so plainly written as in Mr Knightley.'[ch 4]

Mr Knightley is the most gentlemanly of all Jane Austen's characters and, when all the confusion of who loves who is resolved, he marries the novel's heroine.

### *John Knightley*

John Knightley enjoys a close but undemonstrative relationship with his brother George. He is not as friendly and talkative as his brother, and hates visiting and all social occasions. He is a good judge of character and suggests, correctly, that Mr Elton is in love with Emma. Much to her displeasure, he advises her to 'regulate' her behaviour because she appears to be encouraging Mr Elton to think that she loves him in return.

Unlike his brother, John Knightley is impatient with his father-in-law. He is not happy at having to attend the Westons' Christmas Eve party and probably for this reason, he rather unkindly delights in telling Mr Woodhouse that the ground outside is covered in snow. 'This will prove a spirited beginning of your winter engagements, Sir,' he tells him. 'Something new for your coachman and horses to be making their way through a storm of snow.'[ch 15] Despite his brother's assurance that the snow won't prevent them from getting home, Mr Woodhouse and Isabella are so alarmed that they insist on leaving early, with the result that the party breaks up and the evening is spoiled.

Maybe John Knightley can be forgiven for his impatience and irritability as he has to live with a wife who is a nervous and needy character like her father and, like him, is obsessed with her own and her children's health.

John's negative personality traits and ungentlemanly behaviour serve to highlight his brother's superior qualities.

### *Mr Woodhouse*

Mr Woodhouse, a gentleman by birth and conduct, is an affectionate and indulgent father. He is also civil and courteous to everyone and is 'beloved' for his friendliness and his good nature. Mr Woodhouse is greatly respected by the people of Highbury.

Despite these good qualities, Mr Woodhouse has some negative characteristics which affect the lives of others. One of these is his dislike of change, which leads him to make a great deal of fuss about Emma's former governess Miss Taylor leaving their household to marry Mr Weston. 'Poor Miss Taylor,' he says. 'I wish she were here again. What a pity it is that Mr Weston ever thought of her!'[ch 1]

Due to his 'horror of late hours, and large dinner-parties' Mr Woodhouse has his own small circle of friends who are happy 'to visit him on his own terms.'[ch 3] They include Mrs and Miss Bates, and Mrs Goddard, headmistress of the boarding school for young ladies where Harriet Smith lives.

As expected of a gentleman, Mr Woodhouse treats the poor well, especially Mrs Bates and her tiresome, talkative daughter. He is particularly gallant towards women and likes to pay them compliments. Being mindful of the need to visit the newly married Mrs Elton, he tells Emma, 'a bride, especially, is never to be neglected. More is avowedly due to her. A bride...is always the first in company, let the others be who they may.' He explains that this is 'a matter of mere common politeness and good breeding'.[ch 32]

Although he does not like large parties, Mr Woodhouse, unlike his snobbish daughter, does not think of refusing the invitation he receives to the Cole family's party. He is careful not to offend them. 'I should be extremely sorry,' he says 'to be giving them any pain, I know what worthy people they are.'[ch 25]

Despite his good points Mr Woodhouse is selfish. When his older daughter Isabella, her husband and their children come to stay Mr Woodhouse does not want to share them with Mr Knightley, who also wants to see them.

Described as a 'valetudinarian all his life'[ch 1] or a 'sad invalid' as he calls himself, Mr Woodhouse is overly concerned about his health and diet, and Mr Perry, the local apothecary, is a regular visitor at Hartfield. Mr Woodhouse's timidity and nervousness cause problems for others, especially Emma, who has to reassure, placate and soothe him. Her father's dependence on her is one reason she gives for not wanting to marry.

Mr Woodhouse is particularly anxious about taking journeys. When it snows during the Westons' Christmas Eve party he panics, despite Mr Knightley assuring him that it is no more than half an inch deep. 'What is to be done?' he asks Emma. 'What is to be done?'[ch 15]

When she accepts Mr Knightley's proposal of marriage, Emma's first thought is for her father and whether he would give his consent. Mr Woodhouse, predictably, is not happy about Emma marrying. Emma 'could not bear to see him suffering; to know him fancying himself neglected'[ch 55] and due to his selfishness, she feels unable to go ahead with the marriage.

The problem is solved when Mrs Weston's poultry house is broken into one night and her turkeys are stolen. When this happens to other neighbours, Mr Woodhouse becomes frightened. He then allows the marriage to take place because he needs the protection of Mr Knightley, who agrees to move to Hartfield.

Mr Woodhouse's selfishness and neediness spoil his many good, gentlemanly qualities.

### *Frank Churchill*

Frank Churchill, son of Mr Weston by his first wife, is a good-looking young man with perfect manners. He is 'eager to please, smiles a lot' and bows perfectly. Frank has all the 'life and spirit, cheerful feelings, and social inclinations of his father'[ch 24] and, when he finally visits his father, is very attentive to his new stepmother.

Not only does Frank appear to be a gentleman, but he also has the appearance of a hero. Mr and Mrs Weston think Frank would make a good husband for Emma. They are of equal social status and both expect to inherit a fortune. Emma, however, has no plans to marry. She is happy running her father's household and looking after him. Emma takes an immediate liking to Frank Churchill and notices his 'well-bred ease of manner, and a readiness to talk, which convinced her that he came intending to be acquainted with her, and that acquainted they soon must be.'[ch 23]

But Emma suspects that there is something not quite right about Frank. Mr Knightley, who distrusts Frank, points out that he can always find time to visit watering-places like Weymouth but does not visit his father. When Mr Knightley finally meets Frank, his opinion of him does not improve.

The cover-up of Frank's engagement to Jane Fairfax, whom he met recently in Weymouth, begins as soon as he arrives in Highbury. Before Frank's arrival and when he leaves to go to London, he and Jane write to each other. Mrs Elton notices that Jane collects her own letters from the Post Office and offers to send her servant to collect Jane's mail for her. This puts Jane in an awkward position. Although he looks like a hero, the only heroic act Frank performs is rescuing Harriet Smith from the gipsies who are harassing her in the woods near Highbury.

As no-one is aware of their engagement, matches are made for both Frank and Jane. The worst part of the cover-up is Frank's flirtation with Emma, to 'disguise and blind'[ch 30] all about him. People, not unsurprisingly, think that Frank and Emma are in love and Emma decides that he has 'a decidedly warm admiration, a conscious preference for herself'. Emma thinks that she must be 'a little in love with him'.[ch 30] When Mr Knightley detects signs of an attachment between Frank and Jane, Emma confidently asserts that he is wrong.

The secret engagement causes a lot of confusion and misunderstanding. There is much intrigue when Frank sends Jane a piano with no indication of who has sent it. Various suggestions are made as to who the sender might be.

Jane becomes ill and depressed due to the strain of hiding her engagement and the hurt caused by Frank's public flirtation with Emma. It is only when Jane breaks off the engagement and is about to accept the job as a governess that Mrs Elton has found her that Frank reveals the engagement. His father and stepmother are deeply hurt by the revelation. In Emma's words everyone had been 'completely duped'.[ch 46]

Even though he suspected there was something between Frank and Jane, Mr Knightley also suffers as a result of the deception as he thinks that Emma loves Frank.

Frank is remorseful for the pain he has caused Jane and confesses that he has 'behaved shamefully.'[ch 51] He also apologises to Emma, who points out that he has not shown 'that upright integrity, that strict adherence to truth and principle, that disdain of trick and littleness, which a man should display in every transaction of his life.'[ch 46]

Fortunately, Emma did not fall in love with Frank but, as she asks, 'How could he tell what mischief he might be doing? How could he tell that he might not be making me in love with him?'[ch 46]

Frank is another of Jane Austen's characters who purports to be a gentleman but fails to act like one. Jane forgives him and fortuitously, his adoptive mother, who would not have agreed to the marriage, dies. Frank and Jane are the last of the three couples in the novel to be united in marriage.

*Mr Weston*

Mr Weston was born in Highbury of a respectable, but not rich, family. He became a captain in the army and married Miss Churchill, against the wishes of her wealthy, upper-class family, who disowned her. On his mother's death their son Frank was brought up by his childless uncle and aunt, Mr and Mrs Churchill and took their surname.

When he left the army Mr Weston made a fortune in business, bought a house in Highbury and married Miss Taylor, Emma's former governess. Mr Weston is one of the nouveaux riches who have risen into gentility by making money in trade and business. An affable, cheerful, and sociable man, he is well liked in the community. He is described by Isabella Knightley as 'that excellent Mr Weston ... he is one of the very best-tempered men that ever existed.'[ch 11]

Being of a sanguine, optimistic, and positive disposition, Mr Weston is philosophical about Frank's repeated failure to visit him. After the latest disappointment Mr Weston begins to think that Frank's coming two or three months later 'would be a much better plan; better time of year; better weather' and that he would probably be able to stay longer.

Despite not being born a gentleman, Mr Weston always follows the gentlemanly code of conduct. He is kind to Mr Woodhouse and visits him frequently. He considers the feelings of others, as demonstrated by his persuading him to let Emma stay at the Coles' party. 'You would not wish to disappoint and mortify the Coles, I am sure, Sir!' he says, describing them as 'friendly, good sort of people as ever lived,'[ch 25] and who had been Mr Woodhouse's neighbours for ten years. At his Christmas Eve party, although he knows that it is snowing outside, Mr Weston does not mention this as he knows it will cause Mr Woodhouse to fret and worry.

When Frank finally visits him, Mr Weston reminds him that he should call on Jane Fairfax. He thoughtfully points out that when Jane is with the wealthy Campbells, who brought her up, she is the 'equal of everybody she mixed with'. While she is staying with Mrs Bates, 'her poor old grandmother who has barely enough to live on,' he tells Frank that if he does not call on her early, 'it will be a slight.'[ch 23]

Although deeply hurt that Frank concealed his engagement to Jane Fairfax, his father forgives him and accepts it, despite it not being a good financial match for him. The excellent Mr Weston deserves the happiness that his new wife and baby bring him.

•

### *Mr Elton*

Mr Elton, the vicar of Highbury, is very handsome and has 'the most agreeable manners'. Emma, initially, thinks highly of him and considers him to be 'good-humoured, cheerful, obliging and gentle' and to have 'such perfect good temper and good will'.[ch 4] She is amused by his pompous speeches.

Although Mr Elton is 'without any alliances but in trade'[ch 16] he is accepted in gentry circles as he is an educated man with an important role in the community.

Mr Elton is very charming and polite to Emma and her friend Harriet Smith. He contributes a rhyme to a riddle book they are putting together and obligingly offers to take a portrait Emma has painted of Harriet to London to be framed. Mr Elton continues to be charming and obliging because he thinks that Emma is in love with him when she is, in fact, trying to make a match for him with Harriet Smith.

Emma sees another side to Mr Elton when he proposes to her in the coach going home from the Coles' party. At first, Mr Elton will not accept Emma's rejection of his proposal and takes her shocked silence as a sign of encouragement. He is highly affronted when he discovers that Emma thinks that he loves Harriet. 'Everybody has their level,' he tells her. 'I need not so totally despair of an equal alliance, as to be addressing myself to Miss Smith.'[ch 15] Emma, for her part, is astonished that Mr Elton should think himself good enough to propose to her.

After the shock of his rejection, Emma sees that Mr Elton

> ... was proving himself, in many respects the very reverse of what she had meant and believed him; proud, assuming, conceited; very full of his own claims, and little concerned about the feelings of others.[ch 16]

This is not the way a gentleman, or a man of the cloth, should behave.

Even after his marriage Mr Elton continues to hold a grudge against Emma and Harriet. He takes pleasure in publicly humiliating Harriet at the Crown Inn ball. She is the only young lady not dancing and Mr Elton refuses to ask her to dance when Mrs Weston suggests it and 'smiles of glee passed between him and his wife.' When Mr Knightley then asks Harriet to dance, Mr Elton retreats into the card room 'looking very foolish.'[ch 38]

Mr Knightley, who had warned Emma against trying to match Harriet with Mr Elton, is very angry. He is 'warm in his reprobation of Mr Elton's conduct; it had been unpardonable rudeness'[ch 38] and he also criticises Mrs Elton. Mr Knightley sees that the Eltons had 'aimed at wounding Emma too'[ch 38] with their sneering and contemptuous treatment of Harriet. Mr Elton not only behaves badly but he has not set a good example to his parishioners. The amiable, obliging Mr Elton turns out to be a veneer covering a rather unpleasant character.

### *Robert Martin*

Robert Martin is the tenant farmer of Abbey Mill Farm on Mr Knightley's estate. He is 'very neat' in appearance, 'good-natured,' 'amiable' and 'obliging'.[ch 4] Mr Knightley considers Robert to be an 'excellent young man' and even Emma concedes that he is 'very respectable'.[ch 8]

Harriet Smith is a friend of Robert's sister and a welcome visitor at the Martin family's home. Robert proposes to Harriet in a letter, after talking to Mr Knightley about his intentions and receiving his approval.

Emma, who has plans to elevate Harriet into better society, is prejudiced against Robert and tells Harriet that he is not good enough for her. Emma describes him as a 'very inferior creature,' and his family as 'illiterate and vulgar… [He is] the very last sort of person to raise my curiosity. The yeomanry are precisely the order of people with whom I feel I can have nothing to do.'[ch 4]

When Emma reads Robert's letter proposing marriage to Harriet, she is surprised at how well it is written. She admits that 'as a composition it would not have disgraced a gentleman,'[ch 7] and praises the sentiments it expresses.

Mr Knightley tells Emma that he has a 'thorough regard' for Robert and his family and adds: 'I never hear better sense from anyone than Robert Martin. He always speaks to the purpose – open, straightforward and very well-judging.'[ch 8]

Mr Knightley considers that Robert is 'more than her (Harriet's) equal... The advantage of the match is all on her side.'[ch 8]

Although disappointed at Harriet's rejection of his offer of marriage, Robert does not hold a grudge against her. When he and his sister see Harriet in a shop, Robert encourages his sister to speak to her. He approaches her himself to ask how she is and seems to want to shake her hand.

Mr Knightley is right in his judgement of Robert, and Emma is completely wrong in hers. He is far more of a gentleman than other characters who were born into the gentry class.

When Emma has learned not to interfere in other people's lives by matchmaking, Harriet returns to the level of society to which she belongs. When Robert proposes to her a second time, she happily accepts.

### *Mr Perry and Mr Cole*

There are two minor characters in *Emma* who are referred to as 'half-gentlemen'. Jane Austen uses this term to describe men who made their living as, for example, apothecaries, lawyers, in trade, or in business. They were educated men who mixed with the gentry but lacked the breeding and connections to be a gentleman.

Mr Perry, the Highbury apothecary, is described as 'an intelligent, gentlemanlike man whose frequent visits were one of the comforts of his (Mr Woodhouse)'s life.'[ch 2] He appears to tell Mr Woodhouse what he wants to hear, as he agrees with him that wedding cake is probably not good for the digestion, although his children are seen with slices of the Westons' wedding cake.

Mr Cole and his wife have been settled in Highbury for some years and 'were a very good sort of people, friendly, liberal, and unpretending, but on the other hand, they were of low origin, in trade and only moderately genteel.'[ch 25]

On their first arrival in Highbury the Coles 'had lived in proportion to their income' and 'kept little company.'[ch 25] Then, having made a fortune in trade, they had extended their house, taken on more servants, lived more extravagantly and started to mix with the real gentry.

The Coles are accepted by everyone except Emma, who wants to refuse an invitation to their party because they needed to be taught that it was not for them to decide 'the terms on which the superior families would visit them.'[ch 25] When she discovers who else will be going to the party, Emma decides to accept the invitation. Mr Knightley, who is not a snob like Emma, thinks they are 'worthy people'[ch 21] and is happy to accept their hospitality.

The Coles are kind, hospitable, and courteous people. Like Mr Perry, they have all the attributes of gentility, and their conduct is better than that of some characters higher up the social scale, such as Frank Churchill and John Knightley.

*Frontispiece of the 1833 edition of* Northanger Abbey.

# 5

# NORTHANGER ABBEY

*Summary*

Catherine Morland, the seventeen-year-old heroine of *Northanger Abbey,* is the daughter of the Reverend Richard Morland and his wife, who live in Fullerton, Wiltshire. Catherine is invited to go to Bath with her elderly, wealthy and childless neighbours, Mr and Mrs Allen. At the start of the novel Catherine is naïve and innocent, but she learns and grows from her experiences.

Soon after her arrival in Bath, Catherine is introduced by the Master of Ceremonies at the Lower Assembly Rooms to Henry Tilney, a young clergyman from a respectable family.

At the Pump Room Mrs Allen meets Mrs Thorpe, an old school friend. Mrs Thorpe, a widow, is staying in Bath with her three daughters. Her son John is a university friend of Catherine's brother James. Catherine makes friends with Isabella Thorpe whose interests are fashion, gossip, and flirting. The two become inseparable and enjoy reading Gothic horror novels together.

What Catherine does not yet see is that everything about her new friend is false and that she is not a true friend. Isabella's long list of negative character traits include shallowness, hypocrisy, and selfishness. Wherever the friends go in Bath, Catherine looks out for Henry Tilney.

John Thorpe and James Morland appear unexpectedly in Bath in a gig driven recklessly by Thorpe. From their first meeting he is attracted to Catherine, but she takes an immediate dislike to him. Isabella, thinking the Morlands are a wealthy family, decides that James would make a good husband.

Henry Tilney and his sister Eleanor meet Catherine at the next ball. Henry asks Catherine to dance, but she has already promised the first dance to John Thorpe, who then appears. As they are dancing in the same set, Catherine and Eleanor talk to each other and Catherine thinks that they could become friends. Isabella and James Morland dance together.

Catherine would like to see Eleanor again and hopes to meet her at the Pump Room the next morning. Catherine does not go to the Pump Room, however, as her brother, Isabella and John arrive. They insist on taking her for a carriage drive, despite her reluctance to go.

Catherine and Henry dance together at the next ball and she meets his father, General Tilney. Catherine agrees to go for a walk with the Tilneys the following day. On this and two more occasions the Thorpes and James prevent Catherine from seeing the Tilneys, causing her much embarrassment and disappointment. Catherine finally goes with Henry and Eleanor on a carriage drive to Beechen Cliff. She and Henry have a shared interest in literature and enjoy light-hearted banter. They are falling in love.

After a brief courtship, Isabella and James become engaged. John Thorpe suggests that he and Catherine should marry, but she misunderstands his way of proposing.

Isabella is not happy when she discovers that all James's father can give them when they marry is a clerical living worth only £400 a year. Catherine, who has begun to have doubts about her friend, notices a change in Isabella's behaviour. She responds to the attentions of Captain Frederick Tilney, Henry's older brother, who has arrived in Bath. As the heir to Northanger Abbey, Frederick is a more attractive potential husband than James. Isabella flirts openly with Frederick, which distresses Catherine, who is beginning to learn to be more discerning about people and to be aware of their motives.

Catherine notices that General Tilney seems to dominate Henry and Eleanor, and that they appear to be afraid of him, although he is always kind and friendly to her. When the Tilneys leave Bath, Catherine is invited to stay with them at Northanger Abbey. Catherine, whose 'passion for ancient edifices was next in degree to her passion for Henry Tilney,'[ch 17] is excited at the prospect of staying in an abbey. Due to her interest in Gothic novels, Catherine has a romantic image of 'long, damp passages, narrow cells' and a 'ruined chapel'.[ch 17] On the journey to Northanger Abbey, Henry encourages Catherine in her romantic fantasy by telling her frightening stories about things that have supposedly happened there, which she naively believes. When they arrive, Catherine is surprised to discover that much of the Abbey is modern.

That night is stormy and Catherine, remembering Henry's stories, is afraid. She finds a cabinet in her room which contains some old papers that appear to have been concealed. Catherine cannot settle to sleep until she reads the papers, but at that point her candle goes out and she hears receding footsteps. Catherine is so frightened that she gets very little sleep. The next morning, she discovers that the papers are just an old laundry list and berates herself for being so foolish.

Catherine sees a memorial to the late Mrs Tilney in church. Inspired by the horror stories she has read about cruel villains attacking their families, she imagines that the General was responsible for his wife's death or has locked her away somewhere in the Abbey.

Catherine goes looking for the late Mrs Tilney's bedroom, but she is discovered by Henry to whom she explains her fears. He assures her that she is mistaken. Catherine realises the dangers of confusing fantasy with reality and vows not to do so again. She makes a resolution of 'always judging and acting in future with the greatest good sense.'[ch 25] She has learned another lesson on her path from innocence to knowledge.

James sends Catherine a letter informing her that Isabella has broken off their engagement because she has fallen in love with Frederick Tilney. Catherine realises that her doubts about Isabella were not unfounded and vows never to see her again. When Frederick Tilney abandons her, Isabella asks Catherine to help her reconcile with James, but Catherine ignores her request. Now seeing clearly the flaws in Isabella's character, she determines to be more careful when choosing friends in future.

On an excursion to Henry's parsonage, Catherine becomes aware that General Tilney hopes that she will marry Henry. General Tilney leaves for London and on his return, Catherine is surprised to be told to leave Northanger Abbey immediately because the General has remembered an engagement that the family has elsewhere. Eleanor reassures Catherine that she is not to blame for her sudden banishment, which is due to 'some disappointment, some vexation of her father's'.[ch 28] Catherine travels home in a distressed state, fearing that she will never see Henry again.

At home, Catherine is restless and unhappy, but her depression lifts when Henry arrives and proposes to her, leaving her ecstatically happy. Henry explains that John Thorpe had led his father to believe that Catherine was heiress to Mr and Mrs Allen's wealth. He wanted Henry to marry her for her supposed fortune and, in the hope of bringing them closer together, had invited Catherine to Northanger Abbey. While in London the General learned that he had been misled and on his return he banished her from the Abbey and ordered Henry to forget her. The couple agree not to meet again until they obtain the consent of Henry's father to their marriage.

Eleanor's marriage to a rich man pleases her father so much that, with her persuasion, he gives Henry permission to marry Catherine. The young heroine, having completed her emotional and moral education, is now ready to marry the hero.

Isabella, having lost James and been abandoned by Frederick Tilney is alone, as she deserves to be.

### *Henry Tilney*

Henry Tilney has the appearance and character of a hero and a gentleman. He is about twenty-four or twenty-five years old and 'rather tall' with a 'pleasing countenance, a very intelligent and lively eye, and, if not quite handsome, was very near it.'[ch 3] Henry is the parson of the small country parish of Woodston, a few miles from Northanger Abbey, Gloucestershire.

Henry is an affable, modest, polite, witty, learned, and cultured man who, like Catherine, enjoys reading novels. He is also a good dancer. He enjoys a close relationship with his sister Eleanor. Henry and Catherine get on well from their first meeting in Bath Assembly Rooms.

Normally a calm and gentle character, the only time Henry nearly loses his temper is when he is dancing with Catherine and John Thorpe will not stop talking to her. 'That gentleman,' he tells Catherine, 'would have put me out of patience, had he stayed with you half a minute longer. He has no business to withdraw the attention of my partner from me.'[ch 10]

Catherine goes with Henry and Eleanor on a trip to Beechen Cliff, a nearby beauty spot from where the best view of Bath can be seen. Henry patiently teaches Catherine about the picturesque. Their similarity in what Jane Austen calls 'taste' is an early indication that they are meant for each other.

When Henry drives Catherine to Northanger Abbey in his curricle, his driving is contrasted with that of John Thorpe, and it shows the differences in their characters. He drives 'so well, so quietly – without making any disturbance, without parading to her, or swearing at them [the horses].'[ch 20]

When Henry teases Catherine about her romantic expectations of the Abbey, he unwittingly feeds her fantasies by telling her frightening tales of what she may experience there. When Henry surprises Catherine as she is looking for his mother's bedroom and discovers her foolish suspicions about his father, he does not chastise her as she expects. Realising that the Gothic horror novels Catherine has been reading, and possibly his tales of the Abbey, have led to her fantasy, Henry reasons with her gently and kindly. He urges her: 'Remember the country and the age in which we live. Remember that we are English, that we are Christians. Consult your own understanding, your own sense of the probable, your own observation of what is passing around you.'[ch 24]

Catherine sheds 'tears of shame' and runs 'to her room in embarrassment. She recognises Henry's 'astonishing generosity and nobleness of conduct'[ch 25] in never mentioning her suspicions again. She learns the lesson of never mixing fantasy and reality.

Henry is away from home when Catherine is banished from Northanger Abbey. When he discovers what has happened, he finally stands up to his father. He tells him that he intends to propose to Catherine. Henry sets off for Fullerton to make sure Catherine has arrived home safely and apologise for his father's behaviour. His 'pleasing manners and good sense were self-evident recommendations'[ch 31] to Catherine's parents and they give him permission to propose to her. The General grudgingly gives Henry his consent to marry Catherine.

### *John Thorpe*

John Thorpe is the main villain in the novel. He was born a gentleman, although his widowed mother is not well off. John is described as a 'stout [healthy] young man of middling height' with a 'plain face and ungraceful form'.[ch 7] As well as being physically unattractive, he has an unpleasant character. John's many ungentlemanly qualities include being opinionated, boastful, rude, overbearing, uncouth, selfish, and manipulative. He is the antithesis of Henry Tilney, the hero, who is a true gentleman.

When John arrives in Bath with James Morland, he is showing off by driving his gig 'with all the vehemence that could most fitly endanger the lives of himself, his companion and his horse.'[ch 7] Having only just met Catherine, he boasts to her about his gig, pointing out all the fine features and telling her how much he paid for it:

> Curricle-hung you see, seat, trunk, sword-case, splashing-board, lamps, silver moulding, all you see complete; the iron-work is as good as new, or better. He asked fifty guineas; I closed with him directly, threw down the money, and the carriage was mine.[ch 7]

His behaviour does not improve as Catherine witnesses him being disrespectful to his mother and unkind to his sisters. Catherine takes an immediate dislike to John Thorpe and cannot understand why her brother likes him.

Soon after meeting Catherine, John reveals his lack of culture by ridiculing novel reading. His lack of interest in literature is ungentlemanly and is an early indication that he is not destined to marry novel-loving Catherine.

When the Morlands and Thorpes meet at Bath Assembly Rooms John displays more bad behaviour. He has engaged Catherine for the first dance of the evening, but when he arrives he goes straight to the card room and rudely keeps her waiting. Meanwhile, Henry and his sister Eleanor approach Catherine. Henry asks her to dance but she cannot break her promise to John Thorpe, who at that moment comes back to claim her. Catherine hopes Henry will ask her to dance again but he does not. As well as the disappointment of not dancing with Henry, Catherine suffers the humiliation of sitting alone without a partner.

Towards the end of the evening John Thorpe approaches Catherine and uncouthly says 'Well, Miss Morland, I suppose you and I are to stand up and jig it together again.' Catherine pleads tiredness. The boorish Thorpe then suggests that they walk around the room and 'quiz' people, meaning to ridicule or tease them.

> *Come along with me and I will shew you the four greatest quizzers in the room; my two younger sisters and their partners. I have been laughing at them this half hour.*[ch 8]

Catherine excuses herself.

The next morning, Catherine reluctantly goes out with the Thorpes and her brother instead of going to the Pump Room in the hope of finding Eleanor Tilney. She travels alone with John in his gig. It is not appropriate for her to be alone in a vehicle with a young man she hardly knows, but Catherine does not realise this. Either John does not know that this is wrong or, more likely, he takes advantage of Catherine's innocence and naivety.

During the drive John rudely questions Catherine about Mr Allen. 'Old Allen is as rich as a Jew – is not he?'[ch 9] he asks a shocked Catherine and then refers to Mr Allen's goutiness and unjustly accuses him of being an alcoholic.

For the remainder of the journey Thorpe's 'conversation, or rather talk, began and ended with himself and his own concerns.'[ch 9] He has no idea how to behave appropriately. Unsurprisingly, Catherine's initial dislike of her brother's friend is confirmed, and she concludes that he is 'quite disagreeable'.[ch.9]

On two more occasions, John, Isabella and James stop Catherine from keeping her arrangements to meet the Tilneys. John Thorpe lies twice to get Catherine to do as he wants, causing her distress and embarrassment. He seems to take pleasure in her discomfort.

When James and Isabella become engaged, John suggests that he might propose to Catherine. He quotes the song *Going to One Wedding Brings on Another*, but Catherine does not take this as a proposal. She is shocked when John later claims that he had made her an offer and Isabella accuses her of encouraging him. Yet again, Catherine is embarrassed by John's manipulative behaviour.

Catherine's banishment from Northanger Abbey and all the distress this causes her is a direct result of John Thorpe misleading General Tilney into believing that she was heiress to the Allens.

All his lies and manipulation notwithstanding, John Thorpe does not succeed in winning Catherine's affection. The novel ends with her marriage to the hero.

### *James Morland*

As the son of a clergyman, James Morland belongs to the gentry class. He is an honourable young man who is very attached to his sister Catherine. James is also rather naïve and is not a good judge of character. He fails to see his friend John Thorpe's character flaws.

Soon after his arrival in Bath, James asks Catherine what she thinks of his friend.[ch 7] Catherine, who takes an instant dislike to Thorpe, is too polite to tell her brother what she really thinks of him.

James, like Catherine, misjudges Isabella Thorpe and fails for a long time to see her many faults. He tells his sister that Isabella is 'just the kind of young woman I could wish to see you attached to.'[ch 7] James, who has met Isabella previously, begins to fall in love with her. His description of her as having 'good sense' and being 'so thoroughly unaffected'[ch 7] is incorrect. James also fails to realise that Isabella, who believes he belongs to a wealthy family, is only interested in his supposed wealth.

When they dance together at the Assembly Rooms, James allows his feelings for Isabella to cloud his judgement. They unwisely break the rule of not dancing too much with the same partner, thus risking exposure to gossip. Isabella unfairly blames James for this, saying to Catherine, 'I declare it is quite shocking. I tell him he ought to be ashamed of himself,'[ch 10] as if it has nothing to do with her. James becomes engaged to Isabella before he knows her well.

Despite his close and affectionate relationship with his sister, James is thoughtless and unkind to her when, on several occasions, he joins the Thorpes in insisting that she goes out with them against her wishes. This prevents Catherine from keeping her engagements with the Tilneys. James is weak and allows himself to be manipulated by the Thorpes into siding with them against Catherine.

James also lets his sister down by allowing John Thorpe to take her out alone in his carriage. It was considered improper for young ladies to be alone with men they did not know well. Even though Thorpe is his friend, James should have been more careful about the moral reputation of his innocent younger sister, especially as Mrs Allen, who was responsible for her, did not stop Catherine from going. The closeness of the siblings is evident in Catherine's distress and concern when James' engagement is broken because Isabella thinks she has a chance of winning Frederick Tilney.

Both James and Catherine finally realise that they have misjudged the selfish and manipulative Isabella. James blames himself for being too trusting. He is hurt by her duplicity most of all. James remains blind, however, to the true character of John Thorpe. When his engagement ends, he says to Catherine

'I dread the sight of him [John]; his honest heart would feel so much.'[ch 25] In reality, the self-centred John Thorpe is not in the least concerned about the feelings of others.

### *General Tilney*

General Tilney, a minor villain in the novel, is the widowed father of Frederick, Henry and Eleanor and the wealthy owner of Northanger Abbey. He is described as a 'very handsome man of a commanding aspect, past the bloom but not past the vigour of life.'[ch 10] He would, therefore, be deemed a gentleman by birth and appearance.

From the moment Catherine meets the General he is excessively polite, charming, and considerate towards her. Catherine wonders what she has done to deserve this when she hardly knows the General. Catherine notices that, despite his charm, the General 'seemed always a check upon his children's spirits.'[ch 20] This is more evident at Northanger Abbey when Catherine sees that he is a stern, harsh and overbearing disciplinarian who dominates Henry and Eleanor. The General makes Catherine feel uncomfortable.

On the day after her arrival at Northanger Abbey, General Tilney graciously shows Catherine around his park and gardens. He then leaves Eleanor to take her along her late mother's favourite walk. Catherine notices how sad her friend is at the mention of her mother and decides that there must be some mystery about her death. This is the start of Catherine's foolish fantasy that the General was cruel to his wife and may even have murdered her.

During her stay at Northanger Abbey Catherine suspects that the General wants her to marry Henry. This adds to her astonishment when he suddenly terminates her visit. She is sent home 'Without any reason that could justify, any apology that could atone for the abruptness, the rudeness, nay, the insolence of it.'[ch 28] To make matters worse, Catherine is not allowed to say goodbye to Henry. Catherine is forced to make the long journey home alone in a public stagecoach, which was neither safe nor proper. She concludes that she must have done something to offend her host.

Catherine learns the truth when Henry visits her at Fullerton. His father had informed him 'in angry terms of Miss Morland's departure,' and ordered him 'to think of her no more.'[ch 30] Catherine had done nothing wrong apart from being 'less rich' than the General had supposed her to be.

During his visit to London the General had found out that John Thorpe had misled him about Catherine. He was 'Enraged with almost everybody in the world but himself' and sent Catherine home to indicate his 'resentment towards herself, and his contempt of her family'.[ch 30]

Although General Tilney is a thoroughly unpleasant man who does not behave in a manner befitting a gentleman and a man of his status in society, he is not the cruel wife murderer Catherine suspected him to be.

### *Frederick Tilney*

Captain Frederick Tilney, the heir to Northanger Abbey, is another minor villain in the novel. Although a gentleman by birth, Frederick's behaviour is not that of a gentleman. His negative character traits show up his brother's positive ones.

Frederick is described as a 'very fashionable-looking, handsome young man'.[ch 16] Catherine decides that 'his air was more assuming, and his countenance less prepossessing' than Henry's and that his 'taste and manners were, beyond a doubt, decidedly inferior.'[ch 16]

One indication that Frederick is not a true gentleman is that he lacks the ability to dance well. He 'not only protested against every thought of dancing himself, but even laughed openly at Henry for finding it possible.'[ch16]

Frederick forgets his dislike of dancing when he meets Isabella Thorpe at a ball and they dance together, despite Isabella's promise to James that she will not dance while he is absent from Bath. Frederick and Isabella openly flirt and continue to do so after James's return. Catherine is distressed to see how this hurts her brother, but Isabella and Frederick are not concerned. When the rest of his family and Catherine leave Bath for Northanger Abbey, Frederick stays behind.

Isabella, disappointed at the small income she and James will have on marriage, transfers her affection to Frederick. Although he is the reason why Isabella breaks off her engagement to James, Frederick Tilney has no intention of marrying her himself. Catherine learns from Henry that his brother has a habit of flirting with attractive women but that 'his vanities ... have not yet injured himself.'[ch 27] Frederick is the complete opposite to his decent and honourable brother. The most fitting words to describe him are cad and scoundrel.

Inevitably, Frederick rejects Isabella and leaves Bath. She fails in her attempt at a reconciliation with James and gets what she deserves for cheating on him, by losing both of them. Frederick gets away with his selfish behaviour. He is another example of a male character in Jane Austen's novels who, although born a gentleman, fails to act like one.

6

# *PERSUASION*

## *Summary*

Anne Elliot, the heroine of *Persuasion,* is the twenty-seven-year-old daughter of the widowed Sir Walter Elliot of Kellynch Hall in Somerset. Anne's older sister Elizabeth is their father's favourite. Anne and her younger sister Mary are of 'inferior value' to their father. Despite being belittled and disregarded by her father and older sister, Anne has 'elegance of mind and sweetness of character, which must have placed her high with any people of real understanding.'[ch 1] Anne is also very pretty, gentle, and modest.

As Walter Elliot does not have a son, the heir presumptive to his estate and the baronetcy is his cousin William Elliot. Sir Walter and Elizabeth had wanted her to marry William, but he rejected her and became estranged from them.

Sir Walter Elliot cannot live within his means and, on the advice of his land agent Mr Shepherd, he lets Kellynch Hall and moves to Bath, where he can live more economically. Lady Russell, Anne's godmother and a close friend of her late mother, encourages the move. She hopes it will give Anne an opportunity to find a husband, and that it will end Elizabeth's unsuitable friendship with Mrs Clay, the daughter of Mr Shepherd with whom she is living following an unhappy marriage. Mrs Clay has been ingratiating herself with Sir Walter in the hope of marrying him.

Admiral Croft and his wife become the tenants of Kellynch Hall. Their arrival concerns Anne because eight years previously she had briefly been engaged to Mrs Croft's brother, Captain Frederick Wentworth, a naval officer. Anne was persuaded by her father and Lady Russell to break off the engagement because Wentworth had no money and his career prospects were uncertain. He left the country after the break-up. Anne soon regretted her decision which had 'clouded every enjoyment of youth' and led to 'an early loss of bloom and spirits.'[ch 4]

Captain Wentworth's career has flourished since he left, but he was too proud to propose to Anne again when he returned home. She has never met another man who could compare with him and turned down a proposal from the 'highly eligible' Charles Musgrove, who subsequently married her sister Mary.

When Anne goes to stay with Mary at Uppercross Cottage, she is surprised to discover that Frederick Wentworth is staying at Uppercross House with the Musgroves. He is still resentful about the broken engagement. It seems to be expected that he will marry one of the Musgrove daughters, Louisa and Henrietta, who are both infatuated with him. Henrietta's cousin Charles Hayter is upset because he had expected to marry her.

Anne is included in a trip to Lyme Regis to see two navy friends of Captain Wentworth. While in Lyme, Anne twice meets a good-looking man who, as Wentworth notices, clearly admires her.

During a walk along the harbour wall, Louisa Musgrove falls down some steps and is knocked unconscious. While the others panic Anne calmly takes control, calls for a doctor and gets the others to carry Louisa to the inn where they are staying. Captain Wentworth is impressed with the way Anne takes charge. She returns to Uppercross with Wentworth and Henrietta to tell Mr and Mrs Musgrove about Louisa's fall.

When Louisa is on the mend, Anne leaves Uppercross and goes to Bath with Lady Russell. Captain Wentworth also leaves. At her father's house, Anne is surprised to meet the man who had admired her at Lyme. He is her father's cousin William Elliot who, to Anne's surprise, has made up with him. Lady Russell likes William Elliot, who wants to marry Anne, and hopes that he will propose to her, but Anne has reservations about him. Apart from his designs on Anne, William Elliot has heard about Mrs Clay and is anxious to prevent her marrying Sir Walter, which could threaten his inheritance.

Anne visits an old school friend, Mrs Smith, a poor, disabled widow who is in Bath to take the healing waters. The Crofts arrive and give Anne a letter from Mary. This informs her that Louisa has become engaged to Captain Benwick and Henrietta is reconciled with Charles Hayter. This leaves Captain Wentworth, in Anne's words, 'unshackled and free'.
ch 18 The Musgroves arrive in Bath to buy wedding clothes for Henrietta.

Before long, Captain Wentworth returns to Bath to try once more for Anne's hand in marriage but he is prevented from speaking to her by William Elliot. Anne suspects that Captain Wentworth is jealous of William Elliot, but she does not know how to tell him that she still loves him. Mrs Smith tells Anne about rumours of her being engaged to William Elliot and reveals that she knows him to be an evil, cruel man.

Anne meets Captain Wentworth again at the Musgroves' hotel. On overhearing a conversation between Anne and Captain Harville he finds the courage to leave Anne a letter saying that he has never stopped loving her. They are reconciled and, this time, no-one objects to their marriage. Captain Wentworth helps Mrs Smith to recover some of her lost money.

William Elliot, having failed to win Anne, leaves for London with Mrs Clay, whom he has made his mistress to ensure that she no longer presents a threat to his inheritance.

### *Frederick Wentworth*

Frederick Wentworth is a naval officer and, therefore, regarded as a gentleman. He is the most romantic of Jane Austen's heroes.

When he met Anne, Wentworth was a 'remarkably fine young man with a great deal of intelligence, spirit and brilliancy'.[ch 4] They fell in love and became engaged. Wentworth was devastated when Anne broke the engagement. He felt that he had been ill-used and that Anne had shown 'a feebleness of character' in giving him up 'to oblige others.'[ch 7]

In the next few years, Captain Wentworth's naval career flourished and brought him fame and fortune. He was promoted to Commander following his bravery in the Battle of San Domingo. After eight years at sea, he has returned home with a fortune in prize money from capturing enemy ships and cargo. He is one of the new breed of men who took advantage of the opportunities for advancement in the navy. He is now a hero as well as a gentleman.

Captain Wentworth meets Anne again at the Musgroves' home, to which he has been invited because of his kindness to their late son Dick, who was a sailor on one of his ships. Although as a gentleman Wentworth is expected to keep his feelings under control, he cannot hide his continued resentment towards Anne. He shows her 'cold politeness' in contrast to the friendliness he shows to others. He also makes hurtful comments about Anne's appearance, which he knows will be repeated to her.

Wentworth spends too much time with the unmarried Musgrove sisters. This hurts Charles Hayter, the cousin who is expected to marry Henrietta Musgrove, and Anne, who is confused because some of Wentworth's actions make her think that he still has feelings for her. The Musgroves are also misled into thinking that he will marry one of their daughters, a prospect which they find 'extremely delightful'. A gentleman was expected to be careful in the company of unmarried women. Wentworth fails in this respect. He admits that his attentions to Louisa had been 'grossly wrong' and that he was 'hers in honour if she wished it.'[ch 23]

It is difficult for Captain Wentworth to hide his jealousy when he notices William Elliot's admiration of Anne. After seeing how she remains calm and takes charge when Louisa falls off the harbour steps at Lyme Regis, he sees 'everything to exalt in his estimation the woman he had lost' and from then on 'his penance had become severe.'[ch 23] He left Lyme for his brother's house 'lamenting the blindness of his own pride,'[ch 23] which had stopped him from proposing to Anne again when he had returned home before.

When Captain Wentworth returns to Bath to make one more attempt to seek Anne's hand in marriage, he is thwarted by the presence of William Elliot. Anne realises that he is jealous of Elliot. By this time, she knows that Wentworth is a free man again. After hearing Anne say to Captain Harville, 'All the privilege I can claim for my own sex (it is not a very enviable one, you need not covet it), is that of loving longest, when existence or when hope is gone,'[ch 23] he writes Anne a passionate love letter. By doing so Captain Wentworth breaks the rule that a man should not write to an unmarried woman unless he is engaged to her, but he cannot risk losing her again.

When they are reunited, both admit their mistakes. Wentworth regrets his pride even more when Anne tells him that she would have accepted another proposal from him. Anne regrets her lack of judgement and that she meekly allowed herself to be persuaded by others to break her engagement.

Having both learned from their mistakes, the hero and heroine are united in marriage. Captain Wentworth, who, despite his flaws, is a kind man, helps Mrs Smith to sort out her financial affairs and recover enough of her property to provide her with a comfortable living.

### *Walter Elliot*

Although not the villain of *Persuasion,* Sir Walter Elliot is a very unpleasant character. He is a superficial, shallow, vain man and a bad father who, despite his exalted position in society, does not behave like a gentleman.

Sir Walter is a selfish man who does not look after the poor of the parish, as expected of the Lord of the Manor. He is also a spendthrift. Since his prudent wife's death thirteen years earlier Sir Walter has become 'dreadfully in debt'.[ch 1] Attempts to control his spending while retaining the 'dignity' of his position have failed, and he is forced to let Kellynch Hall and move to Bath.

Vanity is Sir Walter's most serious flaw – 'vanity of person and of situation'. He had been 'remarkably handsome in his youth; and, at fifty-four, was still a very fine man.'[ch 1] The countless mirrors at Kellynch Hall testify to Sir Walter's obsession with his appearance.

His other obsession is with his status as a baronet. The only book he ever reads for amusement is the Baronetage where 'he could read his own history with an interest that never failed – this was the page at which the favourite volume always opened.'[ch 1] Sir Walter is extremely proud of his 'ancient and respectable' family.

One of Sir Walter's objections to Frederick Wentworth as a husband for Anne was that it would be a 'very degrading alliance.'[ch 4] He is such a snob that he considers people without the right connections as 'nobodies' and Wentworth fits into this category. Sir Walter is also prejudiced against him because of his disdain for the navy, 'a means of bringing persons of obscure birth into undue distinction, and raising men to honours which their fathers and grandfathers never dreamt of…'[ch 3] He also objects to the navy because a life at sea 'cuts up a man's youth and vigour most horribly; a sailor grows old sooner than any other man; I have observed it all my life.'[ch 3]

When he moves to Bath Sir Walter enjoys being seen with his cousin Lady Dalrymple and her daughter, the Honourable Miss Carteret. Anne, who does not judge people according to their rank, found them 'not very agreeable'. She notes that they possess 'no superiority of manner, accomplishment or understanding'.[ch 16]

Due to his snobbery Sir Walter will not introduce the Crofts to his distinguished cousins. He looks down on this worthy couple and declares his intention to leave them 'to find their own level.'[ch 18]

When Anne goes to visit her friend Mrs Smith her father objects strongly. He does not know Mrs Smith but he dismisses her as a 'poor widow barely able to live ... a mere Mrs Smith, an every- day Mrs Smith, of all people and all names in the world, to be the chosen friend of Miss Anne Elliot.'[ch 17]

He also objects to Anne visiting Mrs Smith because she lives in an unfashionable part of Bath: 'Every thing that revolts other people, low company, paltry rooms, foul air, disgusting associations are inviting to you.'[ch 17] Not only is this cruel to Anne, but failing to treat his social inferiors with respect and dignity is not the behaviour of a gentleman.

Walter Elliot also shows poor judgement. He accepts his cousin William back into the family, does not doubt his explanation for his 'neglect' and the reasons for his marriage. Anne cannot understand why William Elliot has made up with her father because she cannot see what he gains from this. Her father is taken in by his cousin's 'very gentlemanlike appearance, his air of elegance and fashion, his good shaped face, his sensible eye'.[ch 15] Sir Walter does not look beneath the veneer of a gentleman.

At the end of the novel Sir Walter is happy for Anne to marry Captain Wentworth, as he is now in possession of a fortune and a respectable position in society, despite the fact that he owes them to his career in the navy.

Sir Walter Elliot is a good example of a male character who is only superficially a gentleman.

### *William Elliot*

Sir Walter Elliot has three daughters but no son. Under the custom of male primogeniture, therefore, his baronetcy and estate are to pass to his cousin William Elliot, his nearest male relative. Due to his rejection of Elizabeth, William is estranged from Sir Walter and his family and has dishonoured them by speaking of them 'most disrespectfully...most slightingly and contemptuously'.[ch 1]

When William Elliot enters the novel, he is widowed and anxious to make amends with his family to protect his inheritance. William is not handsome, but he is 'agreeable,' and is said to possess 'good understanding, correct opinions, knowledge of the world, and a warm heart. [He is] steady, observant, moderate, candid,' with manners 'so polished, so easy, so particularly agreeable.'[ch 16] He appears to be a gentleman and he owns a curricle – a gentleman's carriage. Outward appearances, however, are deceptive.

William Elliot has heard about Mrs Clay's hopes of marrying Sir Walter, which could lead to the loss of his inheritance, and he is determined to prevent this from happening. He goes to Bath soon after Sir Walter and Elizabeth move there and turns up, unannounced, at their new home in Camden Place. Sir Walter accepts his explanation for his 'neglect' and that it was his late wife who had pursued him, not the other way round. William is so anxious to make up with his cousins that he 'omitted no opportunity of being with them, threw himself in their way, called at all hours.'[ch 21] Another reason for his presence in Bath is to pursue Anne.

Everyone is taken in by William. Anne, at first, can find no fault with him; she is deceived by his gentlemanly behaviour and good manners. Lady Russell also 'could not picture to herself a more agreeable or estimable man.'[ch 16] She is impressed that he, like herself and Sir Walter, places a high value on rank and connections.

It is not long before Anne becomes suspicious of William Elliot. She thinks there is 'something more than immediately appeared'[ch 15] in his sudden wish to make up with her father after so many years. Anne decides that he is 'too perfect' and tries to please everyone while not revealing his true feelings and opinions. After knowing William for a month, Anne feels that she does not really know his character. She is correct in her suspicions because William Elliot is really a devious, calculating opportunist – the opposite to the gentleman he purports to be.

When Anne is told by Mrs Smith that William, who has admired Anne since first seeing her in Lyme Regis, wants to marry her, she realises 'the evil of his attentions' to her and the 'irremediable mischief he might have done.'[ch 22]

Mrs Smith reveals the truth about William Elliot to Anne. He had once been a poor lawyer when her late husband helped him financially and welcomed him to their home. Then he quickly married a woman of low rank for her money. He had never loved his wife and they were unhappy together.

Mrs Smith tells her that he is 'a man without heart or conscience; a designing, wary, cold-blooded being, who thinks only of himself, who, for his own interest or ease would be guilty of any cruelty or any treachery.'[ch 21] He had led Mr Smith into financial ruin. He then failed in his duty to execute Mr Smith's will and responded to his widow's pleas for him to act with 'hard-hearted indifference'[ch 21] leaving her in poverty.

After Mrs Smith's revelation, Anne is wary of William Elliot, who remains devious to the end. After being thwarted in his attempt to marry Anne, he leaves Bath for London taking Mrs Clay with him as his mistress, to protect his inheritance. The scheming couple deserve each other.

### *Admiral Croft and Captain Harville*

There are two minor male characters in the novel who show up the bad behaviour of Sir Walter Elliot and his cousin William. These characters are Admiral Croft and Captain Harville.

Admiral Croft fought at the Battle of Trafalgar and served in the East Indies. Anne liked the Admiral and his wife from their first meeting. Lady Russell, however, does not entirely approve of the Admiral, but she is not a very good judge of character, as shown by her initial judgements of Captain Wentworth and William Elliot.

The Admiral is described by Sir Walter's land agent as 'a most responsible, eligible tenant'.[ch 3] Anne feels that with him as tenant of Kellynch Hall, the parish would be 'so sure of a good example, and the poor of the best attention and relief.'[ch 3]

The Admiral's gentlemanly conduct is genuine, not a veneer to cover negative character traits or deception, as it is with Sir Walter and William Elliot. There is nothing negative about the Admiral. He is friendly, genial, down-to-earth, plain speaking and courteous. His 'goodness of heart and simplicity of character [are] irresistible.'[ch 13] The Admiral is agreeable to everyone he meets, including Anne's self-centred and attention-seeking sister Mary. He wins her over by 'his good-humoured notice of her little boys.'[ch 6] The Admiral is happily married to Captain Wentworth's sister Sophy, who is as good-natured and affable as her husband.

The Crofts are considerate and kind to others, including Anne, even though she broke off her engagement to Sophy's brother. When Anne is tired after a long walk, they make room for her in their gig so they can drive her home. Another example of Admiral Croft's attentiveness to Anne occurs later in the novel when she meets him in Milsom Street, in Bath, and he asks 'Where are you bound? Can I go any where for you, or with you? Can I be of any use?'[ch 18]

Anne frequently sees the Crofts together in Bath when she is riding around in Lady Russell's carriage. The sight of them 'was a most attractive picture of happiness to her.'[ch 18] They have achieved a state of contentment which the shallow, snobbish Sir Walter and his scheming, deceitful cousin could never achieve.

Captain Harville, Frederick Wentworth's friend, is also happily married. A 'tall, dark man with a sensible, benevolent countenance ... perfect gentleman.'[ch 16] Harville is not in good health, after suffering a war wound two years previously. He is described as 'unaffected, warm and obliging'[ch 16] and his wife has 'the same good feelings'[ch 11] as her husband.

When the Harvilles hurry to the spot where Louisa Musgrove was lying after her fall, the Captain, though shocked, 'brought senses and nerves that could be instantly useful.'[ch 12] Louisa and the others are taken to the Harvilles' home and Mrs Harville has Louisa put in her own bed, while 'assistance, cordials, restoratives were supplied by her husband to all who needed them.'[ch 12] Despite having a young family to look after, the Harvilles care for Louisa until she is well enough to go home. Nothing is too much trouble for them.

When Anne leaves the Harvilles' house, she feels that she is leaving 'great happiness behind her'.[ch 11] This is in marked contrast to her feelings on arrival at her father's new home in Bath, which she had entered 'with a sinking heart, anticipating an imprisonment of many months.'[ch 15] and anxiously asking herself when she will leave again.

Parts of Captain Harville's character are believed to have been inspired by Jane Austen's brother Frank. He himself stated:

> I rather think parts of Captain Harville were drawn from myself; at least the description of his domestic habits, tastes and occupations bear a considerable resemblance to mine.

Captain Harville, like Frank, is a warm, good-natured man who gets on with everyone he meets and is a true gentleman.

# ENDNOTES

## PART I: THE MEN IN JANE AUSTEN'S LIFE

*Chapter 1 George Austen*

1. Tucker, George Holbert, *A History of Jane Austen's Family* (Sutton Publishing, 1998), 27
2. Austen-Leigh, J.E., *A Memoir of Jane Austen and Other Family Recollections* (Oxford University Press, 2002), 14
3. Austen-Leigh, William and Richard Arthur, and Le Faye, Deirdre, *Jane Austen, A Family Record* (The British Library, 1989), 53
4. Austen-Leigh, Mary Augusta, *Personal Aspects of Jane Austen* (General Books, Memphis, Tennessee, U.S.A, 2009), 32
5. Hubback, J.H. and Edith C., *Jane Austen's Sailor Brothers* (The Bodley Head, 1905), 16-18
6. Austen-Leigh, J.E., 105
7. Austen-Leigh, William and Richard Arthur, *Jane Austen, Her Life and Letters, A Family Record* (General Books, Memphis, Tennessee, U.S.A., 2010), 33

8. Austen-Leigh, W. and R. A., and Le Faye, 120
9. Ibid, 120
10. Le Faye, Deirdre, *Jane Austen's Letters* (Oxford University Press, 1995), 94
11. Ibid, 95-6
12. Ibid, 97-8

*Chapter 2 James Austen*

1. Austen-Leigh, J.E., 12
2. Austen-Leigh, W. and R. A., and Le Faye, 51
3. Austen, James, *The Loiterer, no.2* (The Loiterer.org)
4. Le Faye, *Jane Austen's Letters*, 61
5. Austen-Leigh, W. and R.A., and Le Faye, 77
6. Ibid, 50
7. Ibid, 91-2
8. Le Faye, Deirdre (*Jane Austen's Outlandish Cousin, The Life and Letters of Eliza de Feullide* (The British Library, 2002), 134
9. Austen-Leigh, W. and R.A., and Le Faye, 92-93
10. Ibid, 92
11. Le Faye, *Jane Austen's Letters*, 16
12. Ibid, 73
13. Ibid, 71-2
14. Ibid, 88
15. Tucker, 107
16. Ibid, 109
17. Le Faye, *Jane Austen's Letters*, 114
18. Ibid, 121
19. Ibid, 137
20. Austen, Caroline, *Reminiscences of Caroline Austen* (The Jane Austen Society, 1986), 22

21. Selwyn, David (editor), *Collected Poems and Verses of the Austen Family* (Fyfield Books, 1996), 50
22. Le Faye, *Jane Austen's Letters*, 340-1
23. Austen-Leigh, J.E., 131
24. Austen-Leigh, W. and R.A., and Le Faye, 232
25. Ibid, 236
26. Austen, Caroline, *Reminiscences of Caroline Austen*, 53
27. Tucker, 114

*Chapter 3 George Austen*

1. Tucker, 115
2. Ibid, 115

*Chapter 4 Edward Austen*

1. Tucker, 119
2. Knatchbull-Hugessen, *Letters of Jane Austen* volume 2, 357
3. Le Faye, *Jane Austen's Letters*, 12
4. Ibid, 8
5. Tucker, 123
6. Ibid, 123
7. Hasted, Edward, The *History and Topographical Survey of the County of Kent.*
8. Le Faye, *Jane Austen's Letters*, 40
9. Ibid, 47
10. Ibid, 42
11. Ibid, 248
12. Austen-Leigh, W. and R.A. and Le Faye, 161
13. Le Faye, *Jane Austen's Letters*, 230
14. Austen-Leigh, J.E., 16
15. Le Faye, *Jane Austen's Letters*, 230

16. Ibid, 28
17. Austen-Leigh, W. and R.A., and Le Faye, 184
18. Ibid, 144
19. Ibid, 144
20. Ibid, 161
21. Ibid, 163
22. Knight, Fanny, *Fanny Knight's Diary*.
23. Le Faye, *Jane Austen's Letters*, 146
24. Ibid, 147
25. Ibid, 161
26. Tucker, 130
27. Austen-Leigh, W. and R.A. and Le Faye, 207
28. Ibid, 171
29. Le Faye, *Jane Austen's Letters*, 196
30. Ibid, 215
31. Knight, Fanny, *Fanny Knight's Diary*.
32. Le Faye, *Jane Austen's Letters*, 229
33. Austen-Leigh, W. and R.A. and Le Faye, 195
34. Ibid, 195
35. Tucker, 164
36. Ibid, 132

*Chapter 5 Henry Austen*

1. Austen-Leigh, W and R.A., and Le Faye, 22
2. Ibid, 24
3. Austen, Caroline, *My Aunt Jane Austen*, 11
4. Le Faye, *Jane Austen's 'Outlandish Cousin'*, 89
5. *Tucker,* 133
6. Le Faye, *Jane Austen's Letters*, 101-2
7. Austen-Leigh, J.E., 16

8. Knatchbull-Hugessen, volume 1, 35-6
9. Austen-Leigh, W and R.A., and Le Faye, 88
10. Le Faye, *Jane Austen's 'Outlandish Cousin'*, 129
11. Ibid, 151
12. Ibid, 152-3
13. Le Faye, *Jane Austen's Letters*, 183
14. Ibid, 207
15. Austen-Leigh, W. and R.A., and Le Faye, 178
16. Le Faye, *Jane Austen's Letters*, 215-6
17. Ibid, 230
18. Ibid, 230
19. Ibid, 231
20. Ibid, 218
21. Ibid, 264
22. Ibid, 271
23. Ibid, 292
24. Austen, Caroline, *My Aunt Jane Austen*, 11
25. Austen, Caroline, *Reminiscences*, 48
26. Austen-Leigh, W. and R.A., and Le Faye, 212
27. Le Faye, *Jane Austen's Letters*, 323
28. Ibid, 327
29. Austen-Leigh, W. and R.A., and Le Faye, 236
30. Austen, Caroline, *Reminiscences*, 57
31. Ibid, 57
32. Midgley, Winifred, *The Revd Henry and Eleanor Austen.*
33. Barlow, Angela, *Eleanor Jackson, The Second Mrs Henry Austen.*
34. Ibid.
35. Ibid.
36. Tucker, 148
37. Le Faye, Deirdre, *Chronology of Jane Austen*, 682.

*Chapter 6 Francis Austen*

1. Tucker, 165
2. Austen-Leigh, W. and R.A., and Le Faye, 61
3. Ibid, 62
4. Hubback, J.H. and Edith C., 16-20
5. Le Faye, *Jane Austen's Letters, 6*
6. Ibid, 7
7. Ibid, 32
8. Ibid, 75
9. Tucker, 172
10. Austen-Leigh, W. and R.A., and Le Faye, 134
11. Hubback J.H. and Edith C., 155-6
12. Ibid, 156
13. Le Faye, *Jane Austen's Letters*, 119
14. Austen-Leigh. J.E., 17
15. Le Faye, Jane Austen's Letters, 175-6
16. Ibid, 217
17. Austen-Leigh, R.A., *Austen Papers*, 284-5
18. Knatchbull-Hugessen, volume 1, 37
19. Ibid, 38
20. Hubback, J.H. and Edith C., 285

*Chapter 7 Charles Austen*

1. Hubback, J.H. and Edith C., 49
2. Le Faye, *Jane Austen's Letters,* 91
3. Ibid, 60
4. Austen-Leigh, J.E., 17
5. Hubback. J.H. and Edith C., 208
6. Le Faye, *Jane Austen's Letters*, 105
7. Austen-Leigh, W. and R.A. and Le Faye, 152

8. Ibid, 152
9. Tucker, 185
10. Ibid, 185
11. Le Faye, *Jane Austen's Letters*, 216
12. Ibid, 216
13. Austen-Leigh, W. and R.A., and Le Faye, 167
14. Le Faye, *Jane Austen's Letters*, 239
15. Ibid, 240
16. Ibid, 287
17. Ibid, 287
18. Le Faye, *A Chronology of Jane Austen*, 505
19. Ibid, 522
20. Austen-Leigh, W. and R.A., and Le Faye, 207
21. Austen, Caroline, *Reminiscences*, 47
22. Austen-Leigh, W. and R.A., and Le Faye, 217
23. Ibid, 226
24. Ibid, 237
25. Ibid, 237-8
26. Ibid, 238
27. Ibid, 238
28. Austen-Leigh, R.A., 271
29. Ibid, 285
30. Tucker, 189
31. Hammond, Margaret, *Admiral Charles Austen*.
32. Tucker, 190
33. Ibid, 180

*Chapter 8 James Leigh-Perrot*

1. Austen-Leigh, J.E., 59
2. Le Faye, *Jane Austen's Letters*, 103

3. Ibid, 154
4. Tucker, 82
5. Le Faye, *Jane Austen's Letters*, 40
6. Ibid, 42
7. Ibid, 82
8. Ibid, 85-6
9. Tucker, 83
10. Austen-Leigh, W. and R.A., and Le Faye, 107
11. Ibid, 107
12. Tucker, 87
13. Ibid, 87
14. Austen-Leigh, W. and R.A., and Le Faye, 108
15. Tucker, 89
16. Ibid, 90
17. Austen-Leigh, W. and R.A., and Le Faye, 110
18. Tucker, 91
19. Ibid, 92
20. Ibid, 93
21. Austen-Leigh, W. and R.A., and Le Faye, 221-2
22. Ibid, 222
23. Freeman, K., *T'Other Miss Austen* 106
24. Tucker, 93
25. Ibid, 93
26. Austen-Leigh, W. and R.A., and Le Faye, 222
27. Tucker, 110
28. Ibid, 94
29. Austen-Leigh, W. and R.A., and Le Faye, 240
30. Ibid, 245
31. Ibid, 245

## *Chapter 9 Two Nephews*

### *George Knight*

1. Le Faye, Jane Austen's Letters, 6
2. Ibid, 15
3. Ibid, 17
4. Ibid, 17
5. Ibid, 26
6. Ibid, 34
7. Ibid, 152
8. Ibid, 149-150
9. Selwyn, David, *Jane Austen, Collected Poems and Verse of the Austen Family,* 56
10. Ibid, 56
11. Knatchbull-Hugessen, Volume 1, 26

### *James Edward Austen-Leigh*

1. Le Faye, Jane Austen's Letters, 20
2. Ibid, 21
3. Selwyn, David, *Fugitive Pieces, Poems of James Edward Austen-Leigh,* 7
4. Austen, Caroline, *Reminiscences,* 25
5. Le Faye, *Jane Austen's Letters,* 132
6. Austen-Leigh, J.E. 66-7
7. Ibid, 66
8. Austen-Leigh, W. and R.A. and Le Faye, 135
9. Austen, Caroline, *Reminiscences,* 23.
10. Austen-Leigh, J.E., 81
11. Ibid, 81
12. Selwyn, David, *Collected Poems of the Austen Family,* 61

13. Le Faye, *Jane Austen's Letters,* 318
14. Ibid, 319
15. Ibid, 323
16. Austen-Leigh, Joan, *My Aunt Jane Austen*
17. Le Faye, *Jane Austen's Letters*, 322
18. Ibid, 327
19. Ibid, 342
20. Ibid, 342
21. Austen-Leigh, W. and R.A., and Le Faye, 225
22. Selwyn, David, *Fugitive Pieces*, 58-9
23. Austen, Caroline, *Reminiscences,* 57
24. Austen-Leigh, W. and R.A., and Le Faye, 240
25. Lane, Maggie, *Another Emma*
26. Austen, Caroline, *Reminiscences,* 64
27. Ibid, 65
28. Bussby, Frederick, *Jane Austen in Winchester*, 1
29. Austen, Caroline, *My Aunt Jane Austen,* 2
30. Austen-Leigh, W. and R.A., and Le Faye, 254
31. Austen-Leigh, J.E., 4
32. Austen, Caroline, *Reminiscences,* 68
33. Ibid, 68

*Chapter 10 Could Jane Have Married?*

1. Le Faye, *Jane Austen's Letters*, 1
2. Ibid, 4
3. Austen-Leigh. J.E., 186
4. Austen-Leigh, W. and R.A., and Le Faye, 87
5. Le Faye, Jane Austen's Letters, 279
6. Ibid, 216
7. Austen-Leigh, W. and R.A., and Le Faye, 97

8. Le Faye, *Jane Austen's Letters*, 19
9. Ibid, 216
10. Austen-Leigh, J.E., 29
11. *Persuasion*, chapter 23
12. Austen-Leigh, J.E., 191
13. Ibid, 191
14. Le Faye, *Jane Austen's Letters*, 286

# BIBLIOGRAPHY

*Unpublished Sources*

Knatchbull, Lady (Fanny Knight) *Diaries 1804-1817* (Kent Count Archives, U951 F24)

*Published Sources*

Austen, Caroline, *My Aunt Jane Austen, A Memoir* (Jane Austen Memorial Trust, 1991)

Austen, Caroline, *Reminiscences of Caroline Austen* (The Jane Austen Society, 1986)

Austen, James, *The Loiterer no.* 2 (The Loiterer.org)

Austen-Leigh, J. E., *A Memoir of Jane Austen and Other Family Recollections* (Oxford University Press, 2002)

Austen-Leigh, Joan, *My Aunt Jane Austen* (Jane Austen Society of North America, publication, 1989)

Austen-Leigh, Mary Augusta, *Personal Aspects of Jane Austen* (General Books, Memphis Tennessee, U.S.A.,2009)

Austen-Leigh, R. A. (editor), *Austen Papers, 1704 -1856* (Spottiswoode and Ballantyne, 1942)

Austen-Leigh, William and Richard Arthur, *Jane Austen, Her Life and Letters, A Family Record* (General Books, Memphis, Tennessee, U.S.A., 2010)

Austen-Leigh, William and Richard Arthur, and Le Faye, Deirdre, *Jane Austen, A Family Record* (The British Library, 1989)

Barlow, Angela, *Eleanor Jackson, The Second Mrs Henry Austen* (Jane Austen Society Report, 2018)

Bussby, Frederick, *Jane Austen in Winchester* (The Sidney Press Ltd., 1975)

De Wolfe Howe, M.A., *A Jane Austen Letter and Other Janeana from an Old Book of Autographs* ( www.mollands.net)

Freeman, Kathleen, *T'other Miss Austen* (Macdonald and Co., London, 1956)

Hammond, Margaret, *Admiral Charles Austen* (Jane Austen Society Report, 1986)

Hasted, Edward, *The History and Topographical Survey of the County of Kent, vol. 7 – Parishes – Godmersham)* British History Online.

Hill, Constance, *Jane Austen, Her Homes and Her Friends* (John Lane, The Bodley Head, 1923)

Hubback, J.H. and Edith C., *Jane Austen's Sailor Brothers* (The Bodley Head, 1905)

Lane, Maggie, *Another Emma (Jane Austen Society Report,* 1983)

Le Faye, Deirdre, *A Chronology of Jane Austen and Her Family, 1600-2000* (Cambridge University Press, 2013)

Le Faye, Deirdre (editor), *Jane Austen's Letters* (Oxford University Press, 1995)

Le Faye, Deirdre, *Jane Austen's 'Outlandish Cousin,' The Life and Letters of Eliza de Feuillide* (The British Library, 2002)

Knatchbull-Hugessen, Edward Hugessen, Lord Brabourne (editor), *Letters of Jane Austen, Volume 1*, and *Volume 2* (Cambridge University Press, 2009)

Midgley, Winifred, *The Reverend Henry and Eleanor Austen* (Jane Austen Society Report, 1978.)

Ray, Joan Klingel, *Jane Austen for Dummies* (Wiley Publishing Inc, 2006)

Selwyn, David (editor), *Fugitive Pieces, Trifles Light as Air, The Poems of James Edward Austen Leigh* (The Jane Austen Society, 2006)

Selwyn, David (editor), *Jane Austen, Collected Poems and Verse of the Austen Family* (Carcenet, 1996)

Tucker, George Holbert, *A History of Jane Austen's Family* (Sutton Publishing, 1998)

# PLACES TO VISIT

**Chawton House**
Chawton, Hants.
GU34 1SJ

**Jane Austen Centre**
40, Gay Street, Bath
BA1 2NT

**Jane Austen's House**
Winchester Road,
Chawton, Hants.
GU34 1SD

# INDEX